Desiring Conversion

B. DIANE LIPSETT

Desiring
Conversion

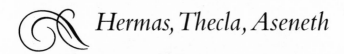 *Hermas, Thecla, Aseneth*

OXFORD
UNIVERSITY PRESS
2011

OXFORD
UNIVERSITY PRESS

Oxford University Press, Inc., publishes works that further
Oxford University's objective of excellence
in research, scholarship, and education.

Oxford   New York

Auckland   Cape Town   Dar es Salaam   Hong Kong   Karachi
Kuala Lumpur   Madrid   Melbourne   Mexico City   Nairobi
New Delhi   Shanghai   Taipei   Toronto

With offices in
Argentina   Austria   Brazil   Chile   Czech Republic   France   Greece
Guatemala   Hungary   Italy   Japan   Poland   Portugal   Singapore
South Korea   Switzerland   Thailand   Turkey   Ukraine   Vietnam

Copyright © 2011 by Oxford University Press, Inc.

Published by Oxford University Press, Inc.
198 Madison Avenue, New York, NY 10016

www.oup.com

Oxford is a registered trademark of Oxford University Press

Library of Congress Cataloging-in-Publication Data
Lipsett, B. Diane (Barbara Diane)
Desiring conversion : Hermas, Thecla, Aseneth / B. Diane Lipsett.
    p. cm.
Includes bibliographical references.
ISBN 978-0-19-975451-9
1. Hermas, 2nd cent. Shepherd. 2. Acts of Paul and Thecla. 3. Conversion—Christianity—History.
4. Desire—Religious aspects—Christianity—History. 5. Joseph and Aseneth.
6. Conversion—Judaism—History. 7. Desire—Religious aspects—Judaism—History.
I. Title.
BS2900.H5L56   2010
229'.9—dc22   2010011241

9 8 7 6 5 4 3 2 1

Printed in the United States of America
on acid-free paper

For my parents
George and Joan Lipsett

Contents

Acknowledgments

I AM PLEASED TO ACKNOWLEDGE MANY WHO HAVE supported me in this project. I presented parts of my analyses in papers for the "Ancient Fiction and Early Christian and Jewish Narrative" section of the Society of Biblical Literature, and benefited from the helpful responses of participants. My anonymous readers for Oxford University Press offered further insights that improved my work. I am grateful for the interest and support of Cynthia Read, Executive Editor at Oxford, and for the steady assistance of Charlotte Steinhardt. My students and colleagues at the Wake Forest University School of Divinity have provided a stimulating environment in which to teach and write. Two of my research assistants, Hilary Floyd and Seth Bledsoe, gave particularly diligent and able help. Jill Crainshaw, Veronice Miles, Lynn Neal, and Phyllis Trible also buoyed me with substantive conversations along the way, as did friends and colleagues beyond Wake Forest, including Catherine Chin, Janice Hamilton, and Suzanne Watts Henderson. I especially thank Stephanie Cobb, whose friendship has made my studies often more possible and always more fun.

The occasion of publishing a first book prompts me to reflect on the remarkable teachers I have had. Patricia Demers and the late Christopher Q. Drummond of the University of Alberta's English Department introduced me to literary analysis as a passionate discipline. During my doctoral work at the University of North Carolina at Chapel Hill, Elizabeth Clark,

Eric Downing, Dale Martin, and Zlatko Plese challenged me with their learning and theoretical versatility; they also astutely critiqued the dissertation from which this study came. I am deeply indebted to Bart Ehrman, my doctoral advisor, teacher, mentor, and friend. My respect for his scholarly achievements is outstripped only by my admiration of his conviviality and gratitude for his exceptional counsel and support.

Most of all, I thank my family. My sons, James and Christopher Wudel, with their candor and curiosity, have been the best cheering section imaginable. Richard Vinson, my husband, has made generous and incisive contributions and lent steadiness and grace through a long process. I dedicate this book to my parents, Joan and George Lipsett, in honor of their resilience and gratitude for their love.

Portions of Chapter 2 were published in *Religion and Theology* 11 (2004), B. Diane Wudel, "The Seduction of Self-Control: Hermas and the Problem of Desire," 39–49. (Copyright Brill, reprinted with permission).

Greek text for *The Shepherd of Hermas* in Chapter 2 is reprinted by permission of the publisher from THE APOSTOLIC FATHERS: VOLUME II, Loeb Classical Library Volume 25, edited and translated by Bart D. Ehrman, pp. 174, 176, 178, 180, 186, 212, 214, 226, 268, 272, 292, 294, 308, 334, 390, 414, 416, 422, 424, 470, Cambridge, Mass.: Harvard University Press, Copyright ©2003 by the President and Fellows of Harvard College. The Loeb Classical Library ® is a registered trademark of the President and Fellows of Harvard College.

Greek text for *Joseph and Aseneth* is reprinted by permission of Koninklijke BRILL NV from Christoph Burchard, *Joseph und Aseneth: Kritisch Herausgegeben*. With assistance from Carsten Burfeind and Uta Barbara Fink. Leiden: Brill, 2003.

Desiring Conversion

ONE

Introduction

We can, then, conceive of the reading of plot as a form of desire that carries us forward, onward, through the text. Narratives both tell of desire—typically present some story of desire—and arouse and make use of desire as a dynamic of signification.[1]

—Peter Brooks

Rather than simple cultural breach, the voiding of a past social self, the language of converts expresses new forms of relatedness. The public aspect of this belonging is perhaps a new identity, a newly inscribed communal self defined through the gaze of others.[2]

—Diane Austin-Broos

F ROM DARKNESS TO LIGHT, FROM BLINDNESS TO SIGHT, from death to life—such tropes are frequent in ancient Christian and Jewish texts that urge or commend *conversion* of the self as fundamental change in piety and identity.[3] Other texts use metaphors of immigration: the proselyte is one who has *come over* from a previous, inferior, even corrupt state of being to the better, more virtuous, more godly new state.[4] Still others, however, depict the transformed self (whether Jewish or Christian) in terms that intersect with a larger Greco-Roman cultural discourse about the problem of the passions, and the oppositions between desire and self-control.[5] When conversion is depicted as transformation from a self abandoned to lust and desire to a self governed by virtue and restraint, then gender frequently becomes a key marker of difference. Luxury, desire, and lust may be associated with feminine fluidity and lack of boundaries; conversion, in contrast, becomes a masculinizing movement toward the closed, composed self, as we shall more fully explore.

More interesting than isolated figures of speech, however, are the tropes and motifs that shape *narratives* of transformed identities. Recent research on conversion betrays a strong literary bent, and a focus on conversion stories, their rhetoric and narrativity.[6] Indeed, many argue that conversion is a phenomenon dependent on narrative's capacity to construct meaning and grant coherence and closure. The particular subject of this study is three ancient conversion tales, drawn from three different literary *corpora:* from the Apostolic Fathers, *The Shepherd of Hermas;* from the Apocryphal Acts of the Apostles, *The Acts of Paul and Thecla;* from ancient Jewish novellas, *Joseph and Aseneth.* Each narrative tells a story of change in the protagonist's identity partly by treating desire and self-restraint, passion and renunciation, as opposed categories. Yet these narratives, like other ancient novelistic literature, also complicate the relations of desire and restraint, deploy gender distinctions in surprising ways, and depict conversion variously as precipitated, driven, or disciplined by desire, even while insisting on sexual self-restraint.

In *The Shepherd of Hermas,* a male Christian householder, Hermas, narrates his own long, diffuse, and erratic movement through receiving revelation, engaging in self-scrutiny, and being urged toward enhanced manliness. Hermas is called "the Self-Restrained," yet his transformation is initiated by an erotically charged encounter with his former mistress emerging from her bath in the Tiber, and culminates in a night-long dalliance with beautiful personifications of virtue. Dating to the late first or early- to mid-second century CE, likely from Rome, *The Shepherd* is in literary form a kind of attenuated apocalypse, but dominated by paraenetic discourse.[7] *The Acts of Paul and Thecla* is a fast-paced tale paying minimal attention to the interiority of the protagonist, yet depicting both desire for restraint and the restraints of desire. In this coherent story inserted into the longer *Acts of Paul,* Thecla is transformed from being an elite, pagan virgin, poised to marry the leading man of her city, to being an ascetic, itinerant Christian missionary and teacher. Her social and religious change is driven by apparent infatuation with the apostle Paul, but also conditioned by her need to actively resist male sexual aggression, and sheltered by the protective acts of other female characters. Dating to the late second century CE, Thecla's story, like the other *Apocryphal Acts of the Apostles,* is sometimes characterized as a kind of antinovel, borrowing yet inverting characteristic motifs and ideologies of the ancient Greek romance.[8] The third story, *Joseph and Aseneth*, tells in often extravagantly figurative language how the beautiful but arrogant virgin, Aseneth, living in cloistered hatred of men and extreme devotion to countless Egyptian gods, came to be the God-venerating, virtuous, radiant wife of the Hebrew patriarch Joseph. Her impassioned desire for Joseph is inextricably interwoven with her turn toward the most-high God. Questions of dating are vexed for this text, though most scholars place it between the first century BCE and first century CE, with one recent proposal for a late-ancient dating. In genre, it is appropriately described as a novel or novella, similar both to pagan Greek romances and to apocryphal writings such as Judith and Tobit, though its sustained revelatory scenes invite comparison to apocalyptic or mystical texts.[9]

One interpreter of Aseneth observes, "The ideal transformation narrative . . . may well be one that utilizes gender as a central component of difference,"[10] and the insight seems applicable to each of these tales. All three suggest that identity transformation is a process of masculinization, whether the protagonist is male or female. All three make female virgins evocative symbols of liminality and desire. All offer distinctive configurations of cultural codes for marriage and for continence or chastity, and all endorse renunciation of erotic consummation (either finally or provisionally) but not the transformative possibilities of desire itself. Close narrative analysis shows that these discrete ancient stories offer intriguing, distinctive developments of the thematic of desire, restraint, and conversion.

To prepare for close literary analysis of these stories, four kinds of initial discussions prove helpful. (1) An overview of how conversion has been and is being studied across disciplines and within the field of ancient Judaism and Christianity helps identify complex features of a concept that is at once cultural and literary. (2) A selective discussion of various ways ancient Greco-Romans (including Jews and Christians) characterized desire as destabilizing and disordering—therefore, a problem of self-mastery for the virtuous, controlled, masculine self—underscores the distinctiveness of ancient views. (3) A further sampling of ancient texts suggests ways that desire is also represented as productive of virtue and good—its transgressive effects having potentially transformative reaches. (4) Finally, a turn to select theories of desire in narrative prepares for analysis of the three ancient conversion tales.

CONVERSION, CULTURAL PASSAGE, AND NARRATIVE

To call these texts conversion tales necessarily raises the question of what associations *conversion* evokes. By identifying some key trends in the last century of scholarship, both on ancient Judaism and Christianity specifically and on religious conversion more broadly, one may elicit a cluster of guiding questions and concepts to bring to particular stories of the changed self.

Discussions of conversion in ancient Christianity and Judaism often still refer to Arthur Darby Nock's magisterial 1933 study, *Conversion*.[11] Nock surveyed ideas of conversion in Greek piety, in Eastern cults, in the Roman Empire, and in philosophic schools, then examined Judaism and Christianity within this broad cultural context. His views were shaped by his Harvard colleague William James, who described conversion as an operation of the subconscious, straining to "straighten out and unify the inner self"[12] and doing so by moving religious ideas (or, in a counter-conversion, irreligious ideas), previously peripheral to the consciousness, into a central, unifying place.[13] Conversion may be gradual and volitional, according to James, or more involuntary and subconscious, marked by self-surrender and seeming sudden, even if resulting from long processes.[14] Nock's working definition is noticeably Jamesean: "By conversion we mean the reorientation of the soul of an individual, his deliberate turning from indifference or from an earlier form of piety to another, a turning which implies a consciousness that a great change is involved, that the old was wrong and the new is right."[15] For Nock, conversion may take place not only *between* forms of piety but *within* one form, appearing as a shift in sectarian identification, or a change from laxity to intensity of observance, or a turn from nominal affiliation to devout attachment. In contrast to *conversion*, Nock defines *adhesion* to be the adoption of "new worships" as useful supplements to rather than substitutes for earlier forms of piety. Conversion was what one did in turning toward a "prophetic religion"; adhesion characterized the affiliation with "traditional religion," and all pagan religions by definition fell into the latter category. Allegiance to the philosophical schools might be analogous to conversion, he concedes, and Lucius' induction into the Isis cult in Apuleius' *The Golden Ass* might approximate the idea, but for Nock, in antiquity, only Judaism and Christianity held out the full possibility of conversion.[16]

James's and Nock's early twentieth-century accounts focused, then, on the individual convert and on conversion as change in consciousness, including ethical reorientation, though with complex social consequences. Their views left some tension between characterizing the convert as recipient (James's "subconscious" as a driving force) or agent (Nock's "deliberate turning"), and tended to emphasize conversion as crisis even while allowing for gradual process.[17] But they concurred in treating new affiliations, intensified affiliations, and disaffiliations as varieties of the same process, and in emphasizing interiority and the individual experience.[18]

More recent analyses across a range of disciplines examine conversion less as a shift in interior commitment than as a change in social identity and social location, modifying both the individual's relation to social groups and, reciprocally, the constitution of those groups into which converts are incorporated.[19] Particularly from social scientific and socio-historical perspectives, conversion may be more about culture than creed, shaped more by social benefit than belief. Some theoretical models have depicted converts as relatively passive, subject to social forces and structures that generate needs and predispositions that serve as causes of conversion.[20] Counter-theories, then, have emphasized the autonomous seeker, willing and rational, with particular investments in social networks and patterns of social identification.[21] Most studies explore conversion not as crisis but as a characteristically lengthy and structured process mediated by complex social and ritual markers.[22] Scholarship on conversion is notably cross-disciplinary, with sociologists, psychologists, anthropologists, literary interpreters, and even neurobiologists of religion referring to and relying on one another's work.[23] Current studies tend to reflect the context of religious pluralism, marked by heightened awareness of religion as a political phenomenon. Anthropologist of religion Austin-Broos offers a complex and evocative description, working with the trope of *passage* in ways that recall the ancient figure of the *proselyte* as one who has "come over":

Conversion is a type of passage that negotiates a place in the world. Conversion as passage is also quest, a quest to be at home in a world experienced as turbulent or constraining or, in some particular way, as wanting in value. The passage of conversion is a passage to some place rather than no place. It is not a quest for utopia but rather for *habitus*. It involves a process of continual embedding in forms of social practice and belief, in ritual dispositions and somatic

experience. Cultural passage generally, and the passage of conversion in particular, are then more than 'travel' . . . , and they are more
than migration. Conversion involves an encultured being arriving
at a particular place.[24]

Even as conversion is theorized by some as a complex cultural passage, so
others attend to how conversion functions as a destabilizing activity in
society—that is, how conversion can mark departure from that which is
politically and socially settled. In the words of one cultural critic and literary interpreter, conversion alters "not only demographic patterns but
also the characterization of belief as communally sanctioned assent to religious ideology."[25] Another urges more such analysis of "the ways in which
conversion is not merely a passive or compliant survival strategy but a
creative form of resistance and even subversion."[26]

Within the study of ancient Judaism and Christianity, the ancient cultural terrain that Nock's study impressively mapped—placing Jewish and
Christian identity alongside civic religion, mystery cults, philosophical
schools—has since been traversed and extended by scholars with a more
multidisciplinary repertoire.[27] Historians and sociologists have examined
the rapid spread of early Christianity by studying broad patterns of social
affiliation—for example, mass conversions or steady patterns of proselytizing that resulted in realigned social identities.[28] So, too, scholars who
debate whether Judaism in antiquity was a missionizing religion focus on
what forms of social identification (including ritual practices) were
entailed in the complex ethno-religious boundary crossing involved in
becoming a Jew.[29] The question of how conversion within both Judaism
and Christianity may have been inflected by gender and social status has
also attracted extensive analysis. Did more women than men convert to
either Christianity or Judaism? Did conversion have different motivations,
processes, benefits, and risks for women than for men, or for higher- than
lower-status persons? A range of scholars examines the evidence for and
social dimensions (including status) of women's attraction to the early
Christian movement.[30] Some of them provide strong reminders that the
evidence for conversion in ancient Christianity and Judaism is textual and
therefore necessarily rhetorical and literary, not immediately available as
social phenomena but shaped by the polemical, hortatory, or narrative
interests of authors and tradents. Lieu remarks, "The gendering of conversion is a matter of rhetorical and not of statistical analysis. The move from

rhetoric to social experience must remain hazardous."[31] Such cautions need not, however, simply discourage the historical questions, but rather underscore the value of careful literary and rhetorical analysis. For, as Elizabeth Clark has argued, literary processes of representation are themselves matters for historical analysis.[32]

Increasingly, then, conversion is being examined in relation to how identity is constructed and contested in discourse, and particularly in narrative, a reflection of a broader turn toward narrative in the social and human sciences.[33] Simply put, stories function to create and refashion identity.[34] Researchers who focus on conversion stories observe that by shaping their own conversion stories in relation to a group's established narrative patterns and strategies, persons incorporate themselves into shared story lines, or resist them. One reviewer of conversion research in the social sciences concludes, "In my view, a new paradigm, what I call the biographical-narrative paradigm—is emerging."[35] Yet the link between conversion and narrative is hardly new. As Paula Fredricksen showed more than twenty years ago, conversion stories, like all stories, follow narrative conventions. The personal integration and coherence manifest in the conversion of a protagonist—in her analysis, Paul and Augustine in autobiographical conversion stories—are the result, in substantial measure, of the power of narrative to construct meaning and to grant coherence.[36] Some of the themes highlighted in conversion research may, then, be helpfully explored as themes of narratives and aspects of narrativity. In story, whether a protagonist's conversion involves passivity or agency, crisis or gradual process, social compliance or resistance, interiority or complex modulations of gender, status, or other forms of social identity—all are functions of narrative strategies, pace, and complications.

RESTRAINING DESIRE

Hermas, Thecla, and Aseneth all undergo the sort of reorientation of identity that may be termed conversion, and in each narrative, desire propels movement in plot and change in character. How, then, did ancient writers construct or construe the operations of desire? Tim Whitmarsh offers a helpful reminder of difference between ancients and moderns: ". . . Greek culture configured sexuality in radically different ways from those of the modern West, focusing upon *eros* as an ethical problem of self-mastery for the desiring subject."[37] Across a range of ancient genres, desire is frequently depicted as a disruptive force, threatening to the equilibrium, judgment, and even health of those affected. To draw from one example, in Chariton's novel *Chaereas and Callirhoe*, Eros has the power not only to afflict characters with debilitating symptoms of love-at-first-sight,[38] but also to reconfigure the social relations of elite families ("Eros likes to win and enjoys succeeding against the odds," the narrator notes).[39] The sway of Eros extends into the public sphere, as he functions as demagogue, compelling the gathered citizens of the city to advocate for the marriage of the hero and heroine: "Who could describe the assembly? It was dominated by Eros."[40] Each of the novel's three most prominent male characters—the Syracusan hero, Chaereas, the noble Ionian, Dionysius, and the Persian king, Artaxerxes—once they encounter the beautiful and noble Callirhoe, are thrown into a struggle between the disintegrative force of desire, and the need to maintain reason, virtue, and the capacity to fulfill their public duties and roles.[41] Dionysius provides a particularly sharp illustration. Smitten with desire, Dionysius reminds himself of his virtue, his age, his masculinity, and his public status, all in the attempt to counter passion: "There was a visible conflict in him now, between reason and passion; desire was flooding over him, but his noble soul tried to bear up against it; as if rising above the waves. . . . This was good sense; but Eros, who took his restraint as an insult, set himself against Dionysius and fanned to greater heat the blaze in a heart that was trying to be rational about love."[42] Rising above the most disruptive effects of desire, he protects the heroine from slavery, provides her the protection of legal marriage, becomes legal father to her child, yet is doomed to become the spurned male within the narrative logic of the romance. When Dionysius' loss of the heroine becomes inevitable, "he tried to endure what was happening to him in a spirit of nobility, drawing on his natural stability of character and his disciplined good breeding," but the struggle proves excruciating.[43]

The more sustained regulatory discourse of the period is found, of course, in the Greco-Roman schools of moral philosophy. Michel Foucault in his influential *History of Sexuality*[44] and many other scholars, before and since, argue that the principal philosophic problem of the age was the problem of the passions, including but not limited to eros. The remedy was a "conversion to the self," ἐπιστρέφειν εἰς ἑαυτόν, achieved through *askesis*; Pierre Hadot explains: "not asceticism, but the practice of spiritual exercises, thought taking itself as its own object of consideration, together with imagination and sensibility."[45] The philosophic schools certainly differed in their views of the constitution of the self and in particular diagnoses of the passions.[46] The Stoic Epictetus, for instance, suggests the most urgent concern is with "desires and aversions,"[47] since it is they that arouse the passions—inappropriate emotions caused by errors of judgment, in particular desire (*epithumia*), fear (*phobos*), intense pleasure (*hedone*), and grief (*lupe*).[48] Passions disturb the inner state and introduce "perturbations, tumults, misfortunes, and calamities; this is the spring of sorrow, lamentation, and envy; this renders us envious and emulous, and incapable of hearing reason."[49] Yet ancient philosophic writers concur in finding the cure for the passions in therapeutic methods, what Foucault calls "strategies" or "techniques" and Hadot terms "spiritual exercises"—ways of turning the governing attention of the self on the self. Philosophers of the Hellenistic period advocated practices of listening, of writing, and of habitual self-reflection, along with practices of abstinence intended to establish independence from the external world.[50] Seneca, for instance, recommends a nightly practice of self-interrogation, asking himself (once his wife is asleep) what ill he has done and what faults he has remedied,[51] along with other disciplines, such as examining one's thoughts, undertakings, companions, and even one's appreciation of the assistance of friendship.[52] Seneca's goal is, "this abiding stability of mind the Greeks call *euthymia*, 'well-being of the soul,' . . . I call it tranquillity."[53] Marcus Aurelius meditates on things he has read and thought, uses reading and writing as disciplinary exercises, resolves not to shirk public or familial duty, and deliberately contemplates the prospect of death.[54] The "invincible governing self" is his goal: "On this account the understanding free from passions is a citadel of refuge; for man has nothing stronger into which to retreat and be thereafter inexpungable."[55] Plutarch advocates similar techniques of self scrutiny for "making progress in virtue": examination of one's thoughts, actions, and dreams; interrogation of one's level of comfort around good people and one's tendencies to excuse personal errors; and the practice of confession.[56]

The goal for the Stoics is a "well-tensed," psychophysical whole—a structured self held in equilibrium; for a Platonist like Plutarch, the goal is stability achieved by the rational part of the self shaping and controlling nonrational desires and appetites.[57] But the philosophers also share a construction of virtue as highly gendered: the self that has achieved masculinity is characterized as active, self-controlled, self-contained; the feminized self, whether anatomically male or female, tends to be characterized as passive, lacking in boundaries, and penetrable.[58] So Philo at one point describes moral progress as "nothing less than the giving up of the female gender by changing into the male, since the female is material, passive, corporeal, and sense-perceptible, while the male is active, rational, incorporeal and more akin to mind and thought."[59]

Philo's *On the Virtues* provides a fascinating example of elite Greco-Roman ethical exhortation, marked by the disciplining of desire, but combined with an exploration of μετάνοια, repentance or conversion, which, in Philo's treatment, resembles the philosophic "conversion to the self," yet goes beyond it to include change or intensification in piety and cultural identification with Judaism. In the section on Manliness or Courage (ἀνδρεία) he declares that when thought is under threat from the tide of the passions (ὑπὸ τῆς τῶν παθῶν φορᾶς), self-control (σωφροσύνη) will lift it high.[60] A key element of humanity (φιλανθρωπία), he urges, is excellence in self-control (ἐγκράτειαν) and the other virtues (ἀρετάς).[61] Clearly linking virtuous self-control with the masculinity encoded in the term ἀνδρεία, Philo interprets scriptural prohibitions of cross-dressing as firm warnings against manly women (ἀνδρογύνους) as well as womanly men (γυνάνδρους).[62]

When Philo turns to μετάνοια, however, to some degree he departs from the usual emphases of Greco-Roman moral philosophers. Some scholars argue that μετάνοια understood as regret, changefulness, or disturbance of equanimity has uniformly negative connotations in pagan Greek writing, but there is some evidence to the contrary.[63] The *Tabula of Cebes* (a Hellenistic moralizing allegory thought to date to around the first century CE) describes μετάνοια as life enhancing and liberating, providing a release from ills and a path to true *paideia*.[64] Whereas Cicero may be cited for the negative Stoic view, "The philosopher surmises nothing, repents of nothing, is never wrong, never changes his opinion,"[65] Musonius Rufus (cited by Aulus Gellius) urges, "The mind . . . of a man who is listening to a philosopher. . . . unless he has completely lost his moral sense, in listening to the philosopher's words must shudder and feel secretly ashamed (*pudeat tacitus*) and repentant (*paeniteat*)."[66] Yet the difference between Cicero and Musonius may lie less in their views of repentance and more in the contrast between Cicero's philosopher and his presumed state of virtue, and Musonius's "man listening to a philosopher." Konstan judiciously notes that *metanoia* is "not a canonical virtue among classical thinkers" because it shows a deficiency in achieved virtue, and can only be a virtue in respect to an earlier state of error or vice.[67]

For Philo, the concepts of repentance and conversion come loaded with scriptural weight and use,[68] and his treatment of μετάνοια melds philosophic emphases with those precedents. The value of repentance for Philo also depends on one's achieved state: μετάνοια may seem to stand second to the virtues, but for any who do not participate in the absolute sinlessness of God or a divine man, repentance shows wisdom.[69] The fundamental turning is toward God.[70] The second, then, is the turn toward orderly self-governance and the abandonment of feminized and feminizing vice: The man who shows repentance passes, "from stupidity to knowledge of that of which ignorance is shameful, from folly to prudence, from lack of self-control (ἀκρατείας) to self-control (ἐγκράτεια), from injustice to justice, from cowardice to daring. For it is excellent and profitable to desert to virtue without turning around, abandoning vice, the treacherous mistress."[71] For Philo, such conversion seems to pertain both to converts to Judaism and to Jews in need of enhanced virtue and piety.[72] Perhaps to counter the associations of μετάνοια with frequent changefulness in an ethical discourse that emphasizes the controlled, restrained self, Philo elsewhere in his writings associates μετάνοια with stability. Repentance is "limited in quantity, and slow and future,"[73] "a firm and saving thing."[74]

The ancient Greco-Roman construction of desire as threat to the stable, virtuous, high-status, masculine self, and therefore in need of mastery or restraint is not only evident in ancient novels, philosophic writings, and theological texts, but is a hallmark of ancient rhetorical invective. In a wide-ranging recent analysis, Jennifer Knust has made plain the polemical and hortatory arsenal available in the ancient world relating to status, sex, and gender—the shaming strategies and polarizing characterizations by which high status, elite men in the agonistic public sphere could find, not only that desire threatened self-mastery, but that *public accusations* of unrestrained lust could threaten their exercise of social power.[75] Medical, literary, and political texts, she shows, provided "mutually reinforcing social codes" about status, sex, and gender, which in turn offered canons for recognizing the truly elite, truly male, truly virtuous.[76] Rhetorical treatises, both Greek and Latin, offered sexualized categories for praise and blame. "In the ancient context, sexual behavior was an important component of the production and maintenance of status. The freeborn, citizen male was thought to be—told he should be, claimed he was—in control of his passions. He avoids excess. He is the active partner in sexual acts. To fail in these areas is to fail as both a man and as a citizen."[77] Through analysis of first- and second-century Christian texts (including *The Shepherd of Hermas* and *The Acts of Paul and Thecla*), Knust shows that Christians very early began to participate in this rhetorical form of competitive power relations. Once they claimed that sexual self-control was the trademark of the Christian movement, slander then became "a potent weapon for distinguishing insiders from outsiders, policing group boundaries, and eliminating rivals."[78]

CONVERTING DESIRE

The destabilizing effects of desire and accompanying demand for self-control are clearly reiterated in a wide range of Greco-Roman texts. Desire prompts regulatory, disciplinary, sometimes conversionary practices in the shaping or reshaping of the self and the group. Yet other texts (or other moments in the same texts) also treat desire as playful and entertaining, or sometimes as productive of transformed selves. Whitmarsh notes, "counterbalancing this centripetal emphasis upon ethical propriety . . . stands a centrifugal pleasure in the indulgent, wandering play of sexuality. . . ."[79] In Chariton's novel, for example, during the revelation scene when Dionysius' love is utterly frustrated and Callirhoe and Chaereas reunited, the narrator underscores how entertaining the play of passions can be: "Who could fitly describe that scene in court? What dramatist ever staged such an astonishing story? It was like being at a play packed with passionate scenes, with emotions tumbling over each other—weeping and rejoicing, astonishment and pity, disbelief and prayers."[80] Certainly, as Simon Goldhill has shown, all the Greek novels stand as examples of the "lures, plays, delights" of ancient erotic narrative.[81]

So, too, do some moral philosophers. Plutarch at times argues, not that self-control restrains passion, but that moral virtue "stands in need of the instrumental ministry of the passions."[82] Indeed, for Plutarch, the experience of erotic desire is analogous to philosophic desire, and he quotes a favorite fragment from Sappho to make the point: "When a young woman has experienced a man, the heat in her eyes gives her away; and when a young man has experienced genuine philosophical progress, these lines of

Sappho's are relevant: 'I am tongue-tied, and delicate fire plays over my skin'—despite which, his gaze is unworried and his eye calm and you would want to hear him speak."[83] For this moralist, desire and restraint are mutually implicated in virtue. Plutarch's *Eroticus*, his dialogue on the merits of boy-love versus marriage, prompted by a rich widow's courtship of a young man, draws from Plato's *Symposium* and *Phaedrus*[84] to argue for the capacity of Eros to improve and elevate the lover: "For the mind (attains virtue and) affection, with the god's help, by traveling on the waves of emotion";[85] "Eros bears us up and directs our way, our kindly mystagogue in this our mystery."[86] Rather than being opposed to self-control, Eros may teach it, Plutarch claims, far better than an external, regulatory, shame-and-fear-driven version of self-control: "Eros, however, possesses within himself such a store of order, control, and faith that, even if he chances to lay hands on an intemperate soul, he turns it away from other lovers, knocks its audacity out of it, breaks its pride and indiscipline, gives it modesty, silence, quiet, and decency, and finally brings it into obedience to a single master."[87]

One scholar of ancient Christianity asks pointedly, and not rhetorically, "What does theology have to say about the place of eroticism in the salvific transformation of human subjects, even of the cosmos itself?"[88] Plutarch offers one kind of answer. Perhaps the ancient Greek novels suggest others. Zeitlin, at least, wonders, "But is more at stake in the narrativisation of desire: the journeys, the ordeals, the *Scheintods* (apparent deaths) and return to life, the constancy of the lovers, the themes of ascent and descent, and hopes of ultimate salvation in an eventual reunion?"[89] My goal here is to turn to three other ancient narratives, and to ask about the place of desire in the salvific transformation of three literary characters.

THE NARRATIVITY OF DESIRE AND CONVERSION

The Shepherd of Hermas, *The Acts of Paul and Thecla*, and *Joseph and Aseneth* all show evidence in their variegated textual traditions, versions, recensions, and (for two of them) reception histories that readers and hearers in antiquity were drawn to these stories. Desire for the tales generated scribes, and then malleable and multiform manuscript traditions, but most of all readers.[90] Peter Brooks, in his *Reading for the Plot*, suggests, "We can, then, conceive of the reading of plot as a form of desire that carries us forward, onward, through the text. Narratives both tell of desire—typically present some story of desire—and arouse and make use of desire as a dynamic of signification."[91] For all three of these texts, although their forms of narrativity may not conform to modern expectations, modern readers do well to explore, not only ancient constructions of gender, desire, and conversion, but ancient constructions of the "textual energetics" of narrative. Again, Brooks, "For the analyst of narrative, these different yet convergent vectors of desire suggest the need to explore more fully the shaping function of desire, its modeling of the plot, and also the dynamics of exchange and transmission, the roles of tellers and listeners."[92]

To help engage the distinct features of these stories, I draw insights from three theoretical approaches helpful in the literary analysis of desire and the changed self. In each case, my goal is not to "apply theory" as an overlay, but to place theoretical considerations alongside the text to see what kind of reciprocal insight, or perhaps interference, results.[93] As will be clear as the analysis proceeds, the story of Hermas is open to a kind of Foucauldian analysis of discursive strategies for self-scrutiny and self-formation in the disciplining of desires. Foucault gestures toward the ways Christian texts constructed a different relation with the self, and the hints are provocative for *The Shepherd of Hermas:* "What is called Christian interiority is a particular mode of relationship with oneself, comprising precise forms of attention, concern, decipherment, verbalization, confession, self-accusation, struggle against temptation, renunciation, spiritual combat, and so on."[94] In the Foucauldian view, disciplinary and self-restraining operations are not finally counter to desire, but mechanisms for the fabrication of pleasure or desire. So the inverse holds: desire is not unregulated, but inculcated by strategies of discipline and restraint. Asceticism, from Foucault's perspective, brings new and previously unavailable desires and satisfactions.

In *The Acts of Paul and Thecla*, the spare, quickly paced narrative, told in the third-person with little access to the interiority of the character, is marked by much movement of seeking, loss, and displacement initiated by Thecla's longing to be in the presence of Paul. Desire is made more problematic, however, in its aggressive eruptions, with Thecla as object, and complicated again as female and maternal figures defer aggressive eros. Analysis of this story may be given point by turning to theorists engaged in psychoanalytic interpretation of narrative. The point is not, of course, to psychoanalyze Thecla. Mieke Bal notes bluntly: "Characters don't have an unconscious, only people do. Psychoanalytic criticism does not, or should not, consist of diagnosing characters but of understanding how texts affectively address the reader on a level that comes close to unconscious preoccupations."[95] For reading *The Acts of Paul and Thecla*, I therefore draw intermittent insights from a selection of literary critics and theorists informed by psychoanalytic views of desire's displacements, movements, and returns.

For the third narrative, I turn from recent theorists to an ancient critic. The ancient author of *On the Sublime*, the literary critic known as "Longinus," explores the paradoxical interrelations of passion and discipline in ways helpful for a reading of *Joseph and Aseneth*.[96] Aseneth's transformation is recounted in a text marked periodically by intense profusions of tropes and by vivid image production. It proceeds by a rhetoric of astonishment that lingers over the disruption of the protagonist by desire, her dissolution of identity, her passionate elevation, and her reconstitution as a transformed self. Longinus is well suited to provide a critical vocabulary for and model of reader response to such literary strategies. Longinus urges an experience of sublime "transport," ἔκστασις, located not merely in the text, but in the reader, transport that comes about through the disciplines of the text and the disciplines of reading. Taken together, these theorists offer discrete ways to see desire as an expressive mode of self-restraint.

THE TEXTURES OF THE TALES

What interests me is the literary particularity of how *The Shepherd of Hermas, The Acts of Paul and Thecla*, and *Joseph and Aseneth* narrate conversion, understood necessarily within the broad cultural possibilities for the construction of desire, restraint, and identity transformation. The study will include comparative analysis, placing each text alongside others to which it has been or may be fruitfully compared. Nevertheless, the primary goal of this study is to offer three particular "glimpses through peepholes" into the large and ongoing construction project of a cultural poetics of desire, to borrow a memorable image and phrasing from an influential study of ancient sexualities.[97] Each analysis is in conversation with scholarship on the texts and related issues. My quotations from the three stories (in Greek and English) are selective but substantive to support the pace of analysis. I use few technical terms from narratology, but attend closely to the texts' structural and stylistic features. I also presuppose narrative coherence, knowing that presupposition must at times be qualified and at times defended for these stories with their fluid textual histories.[98] Though a certain level of paraphrase—of abstraction of the "basic story stuff"—is inevitable, my interest is in the artistic construction into which that story is molded, not merely the events themselves, but the way in which the reader learns about them from the narrator.[99] My goal is to be engaged in "the cogs of narrative" in "the relation of narrative and desire where it takes place, where that relation is materially inscribed in a field of textual practices."[100] Reading strategies are disciplinary, and can be seen as a training of desire—the creation of pleasure through close attention to the how and what of story. If Harpham is right that "resistance . . . is what prevents desire from moving at the speed of light and enables it to do its work,"[101] then perhaps the self-restraint of critical analysis may be construed as a form of resistance that might, in its best moments, enhance the desire and the pleasure of reading these three ancient stories.

TWO

Scrutinizing Desire

Hermas, Metanoia, and Manliness

THE *SHEPHERD OF HERMAS* GETS MIXED REVIEWS from readers. Lane Fox calls it "the jewel of the non-canonical writings."[1] Brown similarly remarks, "Few figures in the Early Church are as delightful or as open-hearted as Hermas."[2] Lawson, on the other hand, calls Hermas "a careless literary composer and a blundering theologian."[3] Hilhorst likewise charges Hermas with literary inconsistency, ethical incongruity, and the narration of improbable events, observing, "he is a dilettante author who simply is unable to compose a balanced work of literature."[4] In antiquity, *The Shepherd* seems to have prompted mostly favorable responses. Manuscript evidence and references by early Christian writers show that *The Shepherd* circulated widely and was much esteemed in some circles, sometimes even treated as scripture.[5] Clement of Alexandria, for instance, quotes *The Shepherd* frequently and favorably in the *Stromateis*, attributing the revelations Hermas received to "divine power."[6] Tertullian, however, dissents: In apparent contempt for the text's less-than-rigorist sexual ethic, he calls Hermas "lover of adulterers" and "shepherd of adulterers."[7]

Written in Rome in the late first or early second century CE (or in stages of composition or editing through that period),[8] *The Shepherd* recounts the revelatory experiences of its narrator and protagonist, Hermas. Most interpreters agree that the text's central concern is with μετάνοια, repentance or conversion, especially for believers who have sinned after baptism. The term, both as noun and verb, pervades all three sections of the narrative—the *Visions, Mandates* or *Commandments,* and *Parables* or *Similitudes*—as does a wider register of language of changing, turning, and renewal. Although some scholars, interested in a history of dogma, have read *The Shepherd* looking for the beginnings of an institutional discipline of penance,[9] μετάνοια here seems not so much a ritual or ecclesial mandate as a broad change of heart and social practice to which the protagonist, his household, and all the saints are called.[10] *The Shepherd* is sometimes said to answer the question of whether repentance is available after baptism by saying, "Yes, but only once." Yet the long, diffuse, varied narrative clearly has other interests beyond giving tidy answers. *The Shepherd* does at key junctures explore limits to μετάνοια: the time available for repentance is limited (*Vis.* 2.2.4–5 [6]); its postbaptismal frequency is limited, indeed, to once (*Mand.* 4.3 [31]); some will prove incapable of it (*Sim.* 8.6.2 [72]); others will prevaricate so long they will find themselves with a less desirable eschatological outcome (*Vis.* 3.7.5–6 [16]; *Sim.* 8.8.3 [74]). Yet throughout, the call to conversion or repentance issued both to and through Hermas is expansive. Limits seem to increase the urgency of the appeal, not curtail it.

Hermas is not merely the messenger of μετάνοια, but the *exemplum.* He narrates an ongoing and somewhat erratic process of self-examination and transformation, sometimes protesting his innocence, sometimes lamenting his corruption, and doing so in dialogue with a series of dream or visionary figures who variously castigate him for stupidity, praise him for virtue, and charge him with responsibility to minister to others. Such transformation of the self may be time limited, but it is also in this text time consuming, prolonged through repeated practices of scrutinizing the self and the community. The narrative offers multiple (indeed, sometimes interminable) discriminations of degrees and kinds of sin and shortcomings among believers, and a proliferation of imagery for envisioning change. In its preoccupation with the reformed self and in its narrative texture, *The Shepherd of Hermas* seems to offer a subelite, Christian counterpart to the more elite Greco-Roman texts that Michel Foucault so influentially studied: "'practical' texts, which are themselves objects of a 'practice.'. . . functional devices that would enable individuals to question their own conduct, to watch over and give shape to it, and to shape themselves as ethical subjects . . ."[11]

Christians in the second century wrote, as is now well recognized, in a social context in which elite ethical discourse was frequently framed by the problem of the passions and the therapy of desire.[12] In its depiction of Hermas's process of conversion or transformation, *The Shepherd* places great emphasis on the virtue of ἐγκράτεια, self-control or self-restraint, and at the same time incorporates surprisingly erotic elements in the narrative. Very early, the first of the heavenly revealer figures calls the protagonist, Ἑρμᾶς ὁ ἐγκρατής, "Hermas, the Self-Controlled" (*Vis.* 1.2.4). Yet this epithet is applied immediately after Hermas has been rebuked for ἡ πονηρὰ ἐπιθυμία, evil desire, arising from the narrative's opening scene, in which he helps his former mistress, Rhoda, out of the Tiber after bathing. Near the end of *The Shepherd*, the tension is sharp again, in the episode Dibelius termed "das Zwischenspiel von den Jungfrauen."[13] Hermas is rejuvenated by a night spent among twelve virgins, personifications of virtue, who dance, play, kiss him, then spend the night with him lying in their midst, praying (*Sim.* 9.11 [88]). The chastely seductive virgins have names: the first is Πίστις, the second, Ἐγκράτεια (*Sim.* 9.15.2 [92]). These erotically suggestive scenes are interludes, uncharacteristic of the tenor of the work as a whole. Indeed some interpreters find them egregiously inconsistent with the text's more conventional ethical concerns.[14] Yet given that the text opens with one such scene, the structure of the narrative suggests that the problem of desire and the relation between desire and self-restraint in the experience of μετάνοια warrant closer attention.

Although the more eroticized scenes in *The Shepherd* are infrequent, the terms ἐγκράτεια and ἐπιθυμία appear frequently; they are indeed workhorse words within this text's register of virtue language. The prominence of noun, adjective, and verb forms of ἐγκράτεια distinguishes Hermas from the relative infrequency of the term in biblical texts.[15] Though in later Christian texts it becomes a technical term for celibacy, the use here is broader.[16] Foucault describes the term's general usage in the moral philosophical tradition: "*Enkrateia*, with its opposite, *akrasia*, is located on the axis of struggle, resistance, and combat; it is self-control, tension, 'continence'; *enkrateia* rules over pleasures and desires, but has to struggle to maintain control."[17] In philosophical discussion, ἐγκράτεια may be related to and yet distinguished from other virtues of self-governance, particularly σωφροσύνη, but also αὐτάρκεια and sometimes ἀνδρεία.[18] The term is prominent, not only in pagan philosophical texts, but in some Jewish and Christian writings, including narratives such as 4 Maccabees, where it is depicted as the power that executes the sovereignty of pious reason over desire: "For reason is the guide of the virtues, but over the emotions it is sovereign. Observe now, first of all, that rational judgment is sovereign over the emotions by virtue of the restraining power of ἐγκράτεια. Ἐγκράτεια, then, is dominance over the desires. Some desires are mental, others are physical, and reason obviously rules over both" (4 Macc 1:32 NRSV, adapted).[19] In Hermas, however, virtue language is relatively undifferentiated. No fine distinctions are made among different terms for moderation, control, governance or even knowledge of the self: ἐγκράτεια seems to be the summary term for such moral-psychological functions, though connections to courage, understood as manliness, are indeed made. Furthermore, unlike in 4 Maccabees or in Philo, in Hermas ἐγκράτεια is related, not to λόγισμος, but to πίστις and καρδία; *The Shepherd* makes no philosophical argument that reason governs passions. The text's language for desire is similarly undifferentiated, with ἐπιθυμία in noun and verb forms being the word of choice.[20]

I propose, then, to examine the distinctive interplay between desire and self-restraint in *The Shepherd of Hermas*, and to do so not merely as an analysis of one motif in isolation, but as an entry point into the text's larger concern with μετάνοια and self-scrutiny. The opposition and interconnection of ἐπιθυμία and ἐγκράτεια also provide a starting place for analyzing the text's many and various dualisms—from its pervasive warnings against διψυχία, doublemindedness, to its multiple and sometimes self-deconstructive binary oppositions. Furthermore, the eroticized treatment of desire and the valuation of self-control bear on the text's constructions of gender: in particular, its repeated exhortations to manliness, often mediated through and sometimes exemplified by female figures. In undertaking this analysis, I will keep in view those readings of *The Shepherd of Hermas* that construe its eroticized elements merely as incidental diversions in an often monotonous narrative, or as titillating, attention-grabbing scenes that are inconsistent with the text's larger ethic, or as borrowings from pagan literature that contrive to make this nonelite text seem more learned. I contend, however, that a plausible, perhaps even compelling, reading of *The Shepherd of Hermas* may take the interplay of ἐπιθυμία and ἐγκράτεια to be linked with the text's larger aims of conversion. It shares with other more philosophic Greco-Roman texts a focus on, in Foucault's words, "the practices by which individuals were led to focus their attention on themselves, to decipher, recognize, and acknowledge themselves as subjects of desire, bringing into play between themselves and themselves a certain relationship that allows them to discover, in desire, the truth of their being, be it natural or fallen."[21] With due cautions about whether "between themselves and themselves" can adequately characterize a text that presupposes revelation and divine accountability, and about how individual this text's concerns are, *The Shepherd of Hermas* invites analysis of the conversion of the self through the narrative scrutiny of desire.

SITUATING *THE SHEPHERD OF HERMAS*

To analyze Hermas, we do well to begin with what kind of text it is and what kind of study it has attracted. *The Shepherd of Hermas* is long, loose, and repetitive. Its Greek style is relatively simple, and both its characteristic syntax and its larger organization are paratactic. Overall, the text manifests a level of language use that Carolyn Osiek has argued is "close to oral thought patterns" and intended for oral proclamation.[22] Apparent theological and literary inconsistencies along with the evidence of the manuscript tradition have led to debates over whether *The Shepherd* is more likely the work of a single author, perhaps working in stages, or of several successive authors. Among the theories of multiple authorship, that of Stanislas Giet has gained the best hearing. Giet postulates three authors and three layers of composition, then explores the implications of reading the text as though it has an internal dialectic between successive authors.[23] Others, however, including Philippe Henne and J. Christian Wilson, have made compelling cases for single authorship and literary unity.[24] Henne, for instance, demonstrates that writers such as Clement of Alexandria and Origen cite Hermas from all sections of *The Shepherd*. Moreover, *The Shepherd*'s prominent concerns—especially its call for μετάνοια and its concern for the needs of the poor and the obligations of the wealthy—are pervasive. Most recent scholars, then, assume that the rambling narrative is the work of a single hand, with some allowing for stages of composition or editing over time.[25]

    The Shepherd has also received considerable attention for the ways it does and does not seem to fit the genre of apocalypse. To some extent, conclusions vary depending on how fixed or fluid an understanding of the genre is employed. Like other literary apocalypses, *The Shepherd* features visions mediated by otherworldly figures, time-limited offers of repentance, warnings of impending tribulation, elaboration of apocalyptic parables, instructions to write the visions so others may read them, and other key elements.[26] Yet it lacks a strong emphasis on imminent eschatology and shows little of the historical and political concerns of many Jewish and Christian apocalypses. Furthermore, its symbolism lacks the intensity and compression that characteristically convey a sense of apocalyptic urgency or crisis. Hermas's visions are explained so fully and at such a relaxed pace that they evoke more tedium than mystery or intensity; his one apocalyptic beast marked with four symbolic colors makes a brief appearance, then collapses quickly into the dust as Hermas hurries by (*Vis.* 4.2.9 [23]). Many scholars have therefore concluded that *The Shepherd* is apocalyptic in form but not in content, or that it is a kind of attenuated apocalypse.[27] Yet recognizable markers of apocalyptic form are present and do shape the reader's expectations, whether satisfying or disrupting them. Carolyn Osiek has offered a nuanced discussion of how the text turns apocalyptic form toward paraenetic function.[28] Edith Humphrey also offers a perceptive summary of the genre debate, emphasizing that in Hermas, as in other apocalypses, the range of literary devices demands participation of the reader in the revelation that unfolds.[29] *The Shepherd* shares with other apocalypses the absorption of various subgenres, including narrative, visions, auditions, wisdom sayings, and parables.

Apart from genre discussions, a long strand of Hermas scholarship has been devoted to tracing other literary parallels. A range of Jewish texts that are dualistic in their moral configurations have been usefully compared to *The Shepherd*, ranging from the Qumran *Manual of Discipline* to the *Testaments of the Twelve Patriarchs* to rabbinic commentaries on the two inclinations in the human heart. Greco-Roman paraenetic literature has also invited comparisons. One text in particular, the *Tabula of Cebes*, has been held up for comparison to *The Shepherd* for its two-ways morality, its feminine personifications of virtue and vice, and its emphasis on μετάνοια.[30] Dating to the early empire, the *Tabula* offers an *ekphrasis* of a tablet on display in the temple of Cronus. The tablet portrays the path into life, which all enter by drinking a cup of deceit. Travelers then proceed to paths and enclosures that represent choices between persisting in deception or finding the path to true παιδεία, leading to knowledge, and ultimately to true happiness. Along the way, feminine personifications represent a range of virtues and vices. Some women represent δόξαι, ἐπιθυμίαι and ἡδοναί (honors, desires, and pleasures) that may lead to either salvation or destruction (VI.2). Two named Ἐγκράτεια and Καρτερία (Self-Restraint and Patience), "radiant and healthy in body," help pull travelers up a steep precipice on the path to Παιδεία (XVI.2). The key to life is an encounter with a feminized Μετάνοια (XI.1). Although scholars roughly a century ago argued that Hermas was literarily dependent on Cebes,[31] the current consensus is that the similarities point to some degree of shared cultural and literary background.[32] Indeed, that conclusion—common background, but not literary dependence—is constant across virtually all history-of-traditions studies of Hermas. It applies also to *The Shepherd's* borrowings from the conventions of pagan bucolic and erotic literature, which will invite further discussion.

Hermas makes his usual literary home among the "Apostolic Fathers"—a collection of noncanonical texts, most of which date approximately to the first half of the second century CE and express theological, ecclesial, and ethical views that are precursors of later orthodoxy.[33] Only one other in this corpus, *The Martyrdom of Polycarp*, is a narrative. Two of them, *1* and *2 Clement*, invite comparison to *The Shepherd* for their emphases on repentance, restraint, and desire. *1 Clement* itself is a letter from the church at Rome to the church at Corinth, addressing some kind of congregational strife that is, in fact, ill-defined (44.6), and the church at Rome writes to urge peace and harmony, εἰρήνη and ὁμόνοια.[34] Repentance and turning, μετάνοια and ἐπιστροφή, are both emphasized at key moments in the letter. Unlike in Hermas, however, it is not desire in its various forms that conditions repentance (erotic motifs are virtually absent in *1 Clement*), but disorder: "pointless toil and strife and the jealousy that leads to death" (9.1).[35] Furthermore, μετάνοια is precipitated not, as in Hermas, by self-scrutiny or revelation, but by the acceptance of church hierarchy and discipline:"Thus you who laid the foundation of the faction should be subject to the presbyters and accept the discipline that leads to repentance, falling prostrate in your heart" (57.1). Overall, Clement recommends repentance, peace, and subordination in place of the self-exalting tendencies that are disrupting communal life.

With *2 Clement*, however, the register of virtue language becomes more similar to *The Shepherd*.[36] This early Christian homily—of uncertain provenance, dating to sometime in the second century—is shot through with warnings about the dangers of fleshly desire, ἐπιθυμία, inimical to God's will and a danger to anyone who wants to attain the kingdom of

God. Those who desire (ἐπιθυμεῖν) to acquire "these worldly things" (τὰ κοσμικὰ ταῦτα) fall away from the way of righteousness (5.6–7). We conquer the soul by refusing to do its evil desires (τὰς ἐπιθυμίας αὐτῆς τὰς πονηράς) (16.2). Having listened to the presbyters in church, the trick is not to get dragged away by worldly desires (τῶν κοσμικῶν ἐπιθυμιῶν) once at home (17.3). Indeed, empty desires (ἐπιθυμιῶν τῶν ματαίων) affect memory and self-awareness; they "darken the understanding" (19.2). The alternative, then is self-restraint, ἐγκράτεια. Though this key virtue is mentioned only twice, its importance is clear early in the text because it stands in first position in a key virtue list: "We should be self-restrained (ἀλλ᾽ ἐγκρατεῖς εἶναι), charitable, and good" (4.3).[37] Then, at the end of the subsequent long section of moral exhortation, before turning to eschatological warnings, the preacher uses ἐγκράτεια as the signal term to summarize all he has so far said:[38] "I do not think I have given trivial advice about self-restraint (ἐγκράτειας). And whoever takes my advice will have no regrets, but will instead save both himself and me, the one who has given the advice" (15.1). The movement from desire to restraint, from waywardness to good works, is conditioned by μετάνοια.[39] Like Hermas, 2 Clement insists that the opportunity to repent is time limited and therefore urgent, yet also steadily available to believers (8.2). Yet for this author, repentance is characterized more by acts of charity than by reflection or interrogation of the self—it is a way to pay God what is due (9.7–8), respond to the sermon (19.1), and disregard sexual difference (12.5–13.1).[40] 2 Clement's moral suasion remains rooted in polarized contrasts. He offers none of the complicating elements we shall find in Hermas, where erotic attraction can be an impulse for transformation and renewal in order to "live to God."

In the last two decades, The Shepherd, like others of the Apostolic Fathers, has also become an intriguing resource for social historians of early Roman Christianity. Less hierarchical in its view of church order than Clement of Rome, The Shepherd has much to say about the dangers of wealth (Vis. 3.6.5–7 [14]), the risks of overindulgence in luxuries (Mand. 12.1–2 [44–45]), and the neglect of reciprocal obligations between rich and poor members of a congregation (Sim. 2 [51]). Hermas is warned by his otherworldly mediators about preoccupations with business, about dishonesty in business, and about the dangers of pagan friendships (Mand. 10.1.4 [40]). These and other elements of the text have prompted insightful study of The Shepherd's evidence for social stratification in Rome in the early second century.[41] Socio-historical and theological study connect in Peter Lampe's recent argument that "*one* aim of Hermas's call to repentance is the reintegration of the secularized wealthy into the active church life, so that financial resources for the care of the Christian poor will flow again."[42]

What kind of text, then, is *The Shepherd of Hermas?* Whether read with other literary apocalypses or other Apostolic Fathers, whether considered a resource for theology or for social history, *The Shepherd* presents itself as a narrative. The point, however obvious, is worth making. Unlike most of the Apostolic Fathers, Hermas is neither epistle nor tractate nor manual nor homily, but story. Granted, it is an odd sort of story, perhaps not riveting to most modern readers. There is, in fact, minimal plot—little action, but much talk. Long passages are given to description, as Hermas relates the visions he is given. Much more is didactic statement, and not merely in the *Mandates* section, though especially there—moral exhortation sometimes delivered directly to Hermas, and sometimes expressed in the second person plural, with the Christian community as intended audience. Significantly, all sections of the story are punctuated by dialogue: by questions and answers that pass between Hermas and his revealers as well as by Hermas's internal debates. Nevertheless, despite the preponderance of talk and minimization of action, Hermas repeatedly inserts indications of changes of setting and the passage of time between episodes—reminders that he is telling a story. And through the long, meandering course of the narrative, Hermas as protagonist is changed. *The Shepherd* merits analysis as a narrative.

One consequence of approaching *The Shepherd* as story is that one may set aside the longstanding attempts to determine which elements of the text may be deemed "autobiographical" and which "fictional."[43] One may still, of course, discriminate between socio-historically plausible and implausible elements (plausible, for instance, that an early Christian might be a freedman; less plausible that a Roman *matrona* would bathe naked in the Tiber) and expect that nonautobiographical narrative may speak to and critique real social circumstances. But scholarly claims of autobiography are not only unverifiable; they are not particularly relevant if a divide is maintained between the categories of human person and of character— that is, if Hermas is approached as narrator and protagonist. Analyzing *The Shepherd* as narrative also encourages one to examine how explicit, didactic statements made in one section of the text may be related to narrative elements elsewhere. For example, the account of μετάνοια offered in the *Mandates* seems complicated and nuanced by the parabolic explorations of it in the *Similitudes*. On the other hand, there is remarkable coherence in the treatment of ἐπιθυμία in both narrative and didactic sections, taken together. Finally, narrative analysis helps explore how the form and function of *The Shepherd* are related—how this tale with its uneven, frequent recapitulations of the processes of dialogue and decipherment depicts the process of transformation that it also explicitly urges. What follows, therefore, is a diachronic reading with close look at selected passages, combined, however, with more synchronic analysis that draws together motifs and emphases from various parts of *The Shepherd*.

THE BATHING WOMAN AND THE EVIL DESIRE

The Shepherd opens with a concise rendering of a provocative scene:

> 1. Ὁ θρέψας με πέπρακέν με Ῥόδῃ τινὶ εἰς Ῥώμην· μετὰ πολλὰ ἔτη ταύτην ἀνεγνωρισάμην καὶ ἠρξάμην αὐτὴν ἀγαπᾶν ὡς ἀδελφήν. 2. μετὰ χρόνον τινὰ λουομένην εἰς τὸν ποταμὸν τὸν Τίβεριν εἶδον καὶ ἐπέδωκα αὐτῇ τὴν χεῖρα καὶ ἐξήγαγον αὐτὴν ἐκ τοῦ ποταμοῦ. ταύτης οὖν ἰδὼν τὸ κάλλος διελογιζόμην ἐν τῇ καρδίᾳ μου λέγων· μακάριος ἤμην εἰ τοιαύτην γυναῖκα εἶχον καὶ τῷ κάλλει καὶ τῷ τρόπῳ. μόνον τοῦτο ἐβουλευσάμην, ἕτερον δὲ οὐδέν.

> 1. The man who raised me sold me to a certain Rhoda in Rome; after many years I became reacquainted with her and I began to love her as a sister. 2. After a certain time I saw her bathing in the Tiber river, and I gave her my hand and drew her out of the river. When I saw her beauty I reasoned in my heart, "I would be blessed if I had a wife of such beauty and character." This was the only thing I intended, nothing more. (*Vis.* 1.1.1–2 [1])[44]

In a succession of relatively brief clauses, the story begins with compressed allusions to the speaker's personal history and slight details of a potentially erotic scene rendered so sparingly and quickly that they are scarcely grasped before being disclaimed. A man helps a beautiful woman out of a river, and the sensual possibilities of the scene are ironically emphasized by the denial of the "more" that Hermas might have thought. The episode echoes bathing scenes from Greek and Roman literature, as many scholars have pointed out.[45] But unlike Teiresias blinded by watching Athena bathing,[46] or Acteon destroyed by glimpsing Diana,[47] or even Chloe aroused by watching Daphnis,[48] here there is no lingering view and no initial delineation of the psychology of desire. A reader recalling other such literary scenes, however, might wonder whether there will be dire consequences for this voyeur. Most scholars argue that Rhoda's river bath is historically implausible, but this apparent borrowing from literature is merged with socially more plausible details. For instance, the text's opening emphasizes status differentiation and a social circumstance not uncommon in early Christianity: Hermas, apparently now a freedman, has in some unspecified past time been Rhoda's slave. There are indications of his emotions and thoughts: he "loves her as a sister"—perhaps loves her without erotic desire, or perhaps "sister" here implies fellow Christian. He insists that the reasonings "in his heart" are licit, but their innocence is quickly challenged. At rapid narrative pace, then, the story's opening lines introduce an erotic scene, realistic details about social status, and explanations or decipherments of the narrator's inner state—all features that will recur in the long, rambling text that follows.

The passage continues by repeating the indefinite chronological marker, "some time later." Hermas describes conditions that further characterize him as a devout person, now being prepared for a revelatory experience: while walking to the countryside, glorifying God's creatures, he falls asleep and is transported by a spirit to an isolated, impassable terrain, where his markedly pious action is to begin confessing his sins. Rhoda, whom he concedes is τὴν γυναῖκα ἐκείνην ἣν ἐπεθύμησα, "that woman whom I desired," appears to him, having crossed, inexplicably, from the social world to become the first of Hermas's heavenly revealers. As she announces that God is angry at him for sinning against her, Hermas protests:

ἀποκριθεὶς αὐτῇ λέγω· εἰς σὲ ἥμαρτον; ποίῳ τρόπῳ; ἢ πότε σοι
αἰσχρὸν ῥῆμα ἐλάλησα; οὐ πάντοτέ σε ὡς θεὰν ἡγησάμην; οὐ
πάντοτέ σε ἐνετράπην ὡς ἀδελφήν; τί μου καταψεύδῃ, ὦ γύναι,
τὰ πονηρὰ ταῦτα καὶ ἀκάθαρτα;

Answering her I said, "Did I sin against you? In what way? Or when have I spoken a shameful word to you? Have I not always regarded you as a goddess? Have I not always respected you as a sister? Why do you falsely accuse me, woman, of these evil and unclean things?" (*Vis.* I.1.7 [1])

With his defense of speech, thoughts, and attitude, Hermas's denials include not just the specific opening incident, but his behavior toward Rhoda "always." The "always" that applies to respecting her as a sister seems in tension with the opening claim that it was upon reacquaintance with her that the sisterly regard began. And the defense that he has regarded her as a "goddess" is curious.[49] Rhoda's laughing, perhaps mocking, response echoes the reference to Hermas's "heart" and the language of desire that Hermas has already used, but now labels that desire as evil: ἐπὶ τὴν καρδίαν σου ἀνέβη ἡ ἐπιθυμία τῆς πονηρίας; "The desire for evil did arise in your heart" (*Vis.* 1.1.8 [1]).[50] Rhoda diagnoses Hermas's predicament as that of the upright man who has intended to do evil.

The opening *Vision*, then, puts desire, self-control, and self-knowledge in problematic relation. Hermas acknowledges that he desired Rhoda, but denies that his desire was anything but innocent. Yet he is, her more authoritative voice from heaven insists, wrong about himself. Perhaps his error is in failing to recognize essentially erotic elements in his desire.[51] Jung, memorably, took this part of the *Shepherd* to show "the repressed erotic impression in the unconscious has activated the latent primordial image of the goddess, which is in fact the archetypal soul-image."[52] Or perhaps "this evil desire" may not be simply sensual—perhaps it implies a desire for status elevation, or a kind of domestic discontent. In any case, problems are raised at the outset: if Christians are as culpable for desires as for deeds,[53] the question of how one can know whether one's desires are innocent becomes acute. At this stage the reader might also wonder, can there be innocent forms of desire? Are all forms of ἐπιθυμία equivalent to ἐπιθυμία πονηρά? Already, a key task of self-scrutiny has emerged for Hermas: "to untwist a sinew of peculiarly private motivation in his own heart."[54] Yet the peculiarly private is not exclusively so. Rhoda's concluding exhortation indicates that if Hermas will pray to God, God will heal a widening circle of sins: Hermas's own, those of his household, and those of all the saints (*Vis.* 1.1.9 [1]). Indeed, movement among those spheres, all in need of μετάνοια, characterizes the remainder of the *Visions*, mediated to Hermas by four successive appearances of a female revealer, all said to represent the church.

As Hermas is left in trembling self-interrogation, there appears, "an elderly woman in a shining garment with a book in her hands," who offers both praise of Hermas's usual character and confirmation of his sin:

ἡ δὲ ἔφη· μηδαμῶς ἐπὶ τὸν δοῦλον τοῦ θεοῦ τὸ πρᾶγμα τοῦτο. ἀλλὰ πάντως ἐπὶ τὴν καρδίαν σου ἀνέβη περὶ αὐτῆς. ἔστιν μὲν τοῖς δούλοις τοῦ θεοῦ ἡ τοιαύτη βουλὴ ἁμαρτίαν ἐπιφέρουσα· πονηρὰ γὰρ βουλὴ καὶ ἔκπληκτος εἰς πάνσεμνον πνεῦμα καὶ ἤδη δεδοκιμασμένον, ἐὰν ἐπιθυμήσῃ πονηρὸν ἔργον, καὶ μάλιστὰ Ἑρμᾶς ὁ ἐγκρατής, ὁ ἀπεχόμενος πάσης ἐπιθυμίας πονηρᾶς καὶ πλήρης πάσης ἁπλότητος καὶ ἀκακίας μεγάλης.

But she said, may this thing never be to a slave of God. But assuredly something did arise in your heart concerning her. To God's slaves, such an intention brings sin; for it is an evil and startling intention to a fully devoted and already approved spirit, if one should desire an evil deed, and especially for Hermas, the self-restrained, who abstains from every evil desire and is full of all simplicity and great innocence. (*Vis.* 1.2.4 [2])

Paradoxically, Hermas is both guilty of desire and exemplary of self-restraint. The tension is not further explored here, however, for the divine charge against Hermas shifts abruptly, away from the episode with Rhoda, and toward the supposed real cause of the Lord's anger: Hermas's domestic negligence, his failure to correct or control his children.

THE *VISIONS*: DECIPHERING HOUSEHOLD, CHURCH, SELF

As the *Visions* continue, various kinds of sins and shortcomings are exposed. The moral instruction is plain, sometimes proverbial, yet carried by shifting vehicles of revelation, virtually all of which demand decipherment: verbal pronouncements require explanation; a mysterious little book is incomprehensible until revelation is offered; a visionary spectacle of a tower under construction warrants an allegorical reading; finally, the variable appearance of the revealer herself bears meaning.[55] All of these media are subsumed in the overarching revelatory framework of dreams or visions, characteristically "mobile, many-faceted, metaphoric."[56]

The insistence on a process of decoding is striking in the diagnosis of Hermas's household. Initially, the elderly lady explains straightforwardly that, as a consequence of parental lenience and excessive affection, Hermas's children have become rebellious and require discipline (*Vis.* 1.3.1–2 [3]). This rather plain instruction then gives way to a mysterious reading of terrifying words from a little book, which have broad application far beyond Hermas's family, some words being intended for the Gentiles and apostates, others for the righteous (*Vis.* 1.3.3–4 [3]). A year later, when the elderly lady makes her second appearance to Hermas, she entrusts another little book to him for copying, which he does letter by letter since he cannot distinguish between syllables, much less elicit meaning (*Vis.* 2.1.4 [5]).[57] Only after a fifteen-day period of fasting and petition is Hermas given understanding of the book's contents, and they turn out to be a far more vehement denunciation of his household. His children are not only rebellious but betrayers of their parents, given to extreme licentiousness and lawlessness (*Vis.* 2.2.2 [6]). His wife is overly talkative, stereotypically so, it seems, perpetrating evil with her speech (*Vis.* 2.2.3 [6]). Hermas himself is now charged, not merely with lenience and excessive affection, but with neglect of both children and wife, then warned against holding grudges against them (*Vis.* 2.3.1 [7]). μετάνοια from the whole heart is required, and the process enjoined upon the household is paradigmatic for the church as well (*Vis.* 2.2.4 [6]), as are the dangers of refusal or denial (*Vis.* 2.2.8 [6]). Response is urgent: Revelation will lead to forgiveness for those who have sinned μέχρι ταύτης τῆς ἡμέρας, "until this day" if they "repent from their whole heart and remove doublemindedness from their heart" (*Vis.* 2.2.4 [6]). Further sinning "once this day has been determined/appointed," however, will preclude salvation. The phrase "this day," then, may indicate the narrative present, or may serve as a less definite eschatologically appointed day. In either case, "repentance/conversion has a limit point (τέλος) for the righteous" and that limit will come sooner than the last day, the final limit for the outsiders/gentiles (τοῖς ἔθνεσιν) (2.2.5 [6]). Household trouble, however prosaic, is in this text a topic for urgent revelation and decoding.

Deciphering the church is far more intricate. The old woman revealer, whom Hermas mistakes for the Sybil, herself represents the church, and so, too, does the tower which she explains to him. The church both reveals and is that which is revealed.[58] In *Vision* 3, Hermas views the square tower being constructed by six young men, and the many kinds of stones, representing types of people, who may or may not be incorporated into the building. The long, allegorizing interpretation (though not nearly as long as the later *Similitudes*) distinguishes some as wholly admirable—the particularly eminent apostles, bishops, teachers, and deacons, as well as those who have suffered on account of the name of the Lord—and others as wholly contemptible—those who have completely abandoned God and no longer consider repenting. Many, however, are of mixed status: some who have sinned but wish to remain; others who know the truth but do not remain; others who are partly righteous, partly lawless; still others who have both faith and wealth. In a more economical text, some such categories could surely be combined. In Hermas, however, multiplication of distinctions seems the point of this first allegory. The length of the interpretation helps convey that the relation of individuals to the church, and their need, capacity, or eligibility for μετάνοια, is not self-evident but requires both scrutiny and revelation.

The figure of the elderly woman is variously interpreted by two young men, who make brief appearances. Hermas is first told that she appears old because the church was created before anything else (*Vis.* 2.4.1 [8]). Later, however, he asks why she has appeared to him in progressively younger forms and is told by a second male revealer that the church, experiencing personal and communal transformation, is being rejuvenated: "And so those who completely repent will become new and well-established (νέοι ἔσονται καί τεθεμελιωμένοι, those who have repented from their whole heart" (*Vis.* 3.13.4 [21]). The rejuvenation of the elderly lady serves as figure for both individual and communal repentance.[59] That the church is both tower and woman, and that the woman is variously explained and fluid in form provides a vivid instance of how polyvalent *The Shepherd*'s imagery can be.[60]

Allegorical figures, cryptic writings, and individual desires all, it seems, demand interpretation. Yet in the *Visions* section of *The Shepherd*, interpretation seems a strenuous, unpredictable, and sometimes risky business. Some interpretations come to Hermas after periods of fasting and prayer, others only after periods of waiting, still others only after sharp rebukes for requesting them. Even strategies that seem unfailingly commendable in a Christian text, such as confession of sin, can be unpredictable here. The first time Hermas describes himself confessing his sins, he is unaware of the one sin he has apparently just committed (*Vis.* 1.1.4 [1]). Later, as he confesses his sins, he is rebuked and told to begin praying for righteousness as well (*Vis.* 3.1.5 [9]). Yet the unevenness of this narrator-protagonist's attempts to gain understanding further emphasizes the practices of self-scrutiny and corporate scrutiny that are being employed.

VISIONS OF MANLINESS

Neither Rhoda nor Hermas's desire for her are explicitly mentioned again in *The Shepherd*. The scene nevertheless affects a reading of what follows. The opening interaction not only initiates the subsequent decipherment of self, household, and church, but also heightens sensitivity to the gender dynamics of the text. Manliness is emphasized early in the *Visions*, and receives particular emphasis in three passages. As the first *Vision* concludes, the elderly lady, smiling, issues her parting charge: ἀνδρίζου, Ἑρμᾶ, "Be a man," "Play the man," or "Be courageous, Hermas" (*Vis.* 1.4.3 [4]). Coming at the close of the episode in which Hermas has faced Rhoda's accusations of evil desire and the church's accusations of failure to govern his household, manliness here seems to entail both the role of *pater familias*[61] and the challenge to grapple with the problem of desire. The connection between manliness and control of desire is then reinforced in *Vision* 3 as Hermas is offered a view of seven women supporting the tower that is under construction. After Faith, the second in order and seemingly in importance is Ἐγκράτεια, a reminder that the protagonist has already been called, Ἑρμᾶς ὁ ἐγκρατῆς (*Vis.* I.2.4 [2]). This feminine personification models manliness, both in appearance and action:[62]

> ἡ δὲ ἑτέρα, ἡ περιεζωσμένη καὶ ἀνδριζομένη, Ἐγκράτεια καλεῖται· αὕτη θυγάτηρ ἐστὶν τῆς Πίστεως. ὃς ἂν οὖν ἀκολουθήσῃ αὐτῇ, μακάριος γίνεται ἐν τῇ ζωῇ αὐτοῦ, ὅτι πάντων τῶν πονηρῶν ἔργων ἀφέξεται, πιστεύων ὅτι ἐὰν ἀφέξεται πάσης ἐπιθυμίας πονηρᾶς, κληρονομήσει ζωὴν αἰώνιον.

> The next, wearing a belt and behaving like a man, is called Self-Restraint; she is the daughter of Faith. Whoever follows her will be blessed in his life, because he will abstain from all evil deeds, believing that if he abstains from every evil desire, he will inherit eternal life. (*Vis.* 3.8.4 [16])

Her work, or rather, her beneficent effect, is described as opposition to evil desire. One more passage in *Vision* 3 further enhances the delineation of manliness. In the course of explaining why the elderly lady revealer has looked younger with each appearance, Hermas is asked to consider the plight of a hopeless older person facing bodily weakness and poverty; receiving news of an inheritance, the old man grows strong, stands, is rejuvenated in spirit, "And he no longer sits, but acts like a man (ἀνδρίζε-ται)" (*Vis.* 3.12.2 [20]). Becoming manly enables the weakened older man to set aside his μαλακία, his softness or effeminacy (*Vis.* 3.12.3 [20]).[63] Notably, becoming manly is likened to the transformation that accompanies receiving revelation: You (plural) are like this, the young man mediating revelation says, when you are hearing the revelation that the Lord has been revealing to you (*Vis.* 3.12.2 [20]). Throughout the *Visions*, acting the man involves strength, vigor, readiness to work, readiness to receive revelation, and, emphatically, self-control over evil desires.[64]

The manliness motif in *The Shepherd* has been astutely analyzed by Steve Young, who traces ways that Hermas's transformation is aided by the feminine figures, in the *Visions* as mediators, later as companions.[65] Rhoda, Young argues convincingly, is progressively displaced in the text. His characterization of Rhoda as role model seems a bit overstated, since she is introduced in the text as object of desire, not object for emulation. Yet the succession of female figures does provide an ironically feminized transformation to masculinity, at least until the male shepherd takes over in *Vision* 5 as mediator. The elderly lady's voice replaces Rhoda's in *Vision* 1; Hermas, formerly Rhoda's slave, is shown the benefits of "serving as a slave" to the seven virtues represented by the women around the tower (*Vis.* 3.8.8 [16]); and *Vision* 4 represents the church as a youthful bride, veiled and dressed in white (*Vis.* 4.2.2 [23]), a modest object of admiration nicely supplanting the bathing Rhoda and Hermas's desire for "such a wife" (*Vis.* 1.1.2 [1]). The displacement, however, does not seem to function as a redirection of desire; that is, throughout the *Visions*, the female figures are not eroticized, not described as beautiful or seductive. Even when Hermas finds himself in a secluded spot with a couch draped in linens, awaiting an appointment with a female revealer, his fears are quickly quieted and the exchange that takes place turns into a discussion of why only the persecuted are worthy to sit on the lady's right side (*Vis.* 3.1 [3]). The real-world displacement of Rhoda, of course, is with Hermas's own wife, whom he is urged to neglect no longer (*Vis.* 2.3.1 [7]), but even that relationship may soon be celibate

(*Vis.* 2.2.3 [6]). In the *Visions* of *The Shepherd of Hermas*, desire seems to be supplanted by the revelatory process and the virtue of ἐγκράτεια rather than replaced with alternate forms of desire; the *Mandates* and the *Similitudes*, however, will complicate this pattern.

In the last of the *Visions*, female revealers are replaced by the honorable-looking man dressed as a shepherd, whom Hermas identifies as' ὁ ἄγγελος τῆς μετανοίας, the angel of repentance (*Vis.* 5.7 [25]). Despite the earlier emphasis on repentance as time limited and urgent, the process is evidently of long duration: this representative of the believer's transformation will live with Hermas for the rest of his life (*Vis.* 5.2 [25]). In a candid admission of the text's repetitiveness, the shepherd claims that his mission is to reiterate what Hermas has already seen. And in a gesture toward the text's intended function, Hermas is given yet another writing task, now recording not mysteriously encoded words, but ἐντολὰς καὶ παραβολάς, commandments and parables, or (as translators of Hermas have often rendered the terms) mandates and similitudes, which may be kept through a repetitive process of reading and repentance (*Vis.* 5.7 [25]).

THE *MANDATES:* DUALISMS MULTIPLY AND DIVIDE

In the *Mandates* section, the narrative alternates between didactic presentation in the shepherd's voice (with occasional reminders that Hermas is relating the shepherd's words) and periodic interjections of dialogue. The strong emphasis on ἐγκράτεια and ἐπιθυμία continues. The two terms stand at the beginning and end, respectively, of the shepherd's commandments. *Mandate* 1 begins with three commands: believe God is one, fear God, and φοβηθεὶς δὲ ἐγκράτευσαι, "as you fear, be self-restrained." The command to be self-restrained stands out as distinctive when grouped with the more conventional, more biblically familiar pair that precede it. ἐπιθυμία, then, is the subject of the shepherd's closing words in the *Mandates*—or rather, of both apparent "conclusions." In the midst of *Mandate* 12, the shepherd summarizes, "And everyone enslaved to good desire (τῇ ἐπιθυμίᾳ τῇ ἀγαθῇ) will live to God," and Hermas remarks, "and so he finished the twelve mandates" (*Mand.* 12.3.1 [46]). Summary statements in *The Shepherd* rarely preclude more talk, however, so after several more sections, the angel of repentance again concludes, emphasizing desire: "And all who purify their hearts from the empty desires of this age (ἀπὸ τῶν ματαίων ἐπιθυμῶν τοῦ αἰῶνος τούτου) will also guard them, and they will live to God" (*Mand.* 12.6.5 [49]).

With ἐγκράτεια at their head and ἐπιθυμία at their close, the *Mandates* between are marked by repeated dualisms.[66] Underlying them is the cosmic opposition between God and the devil, with contrary spirits arranged around each. There is spatial dualism—two ways in which people may walk: the just in a straight, level path; the unjust in a crooked, hard path.[67] Many virtues and vices are presented as tidy oppositions: righteousness versus wickedness (1.1), truth versus lies (3), patience versus irascibility (5), cheerfulness versus grief (10), false prophets versus true prophets (11).[68] Doublemindedness, διψυχία, is strongly proscribed (9)—in an ethically dualistic world, one must not doubt or waver.[69]

When the *Mandates* turn explicitly to matters of sexuality (*Mand.* 4), they address the ethical concerns of the married, male householder: adultery (committed by the wife, that is), divorce as a consequence of adultery, and remarriage after such a divorce or after a spouse's death.[70] Strict marital fidelity is unequivocally required, with advice that resonates with *The Shepherd*'s opening scene: Hermas is enjoined not to allow anything to rise up in his heart concerning someone else's wife, or similar evils, and to remember always his own wife (*Mand.* 4.1.1 [29]). Interestingly, the *Mandate*'s explicit discussion of μετάνοια (chapters 2 and 3) is embedded within the discussion of marriage protocols (chapters 1 and 4), an order that has led some interpreters to suggest that the text has suffered rearrangement.[71] Yet, as with the opening scene, perhaps issues of sexuality provide particularly probing instances of the need for and processes of transformation: "'To repent,' he said, 'is a great understanding' (σύνεσίς ἐστιν μεγάλη)" [4.2.2 (30)]. The text sets up a clear homology between its instructions on marital reconciliation and its instructions on repentance.[72] How many times should a husband take back an adulterous wife? Once, for μετάνοια ἐστιν μία, "there is one repentance" (4.1.8). How many times may a believer who has been corrupted return to God? Once, for μίαν μετάνοιαν ἔχει, "he or she has one repentance" (4.3.6 [31]). To sin and repent repeatedly, however, brings no benefit (4.3.6 [31]). The possibility of repentance and restoration complicates the *Mandates*' oppositional categories by creating a means for crossing them, at least once.

In other respects also, the dualistic tendencies of the *Mandates* are not so tidy. The shepherd's teachings often trace the "inner workings" of the virtues and vices, linger over the inner divisions of the heart or soul. The shepherd warns that there are two spirits within humans: a holy spirit, identified by patience and spaciousness, who may be cramped or crowded out by the presence of the evil, irascible spirit (*Mand.* 5.2 [34]). One must keep an eye on the interior self. Furthermore, a person has, the shepherd says, not only an externalized choice between two ways in which to walk (*Mand.* 6.1.2–5 [35]), but two angels within—one righteous, one wicked— an observation that makes Hermas interject that he needs to know their "inner workings" since they both dwell with him (6.2.2 [36]).[73] With another strong echo of the "thought rising up" language of Rhoda's accusation (*Vis.* 1.1.8 [1]), the shepherd insists that even a thought from the wicked angel rising up in the heart of an extremely faithful man will compel him to sin, just as a thought from the righteous angel in an extremely wicked man or woman will compel a good act (6.2.7–8). Knowledge of the self as doubled and divided heightens the need to explore "inner workings," to discern how dualities are to be accepted, exploited, or resisted.

Whereas in the earlier *Visions*, ἐγκράτεια and ἐπιθυμία seemed to form an opposed pair in agonistic relation, in the *Mandates*, the shepherd complicates that dualism by asserting that they, too, are twofold. *Mandate* 8 begins,

> Εἶπόν σοι, φησίν, ὅτι τὰ κτίσματα τοῦ θεοῦ διπλᾶ ἐστι· καὶ γὰρ ἡ ἐγκράτεια διπλῆ ἐστιν. ἐπί τινων γὰρ δεῖ ἐγκρατεύεσθαι, ἐπί τινων δὲ οὐ δεῖ.

> "I told you," he said, "that the creations of God are twofold, for self-restraint is also twofold. For it is necessary to exercise self-restraint from some things, but not necessary from other things." (*Mand.* 8.1 [38])

Two rather conventional vice lists follow to explain when ἐγκράτεια *is* to be exercised, and two virtue lists to explain ἃ δὲ δεῖ σε μὴ ἐγκρατεύεσθαι, "those things from which you must not restrain yourself . . ." (*Mand.* 8.7 [38]). Some elements are less typical of moralists' vice and virtue lists and more characteristic of Hermas's distinctive ethical concerns. Behaviors that disrupt Christian community include not only decalogue proscriptions like adultery, robbery, and false witness, but also "evil luxury, many kinds of food and the extravagance of wealth" (*Mand.* 8.3 [38]). Recommended virtues include not only love, righteousness, and truth, but the socially concrete acts of "serving widows, looking after orphans and those in need, redeeming God's slaves from distress, being hospitable (for doing good is sometimes discovered in the practice of hospitality) . . ." (*Mand.* 8.10 [38]). It is not clear why the text offers two of each kind of list, except that the strategy conforms to the text's principle of copiousness: There is always something more to say about vice or virtue. What seems most noteworthy in *Mandate* 8, however, is that the key ethical standard of ἐγκράτεια must itself be scrutinized with respect to its objects. Whereas the kind of ἐγκράτεια involved in avoiding evil is a combative self-mastery, the kind of ἐγκράτεια involved in doing good is a release of restraint, a release of control, a simple movement into the doing of good without resistance or particular self-effort: ἐὰν τὸ ἀγαθὸν ποιῇς καὶ μὴ ἐγκρατεύσῃ ἀπ᾽ αὐτοῦ, ζήσῃ τῷ θεῷ, καὶ πάντες ζήσονται τῷ θεῷ οἱ οὕτω ποιοῦντες, "If you do good and do not restrain yourself from it, you will live to God, and everyone who acts in this way will live to God" (*Mand.* 8.12 [38]). Perhaps for *The Shepherd*, the doing of good does not admit of excess, and, therefore, does not require self-mastery. For Hermas, paradoxically, one form of ἐγκράτεια maintains control; another form yields it.

The *Mandates* then underscore that there are also two forms of ἐπιθυμία. According to *Mandate* 12, desire in all its manifestations is not evil *per se*. Rather, one must hate evil desire and instead choose good desire. The specification of ἐπιθυμίαν τὴν ἀγαθὴν καὶ σεμνήν, "good and reverent desire," occurs here for the first time in *The Shepherd*. Its occurrence highlights the fact that throughout the text, ἐπιθυμία is virtually always qualified, specified as "desire for evil" or "desires for women" or "desires of this age"—its negative associations carried by the modifiers. "Clothing" is the metaphor for appropriation of good desire. Eschewing evil desire is more vividly imagined as breaking a wild horse:

1. Λέγει μοι· ἆρον ἀπὸ σεαυτοῦ πᾶσαν ἐπιθυμίαν πονηράν, ἔνδυσαι δὲ τὴν ἐπιθυμίαν τὴν ἀγαθὴν καὶ σεμνήν· ἐνδεδυμένος γὰρ τὴν ἐπιθυμίαν ταύτην μισήσεις τὴν πονηρὰν ἐπιθυμίαν καὶ χαλινα-γωγήσεις αὐτὴν καθὼς βούλει· 2. ἀγρία γάρ ἐστιν ἡ ἐπιθυμία ἡ πονηρά, καὶ δυσκόλως ἡμεροῦται·

1. He said to me, "Remove every evil desire from yourself, and clothe yourself with the good and holy desire, for if you have clothed yourself with this desire you will hate the evil desire and will guide it with a bridle just as you intend. 2. For the evil desire is wild, and tamed with difficulty. (12.1.1–2a [44])

Evil desire's wildness is finally capable, not just of throwing riders, but of consuming them:[74]

φοβερὰ γάρ ἐστι, καὶ λίαν τῇ ἀγριότητι αὐτῆς δαπανᾷ τοὺς ἀνθρώπους· μάλιστα δὲ ἐὰν ἐμπέσῃ εἰς αὐτὴν δοῦλος θεοῦ καὶ μὴ ᾖ συνετός, δαπανᾶται ὑπ' αὐτῆς δεινῶς. δαπανᾷ δὲ τοὺς τοιούτους τοὺς μὴ ἔχοντας ἔνδυμα τῆς ἐπιθυμίας τῆς ἀγαθῆς, ἀλλὰ ἐμπεφυρμένους τῷ αἰῶνι τούτῳ. τούτους οὖν παραδίδωσιν εἰς θάνατον.

For it is fearsome, and consumes people with its extreme wildness; but especially, if a slave of God, being senseless, falls into it, that one will be terribly consumed. It consumes such as are not clothed with the good desire, but are mixed up in this age. These therefore will be handed over to death. (12.1.2b [44])

As the revealer articulates the kind of works characteristic of the evil desire, he again recalls *The Shepherd's* opening scene, and also closely echoes the vices that are the object of necessary ἐγκράτεια in *Mandate* 8:

Πάντων προέχουσα ἐπιθυμία γυναικὸς ἀλλοτρίας ἢ ἀνδρὸς καὶ πολυτελείας πλούτου καὶ ἐδεσμάτων πολλῶν ματαίων καὶ μεθυσμάτων καὶ ἑτέρων τρυφῶν πολλῶν καὶ μωρῶν· πᾶσα γὰρ τρυφὴ μωρά ἐστι καὶ κενὴ τοῖς δούλοις τοῦ θεοῦ.

Above all is the desire for someone else's wife or husband, and for the extravagance of wealth and for many useless foods and intoxicating drinks, and other numerous and foolish luxuries. For every luxury is foolish and empty for God's slaves. (12.2.1 [45])

Imagery of clothing and horse taming yields to military conflict, then, as Hermas is urged to arm himself with the fear of God and actively resist evil desire, which will flee for fear of such a weapon. Good desire, on the other hand, invites not resistance, but submission, even enslavement. *The Shepherd* offers a military parable of conquest, surrender, and enslavement:

σὺ οὖν νῖκος λαβὼν καὶ στεφανωθεὶς κατ' αὐτῆς ἐλθὲ πρὸς τὴν
ἐπιθυμίαν τῆς δικαιοσύνης, καὶ παραδοὺς αὐτῇ τὸ νῖκος ὅ ἔλαβες·
δούλευσον αὐτῇ καθὼς αὐτὴ βούλεται. ἐὰν δουλεύσῃς τῇ ἐπιθυμίᾳ
τῇ ἀγαθῇ καὶ ὑποταγῇς αὐτῇ, δυνήσῃ τῆς ἐπιθυμίας τῆς πονηρᾶς
κατακυριεῦσαι καὶ ὑποτάξαι αὐτὴν καθὼς βούλει.

Therefore, when you seize victory against it and are crowned, come
to the desire of righteousness, and give to her the crown which you
took. Serve as slave to it, just as it wishes. If you serve the good
desire as slave and in submission to it, you will be able to dominate
the evil desire and subdue it just as you wish. (*Mand.* 12.2.5 [45])

The freedman who began his narrative with an account of unwitting
desire for the one to whom he was formerly enslaved, who was urged by
the woman-church revealer to enslave himself to personified virtues led
by Faith and Self-Restraint (*Vis.* 3.8.8 [16]), is now again urged to serve as
a slave of desire—carefully qualified, of course, as *good* desire. The result is
a paradoxical manliness of subjection: dominance and strength come from
servitude.

In the *Mandates'* prolonged didacticism, where does the protagonist
continue to emerge? Hermas initiates questions, most memorably the
question about an adulterous wife, but others as well. He pointedly admits
that he is aware of the duality of spiritual entities that dwell with him.
There are occasionally surprising twists in the conversation. After the
shepherd's exhortation to "Love the truth," Hermas interrupts with
abject and sweeping self-condemnation, saying that he has never in his
life spoken a single true word, but has always portrayed his lies as truth to
others (3.3–3). Paradoxically, the shepherd commends him for truthful
self-incrimination about lies, and promises that the lies may become
trustworthy when the truthful confession of lies is found true (3.3.5). At
the close of the *Mandates*, Hermas expresses doubt about his ability (or
anyone's) to meet the standards therein. The shepherd's response is
extreme, so angry that his appearance changes frighteningly. Then, inexplicably, he relents, "and began speaking to me more gently and cheerfully, and he said, 'You foolish, senseless, and doubleminded man . . . '"
(12.4.1–2). If these are the gentle, cheerful words, one can scarcely imagine the angry ones. The exchange introduces a small drama (and perhaps
humor) into the lengthy paraenetic instruction. The dialogic elements in
the *Mandates* work to remind the reader that Hermas is not merely

receiving instruction, but undergoing transformation—an active, though erratic, discursive process.

RESTRAINT, EXTRAVAGANCE, AND COMMUNITY FORMATION

As the shepherd begins to communicate through similitudes or parables, the subgenre is not altogether new. Parabolic elements have been used in the *Mandates*, and ethical commandments continue through the *Similitudes*. Here, however, the moralizing, allegorizing, deciphering tendencies already evident earlier in *The Shepherd* are extended, relaxed, and elaborated significantly. One need not expect pithy Gospel-style parables. Yet some imagery from the Gospels does appear: slaves and landlords, sheep and shepherds, agricultural fields, lords who make unexpected visits. The first four of the *Similitudes* are relatively brief, at least by the text's diffuse standards. The first two—the slaves of God living in a foreign land, and the elm tree and the vine—both have as their tenor exhortations for the right use of wealth and the vital interdependence of rich and poor. Here, as in the *Mandates* with their complications of ἐγκράτεια and ἐπιθυμία, restraint or abstinence is not represented as a good in itself; ethical choices must be made about what Hermas and his community withhold themselves from or give themselves to. Even extravagance may be transmuted. The shepherd urges rich Christians to spend their wealth on widows, orphans, and those in distress, then concludes:

> 10. αὕτη ἡ πολυτέλεια καλὴ καὶ ἱλαρά, λύπην μὴ ἔχουσα μηδὲ φόβον, ἔχουσα δὲ χαράν. τὴν οὖν πολυτέλειαν τῶν ἐθνῶν μὴ πράσσετε· ἀσύμφορον γάρ ἐστιν ὑμῖν τοῖς δούλοις τοῦ θεοῦ· 11. τὴν δὲ ἰδίαν πολυτέλειαν πράσσετε, ἐν ᾗ δύνασθε χαρῆναι· καὶ μὴ παραχαράσσετε μηδὲ τοῦ ἀλλοτρίου ἅψησθε μηδὲ ἐπιθυμεῖτε αὐτοῦ· πονηρὸν γάρ ἐστιν ἀλλοτρίων ἐπιθυμεῖν. τὸ δὲ σὸν ἔργον ἐργάζου, καὶ σωθήσῃ.

> 10. This extravagance is fair and cheerful; it holds neither grief nor fear, but joy. So do not practice the extravagance of the Gentiles, for it is unprofitable to you, God's slaves. 11. But do practice your own extravagance, in which you can rejoice; and neither debase nor touch nor desire that which belongs to someone else; for to

desire what belongs to another is evil. Do your own work, and you will be saved. (*Sim.* 1.10–11 [50])

One may abandon oneself to a ministry to the poor, luxuriate in supporting widows and orphans. Extravagance, luxury, loss of restraint—all manifest the problematics of desire,[75] and in the ethical practice advocated by the *Shepherd of Hermas*, all may be redeemed by redirection to virtuous objects or ends. Graydon Snyder remarks, "The Christian life is not negative discipline but positive release and enjoyment of the power of the holy Spirit. Such luxuries are good . . ."[76] In particular, "indulgence" of such desires is incumbent upon wealthy Christians, who are invited in *Similitude* 2's image of the elm and the vine to recognize their symbiotic interdependence with poor Christians.[77] The second parable culminates in an extraordinary beatitude, a blessing on the wealthy unusual in early Christian discourse: "Blessed (μακάριοι) are those with possessions who understand that they have been made wealthy from the Lord; for the one who understands this will be able to minister something good" (*Sim.* 2.10 [51]). Again, renunciation is a qualified value in this text.

Many of the parables depict tasks of community discernment, emphasizing that differences are sometimes difficult to ascertain. Just as one cannot easily tell from bare trees in winter which are alive and which are not, so, too, sinners and righteous persons can look deceptively similar (*Sim.* 3 [52]). Budding trees may be distinguishable from withered trees in the spring, but one must wait for summer to know which will truly be fruitful (*Sim.* 4 [53]). The most extended elaboration of how difficult it is to discriminate among kinds of Christians and to determine to what degree each is righteous or not comes in *Similitude* 8. Hermas is given a vision of an extraordinary willow tree, "that spread its shade out over plains and mountains; and all those who have been called by the name of the Lord came under the shadow of the willow" (*Sim.* 8.1 [67]). A glorious angel cuts sticks from the willow, distributes them to people in its shade, then takes them back. The sticks have become varied: some moth-eaten, some withered, some split, some green, some budding—the distinctions are multiple. Time passes, and the similitude continues, and people who have planted their sticks in the ground are now asked to show them for discrimination of their state, to see whether growth can be renewed in them (*Sim.* 8.4 [70]). Hermas is no mere spectator, but is told to put on an apron and assist in the sorting (8.4.2–3 [70]). The multiplication of discriminations seems itself to be the point of the parable—the varying ratios of vitality and corruption are allegorized as representing particular kinds of transgressions that require repentance (*Sim.* 8.6–11 [72–77]).

The three parables between *Similitude* 4 and 8 also warrant attention, as they reiterate similar themes, yet take some surprising turns. *Similitude* 5 begins with instruction to Hermas about fasting: Proper and improper means of fasting can be confused if fasting is not rooted in communal charity and support (*Sim.* 5 [54]). The instruction on fasting then introduces a parable of a vineyard owner, his slaves, and his son. One particular trustworthy slave entrusted with the vineyard in the owner's absence surpasses the work expected of him and is honored by the owner, being made a son. When Hermas asks to have the parable explained, the shepherd first gives an explanation about what constitutes a proper fast, then surprisingly offers a second interpretation that bears on the text's view of manliness. The Son of God, startlingly, is represented in the parable not by the son (who represents the Spirit), but by the slave who was especially honored. With a fluid pneumatology and christology, the shepherd explains:

> 5b. αὕτη οὖν ἡ σάρξ, ἐν ᾗ κατῴκησε τὸ πνεῦμα τὸ ἅγιον, ἐδούλευσε τῷ πνεύματι καλῶς ἐν σεμνότητι καὶ ἁγνείᾳ πορευθεῖσα, μηδὲν ὅλως μιάνασα τὸ πνεῦμα. 6a. πολιτευσαμένην οὖν αὐτὴν καλῶς καὶ ἁγνῶς καὶ συνκοπιάσασαν τῷ πνεύματι καὶ συνεργήσασαν ἐν παντὶ πράγματι, ἰσχυρῶς καὶ ἀνδρείως ἀναστραφεῖσαν, μετὰ τοῦ πνεύματος τοῦ ἁγίου εἵλατο κοινωνόν.

> 5b. And so this flesh, in which the Holy Spirit dwelled, served the Spirit well, walking in reverence and purity, in no way defiling the Spirit. 6a. And so having lived well and purely, cooperating with the Spirit and working together in every work, behaving in a strong and manly way, he chose it to be a partner with the Holy Spirit. (*Sim.* 5.6.5b–6a [59])

The passage suggests an adoptionist Christology,[78] but its interest seems to lie at least as much in the possibility of how flesh and spirit may function, not as polarities, but as a unitive whole, an emphasis that seems at least as much about anthropology as about christology.[79] Indeed, the conclusion the shepherd goes on to draw, is that "All flesh that has been found undefiled and spotless, and in which the Holy Spirit has dwelled, will receive a reward" (*Sim.* 5.7 [60]). Manliness here may be construed as the self-restrained conduct of the flesh that suits it for the indwelling of Spirit.

Similitudes 6 and 7 add further complications to the notion that appearances are deceptive and μετάνοια is vital. Despite the *Mandates'* previous endorsement of cheerfulness and condemnation of bitterness, and despite the text's general pattern that personifications of good appear attractive if not glorious, the shepherd here shows Hermas a young, cheerful shepherd dressed in yellow whose flock is luxuriously fed, frisky, and cheerful (*Sim.* 6.1 [61]) and a second large shepherd with a wild appearance, a bitter look, and a subdued flock (*Sim.* 6.5 [65]). The attractive shepherd turns out to be the angel of luxury and deceit; the wild one is the angel of punishment. The moral, simply put, is that punishment should be preferred to pleasure if μετάνοια is to be had. The exposition of the parable spills into *Similitude* 7, where Hermas complains that the angel of punishment has taken up residence in his own disordered household, and that given that they have all now repented from the whole heart, the affliction should be over. At this point in this very long narrative, the reader may find little surprise and perhaps wry humor in the shepherd's response: that repentance doesn't work immediately (εὐθύς). For μετάνοια to be "strong and pure," it must bring hardship, involve the whole household, and take time (*Sim.* 7.4–6 [66]).

By the time *The Shepherd* reaches *Similitude* 9, which stretches for a third of the length of the entire text, readers unconvinced by Giet's arguments for multiple authorship will nevertheless agree with his characterization that ". . . l'auteur est un moraliste dont la manie didactique brave la monotonie et la fatigue . . ."[80] In *Similitude* or *Parable* 9, erotic motifs emerge again, and the tension between desire and self-restraint is vividly dramatized. Although Hermas begins in his familiar role of watcher and auditor, part way through he becomes participant in the enactment of the parable. Here, the shepherd promises to reveal to Hermas a more accurate version of what he learned earlier through the Church in virgin form: the construction of the tower from *Vision* 3 is now retold, with significant differences and developments. Alerting both Hermas and the readers to the likelihood that erotically charged events may ensue, the shepherd takes his charge "out to Arcadia, to a certain mountain shaped like a breast . . ." (*Sim.* 9.1.4 [78]). The shepherd shows Hermas a plain surrounded by twelve mountains, whose physical appearance and conditions for life are carefully described. In this bucolic setting, a tower is being constructed on a rock in the midst of the plain, and around the tower are stationed twelve virgins (recalling the seven women whom Hermas encountered in *Vision* 3). The description of their dress, appearance, and demeanor is carefully rendered.

> 3. κύκλῳ δὲ τῆς πύλης εἱστήκεισαν παρθένοι δώδεκα. αἱ οὖν τέσσαρες αἱ εἰς τὰς γωνίας ἑστηκυῖαι ἐνδοξότεραί μοι ἐδόκουν εἶναι· καὶ αἱ ἄλλαι δὲ ἔνδοξοι ἦσαν. εἱστήκεισαν δὲ εἰς τὰ τέσσαρα μέρη τῆς πύλης, ἀνὰ μέσον αὐτῶν ἀνὰ δύο παρθένοι. 4. ἐνδεδυμέναι δὲ ἦσαν λινοῦς χιτῶνας καὶ περιεζωσμέναι ἦσαν εὐπρεπῶς, ἔξω τοὺς ὤμους ἔχουσαι τοὺς δεξιοὺς ὡς μέλλουσαι φορτίον τι βαστάζειν. οὕτως ἕτοιμαι ἦσαν· λίαν γὰρ ἱλαραὶ ἦσαν καὶ πρόθυμοι. 5. μετὰ τὸ ἰδεῖν με ταῦτα ἐθαύμαζον ἐν ἐμαυτῷ, ὅτι μεγάλα καὶ ἔνδοξα πράγματα ἔβλεπον. καὶ πάλιν ἠπορούμην ἐπὶ ταῖς παρθένοις, ὅτι τρυφεραὶ οὖσαι οὕτως ἀνδρείως εἱστήκεισαν ὡς μέλλουσαι ὅλον τὸν οὐρανὸν βαστάζειν.

3. Around the gate stood twelve virgins. The four who stood at the corners seemed to me to be more glorious, though the others were also glorious. They stood at the four sides of the gate, with two virgins between them. 4. And they were dressed in linen tunics and attractively girdled, their right shoulders bare, as if they were about to bear a load. Thus they were ready. For they were extremely cheerful and eager. 5. After I had seen these things, I wondered within myself, because I was seeing great and glorious things. And again I was at a loss concerning the virgins, for although they were delicate, they stood like men as though they were prepared to bear the whole world. (*Sim.* 9.2.3–5 [79])

The seven γυναῖκες (*Vis.* 3) now become twelve παρθένοι. The virgins are not merely girdled, but attractively so; with their bared right shoulders, their appearance is both glorious and delicate. Whereas in *Vision* 3, only the woman called Ἐγκράτεια was said to look and act like a man, here all twelve stand in a courageous or manly fashion.[81] The virgins' function, then, is to carry rocks to help six men build the tower. And the shepherd later emphasizes that their role is essential to the transformation of the stones, representing individual believers, into fit elements with which to build the tower, the church: "For if . . . they are not carried through the gate by the hands of these virgins, they cannot change their colors" (*Sim.* 9.4.8 [81]).

As the Lord of the tower arrives to oversee its construction, Hermas receives lengthy explanations of which of the initially rejected stones can be sufficiently reshaped to fit into the building. Then, twelve more female figures make a striking appearance, drawn in careful contrast to the previous twelve (*Sim.* 9.9.5 [86]). Whereas the first are virgins (παρθένοι), these are women (γυναῖκες). Those were dressed in linen tunics, belted, with one shoulder bare; these are in black garments, belted, with both shoulders bare. Whereas the former stood in a delicate, yet brave or manly manner, these seem savage, with loose hair. Though the virgins are said to be "glorious," the women are not ugly, but "extraordinarily beautiful." Their function is the obverse of the other group: they carry away from the tower stones that have been rejected and deemed irremediable. Yet despite being load bearers, they do not merit the highly valued term, "manly."[82] Vividly sketched and clearly attractive, both the delicate-yet-manly virgins and the savage women serve as images of desire that pull, quite literally, in opposite directions in the text's view of Christian formation.[83]

The erotic possibilities of the group of twelve virgins are then made acute as the shepherd leaves, and Hermas finds himself left alone with the virgins for a day and a night. Hermas the *Enkratic* is nervous, perplexed about what to do, whether to stay, how to conduct himself:

2. λέγω αὐταῖς· ἐκδέξομαι αὐτὸν ἕως ὀψέ· ἐὰν δὲ μὴ ἔλθῃ, ἀπελεύσομαι εἰς τὸν οἶκον καὶ πρωῒ ἐπανήξω. αἱ δὲ ἀποκριθεῖσαι λέγουσί μοι· ἡμῖν παρεδόθης· οὐ δύνασαι ἀφ᾽ ἡμῶν ἀναχωρῆσαι. 3. ποῦ οὖν, φημί, μενῶ; μεθ᾽ ἡμῶν, φασί, κοιμηθήσῃ ὡς ἀδελφός, καὶ οὐχ ὡς ἀνήρ. ἡμέτερος γὰρ ἀδελφὸς εἶ, καὶ τοῦ λοιποῦ μέλλομεν μετὰ σοῦ κατοικεῖν· λίαν γάρ σε ἀγαπῶμεν. ἐγὼ δὲ ᾐσχυνόμην μετ᾽ αὐτῶν μένειν.

2. I said to them, "I will wait for him until evening, but if he does not come, I will go home and return in the morning." But they said to me in reply, "You were handed over to us; you cannot leave us." 3. "Where, then," I said, "will I stay?" They said, "You will sleep with us as a brother and not as a husband. For you are our brother, and from now on we are going to live with you, for we love you exceedingly." But I was ashamed to remain with them. (*Sim.* 9.11.2–3 [88])

In response to Hermas's shame, the virgins initiate a kind of holy dalliance, playful and sensual:

4. καὶ ἡ δοκοῦσα πρώτη αὐτῶν εἶναι ἤρξατό με καταφιλεῖν καὶ
περιπλέκεσθαι· αἱ δὲ ἄλλαι ὁρῶσαι ἐκείνην περιπλεκομένην μοι
καὶ αὐταὶ ἤρξαντό με καταφιλεῖν καὶ περιάγειν κύκλῳ τοῦ πύργου
καὶ παίζειν μετ᾽ ἐμοῦ. 5. κἀγὼ ὡσεὶ νεώτερος ἐγεγόνειν καὶ ἠρξάμην
καὶ αὐτὸς παίζειν μετ᾽ αὐτων· αἱ μὲν γὰρ ἐχόρευον, αἱ δὲ ὠρχοῦντο,
αἱ δὲ ᾖδον· ἐγὼ δὲ σιγὴν ἔχων μετ᾽ αὐτῶν κύκλῳ τοῦ πύργου περι-
επάτουν καὶ ἱλαρὸς ἤμην μετ᾽ αὐτῶν. 6.ὀψίας δὲ γενομένης
ἤθελον εἰς τὸν οἶκον ὑπάγειν· αἱ δὲ οὐκ ἀφῆκαν, ἀλλὰ κατέσχον
με. καὶ ἔμεινα μετ᾽ αὐτῶν τὴν νύκτα, καὶ ἐκοιμήθην παρὰ τὸν
πύργον.

4. And the one who seemed to be first among them began to kiss
me and embrace me, and the others, seeing her embrace me,
began to kiss me themselves, and to lead me around the tower and
play with me. 5. And it was as if I had become younger, and I
myself began to play with them; for some were doing choral
dancing, and others dancing, and others singing. But I kept silence
with them, walking around the tower with them and I was
cheerful with them. 6. When evening came, I wanted to return
home. But they would not permit me, but kept me back. I stayed
through the night with them and slept beside the tower. (*Sim.*
9.11.4–6 [88])

Hermas's reluctance, his repeated attempts not to be alone with these
virgins, is an apt expression of concern to protect his male integrity.[84]
He insists, therefore, that the inescapable interaction with the virgins is
emphatically chaste.

7. ἔστρωσαν γὰρ αἱ παρθένοι τοὺς λινοῦς χιτῶνας ἑαυτῶν χαμαί,
καὶ ἐμὲ ἀνέκλιναν εἰς τὸ μέσον αὐτῶν, καὶ οὐδὲν ὅλως ἐποίουν εἰ
μὴ προσηύχοντο· κἀγὼ μετ᾽ αὐτῶν ἀδιαλείπτως προσηυχόμην
καὶ οὐκ ἔλασσον ἐκείνων. καὶ ἔχαιρον αἱ παρθένοι οὕτω μου
προσευχομένου. καὶ ἔμεινα ἐκεῖ μέχρι τῆς αὔριον ἕως ὥρας
δευτέρας μετὰ τῶν παρθένων.

7. For the virgins spread out their linen tunics on the ground, and
made me lie down in their midst, and they did nothing whatsoever
except pray; and I prayed with them unceasingly, and not less than
they. And the virgins rejoiced that I was praying thus. And I stayed
there until about eight o'clock the next morning, with the virgins.
(*Sim.* 9.11.7 [88])

Both Otto Luschnat and Martin Dibelius have noted rich parallels in pagan literature to this scene's images of rejuvenation as a consequence of cultic dance or an encounter with the Muses.[85] Tracing possible sources, however, does not fully account for how the scene functions in *The Shepherd*. And, indeed, it is here that some interpreters conclude that it simply does not function—that it is included as a titillating, attention-grabbing ploy that runs counter to the text's larger paraenetic function.[86] Yet *Similitude* 9 seems integrally connected to themes and motifs evident throughout. Hermas's rejuvenation in this scene echoes the rejuvenation of the revealer-church described in the *Visions*, a transformation described as a return of manliness. Furthermore, the scene has links to the opening erotic scene with Rhoda. In part, there are similarities: Hermas is encountering attractive female figures; he disclaims any thought or action beyond innocent ones; and the emphasis falls on his love for Rhoda "as a sister" and on the virgins' love for him "as a brother." Yet the contrasts are striking too: the encounter with the bathing Rhoda involves a real woman and a brief interaction, whereas the encounter with the virgins involves visionary figures in an extended interaction including kissing, dancing, playing, and lying near one another. Whereas Hermas protests to Rhoda, perhaps inappropriately for a Christian, that he has regarded her as a "goddess," the virgins in fact hold an appropriate status as agents or representatives of divine attributes or purpose. These multiple echoes and reversals seem deliberate narrative strategies. And they are reinforced by the contrasting outcome of the two episodes: in *Vision* 1, Hermas's claim of innocence is refuted by the narrative's more authoritative voices. Yet in *Similitude* 9, when the Shepherd returns, Hermas's claim of innocence after a longer and more fully articulated dalliance is confirmed and approved. If *The Shepherd of Hermas*'s opening vision raised questions about whether innocent desire is possible, perhaps its penultimate similitude answers in the affirmative.

Verbal echoes and narrative interconnections exist also between *Similitude* 9 and *Mandate* 12. As Hermas asks the shepherd to interpret the images of the women, both those in white and those in black, the ensuing explanation insistently recalls the "two desires" of *Mandate* 12. Just as the mandate urges, "clothe yourself with the desire that is good and holy," so the shepherd now explains, "They [the virgins] . . . are holy spirits; and there is no other way a man can be found in the kingdom of God other than that they clothe him with their clothes" (*Sim.* 9.13.2

[90]). The description of the savage women in black also recalls the earlier *Mandate:*

8. μετὰ οὖν χρόνον τινὰ ἀνεπείσθησαν ὑπὸ τῶν γυναικῶν ὧν εἶδες μέλανα ἱμάτια ἐνδεδυμένων, τοὺς ὤμους ἔξω ἐχουσῶν καὶ τὰς τρίχας λελυμένας καὶ εὐμόρφων. ταύτας ἰδόντες ἐπεθύμησαν αὐτῶν καὶ ενεδύσαντο τὴν δύναμιν αὐτῶν, τῶν δὲ παρθένων ἀπεδύσαντο τὸ ἔνδυμα καὶ τὴν δύναμιν. 9a. οὗτοι οὖν ἀπεβλήθησαν ἀπὸ τοῦ οἴκου τοῦ θεοῦ καὶ ἐκείναις παρεδόθησαν· οἱ δὲ μὴ ἁ πατηθέντες τῷ κάλλει τῶν γυναικῶν τούτων ἔμειναν ἐν τῷ οἴκῳ τοῦ θεοῦ.

8. Then, after some time, they were seduced by the women you saw dressed in black garments, with the bare shoulders and loosened hair and lovely figures. Seeing them, they desire them and put on their power, taking off the clothing and power of the virgins. 9a. Having been cast out of God's house, these were handed over to those women. But the others who were not led astray by the beauty of these women remained in God's house. (*Sim.* 9.13.8–9a [90])

Both evil desire and the women in black are called "savage." The one attracted to either is "handed over." And yet hope remains for those who have been seduced: one may renounce desire for the women in black, and return to the virgins (*Sim.* 9.14.1–2 [91]). As the shepherd goes on to name the virgins and the savage women, once again the key virtue of ἐγκράτεια, as in *Vision 3*, appears second only to faith in the text's understanding of virtue. The four most prominent of the virgins are Faith, Self-Control, Power, and Patience; the four most prominent of the seductive women are Unbelief, Self-Indulgence, Disobedience, and Deceit (*Sim.* 9.15.1–3 [92]). The links among *The Shepherd's* opening scene, its middle section of instructive mandates, and the erotic similitude near the text's close suggest that this author is striving, not to incorporate gratuitously titillating elements, but to give a coherent view of desire and its force in Christian ethical experience.

As the narrative comes to its close, the most glorious angel of revelation, one of the figures for Christ, arrives—the culmination of the succession of revealers. He reproves Hermas for despising the shepherd, Hermas protests his innocence, and the angel then confirms that Hermas has indeed not transgressed (10.1.3–2.2 [111–112]). The scene recapitulates the

many times Hermas's revealers have alternated abruptly between castiga-
tion and praise, and the recurrent narrative pattern seems in part to underscore the protagonist's cheerful perseverance in seeking understanding and
change.[87] But the scene of accusation, protest and vindication also inverts
the opening scene with Rhoda, with its accusation, protest, and confirmed
accusation. The glorious angel also reiterates that, once Hermas's house is
freshly cleaned, the virgins will come to live with him as his ongoing
helpers. Here, the text that began by depicting Hermas's desire for a certain kind of wife, and went on to draw attention to his obligation to
establish domestic order and control, is again offering a kind of domesti-
cation of desire. The proper sphere in which Hermas will interact with
chastely seductive virtues is not the dream world of Arcadia, but the real
life of a Christian householder and his house-church. And this domestica-
tion of desire is, then, an integral part of the reiterated call to manliness:
*viriliter in ministerio hoc conversare, omni homini indica magnalia domini, et
habebis gratiam in hoc ministerio;* "Carry out your ministry manfully; pro-
claim the Lord's mighty acts to every person, and you will find favor in
this ministry" (10.4.1 [114]).[88] The final scene remains open-ended; the
glorious angel takes the shepherd and virgins with him as he leaves, but
says he will send them back—preparing, perhaps, for yet another sequel or
addition to this already copious story.

CHRISTIAN SELF-FORMATION
ACCORDING TO HERMAS

By what narrative means, then, do we get from the opening incident with
a naked woman, disputed innocence, and evil desire, to a closing endorsement of the manly virtue of Hermas as he prepares to put on the virgins'
clothing and welcome them to live with him? In her subtle reading of *The
Shepherd of Hermas*, Patricia Cox Miller has argued that Hermas's salvific
transformation is effected by dreams, which bring about repentance
understood as a change of consciousness. She suggests, "He now knows
that he is implicated in the salvific process; no longer a passive confessor of
sin, he is an active interpreter of his world, which he has learned to read as
a parable."[89] Miller's analysis of salvation by dreams is compelling. Perhaps,
however, the range of techniques of self-scrutiny is still more varied
and elaborated—not only dreams and visions, but reading and writing,

symbolic action—twig sorting, dancing and kissing, house cleaning, and more—and long, repetitive, circuitous dialogue. Throughout *The Shepherd* and to the end, Hermas's inclination to confess recurs, though it alternates as well with expressions of fear, self-defense, ignorance, and simple curiosity. His interlocutors also respond to him variously—with anger, cheerfulness, rebuke, encouragement. The progress Hermas makes as an interpreter of himself, his community, and his world, is neither quick nor steady. Nevertheless, the text inscribes an ongoing, albeit precarious, process of acute self-examination and relentless questioning, not in dialogue with a code of conduct but with the series of dream figures and with himself. *The Shepherd of Hermas* indeed depicts a process of salvation by dreams, but also salvation by an elaboration of techniques of self-scrutiny. Even the text's allegorical technique, its seeming inability to stop elaborating images or figures that represent believers who are partly righteous and partly not (be they represented by twigs, or stones, or mountains), may be part of the task of constant scrutiny of the self and of the community. Foucault's characterization is apt: "Christianity requires another form of truth obligation different from faith. Each person has the duty to know who he is, that is, to try to know what is happening inside him, to acknowledge faults, to recognize temptations, to locate desires; and everyone is obliged to disclose these things either to God or to others in the community, and, hence, to bear public or private witness against oneself. The truth obligations of faith and the self are linked together. This link permits a purification of the soul impossible without self-knowledge."[90] Though Foucault seems to have in view more explicitly ascetic Christian texts than Hermas, from somewhat later decades and centuries, his description of the type of self-examination he sees as distinctive to Christianity seems apt for *The Shepherd* also: "the examination of self with respect to the relation between the hidden thought and an inner impurity. At this moment begins the Christian hermeneutics of the self with its deciphering of inner thoughts."[91]

For *The Shepherd of Hermas* the experience of *metanoia* and the cultivation of manliness involve not so much the suppression of desire as the choice of its proper object, and even abandonment to the right kind of desire. Self-restraint, integral to both manliness and *metanoia*, requires self-observation and self-criticism on the way to changed consciousness. The opening scene with Rhoda with its erotic potential introduces metonymically a broader discourse of virtue. The narrator/protagonist begins, then, with the elusive experience of the intention—the dangerous thought teetering between evil act and innocence. Female personifications first appear as erotically neutral, but by the final section of the text they are erotically evocative, and thereby provide a kind of substitution through tropes as a means of recovering the possibilities of desire. ἐγκράτεια, then, turns out to be not simply the denial of ἐπιθυμία but the mechanism for its decipherment and condition for its enactment. For the *Shepherd of Hermas*, iterative forms of resistance and restraint discipline a release of desire. The *Shepherd of Hermas* in the end seems to narrate the key task in Christian self-formation, not as the suppression or repression of desire but as a conversion that leads finally to the seductions of virtue, the luxuriousness of good deeds, the manly surrender to holy desire.

THREE

Thecla Desiring
and Desired

❦ T O TURN FROM *THE SHEPHERD OF HERMAS* TO another second-century tale, *The Acts of Paul and Thecla*, is to move from a long, meandering text whose story line gets submerged in extended dialogue to a brief tale with a fast-paced plot, spare structure, and minimal comment from the narrator. Yet in broad strokes, the two narratives share at least one similarity: the protagonist experiences personal and social transformation construed as both Christianization and masculinization, marked by ἐγκράτεια, yet initiated by a paradoxical experience of desire. The much discussed Thecla tale is a two-part yet cohesive story found within the longer apocryphal *Acts of Paul*,[1] and is titled in some manuscripts "The Passion of the Holy Protomartyr Thecla," or "The Acts of Paul and Thecla." The *Acts of Paul* may be securely dated before 200, though how much earlier is debated.[2] Tertullian, in his treatise *De baptismo*, written between 198 and 206, complains that contemporary readers are appealing to the *Acts of Paul* to claim Thecla's example as a license for women's teaching and baptizing. The story of Thecla was clearly popular in antiquity—surviving in a wide range of versions and manuscripts[3] and reinterpreted in a fascinating range of later texts, art, artifacts and cults, the scholarship on which continues to grow.[4]

Though the reader meets Thecla as a cloistered, passive, beautiful and pagan virgin betrothed to Thamyris, leading man of Iconium, her attachment to the apostle Paul, and through him to Christ, transforms her into a courageous confessor, survivor of martyrdom, and preacher of the gospel. Like the Pauline traditions it is appropriating, both episodes of Thecla's story express transformation as an operation of both πίστις, faith,[5] and ἀνάστασις, resurrection.[6] Thecla is never said to repent in this tale, never shown to be repudiating any other deities or any prior unethical behavior. Rather, at the first hearing of Paul's words, she "pressed on the faith rejoicing exceedingly" (7). Her story anticipates ἀνάστασις, resurrection, as she not only twice escapes literal death, but *rises up*, transformed in her pagan, gendered, social self.[7]

Thecla's growth in agency and autonomy has been astutely analyzed by more than one interpreter.[8] Hints of transvestitism—Thecla offers to cut her hair in order to travel with Paul and eventually sews her mantle into a man's cloak—suggest that her movement into the public sphere may be construed as a form of acquired manliness. At the same time, the initial stage of Thecla's transformation is rendered in the narrative through symptoms of apparent lovesickness. Captivated by a sermon of Paul overheard from her neighbor's house, Thecla gazes fixedly from her window, refuses to eat, to sleep, to speak. Ancient folklore, literature, and medicine mark these as conventional signs of desire.[9] So, too, do the ancient Greek romances, whose heroes and heroines suffer similarly. Philetus tells Daphnis and Chloe, "I was young myself once and fell in love with Amaryllis. I forgot to eat; I didn't drink; I couldn't sleep . . ."[10] Clitophon, enamored of Leucippe, eats like a man in a dream, experiences smoldering fires and sickness of heart, and cannot sleep.[11] Chariklea, in *An Ethiopian Story*, becomes motionless and refuses to say a single word, and her condition is readily interpreted by "a learned physician": "'Is it not plain even to a child,' he said, 'that her disease is one of the soul and that we have here a clear case of love sickness?'"[12] Similarly, other characters in Thecla's tale diagnose her as lovesick, but with a paradoxical twist: she is smitten with a preacher of ἐγκράτεια and sexual renunciation.

Some who analyze gender construction in *The Acts of Paul and Thecla* treat Thecla's desire as a borrowing of novelistic convention that is relatively unimportant compared to her growth in manliness. Willi Braun, for instance, remarks, "Of course, the story does insinuate that Thecla's desire to follow Paul is motivated by a romantic, perhaps erotic, interest in Paul (40), but this *topos* of the romance novel is not exploited in such a way that it counters the plot of Thecla's masculinization."[13] Desire in this reading is more or less incidental *topos*, whereas gender transformation is plot. To some degree such a distinction may seem warranted, for in the tale's second half, set in Antioch, Thecla's desire does seem displaced or at least submerged. Yet here, even more than in the story's first half, Thecla becomes the pursued *object* of desire. The predatory violence of enflamed males serves as another all-too-recognizable form of literary lovesickness and recalls familiar scenes from ancient romances.[14] Furthermore, two maternal figures are also drawn to Thecla, representing forms of maternal desire that can either reject or protect. Indeed, throughout the narrative, Thecla, desiring and desired, seems both to animate and to disrupt the social order.[15] I propose, then, a reading of *The Acts of Paul and Thecla* that foregrounds the construction of desire, recognizing that desire is necessarily implicated in the construction of gender and sexuality. Here a nexus of topics in Thecla's story invites attention: desire, restraint, and narrative transformation as they intersect with masculinity, virginity, and maternity.

For reading *The Acts of Paul and Thecla*, I draw intermittent insights from a range of literary interpreters informed by psychoanalytic views of desire's displacements, movements, and returns, all of whom recur in some way to Freud or Lacan—readers such as Roland Barthes, Peter Brooks, Judith Butler, and Julia Kristeva. For Freud, repression takes place in the confrontation between a desire, or impulse, or instinct, and a resistance that works in accord with cultural imperatives to deny desire in order to maintain an acceptable existence for the self. Yet repression is not simply a frustration of desire. "The satisfaction of an instinct under repression is still possible."[16] Repression sets up a movement, a displacement of impulse or desire. For Lacan as for Freud, the primal gratification is always foreclosed,[17] and the subject is split, driven by desire, which, ferretlike, goes underground, moving furtively and persistently.[18] Desire's aims, therefore, are not transparent in the objects it seeks, but cloaked or displaced. As Judith Butler helpfully recasts Lacan: "If desire is irreducible to appearance, then it is also true that however desire appears to the subject is not necessarily the true aim and trajectory of desire. That true aim is, by definition, foreclosed. The subject may well be the last to know, if he or she ever does, what it is that he or she desires. The subject is constituted in the dislocation of desire."[19] Such theoretical constructs may prove helpful to place alongside the story of a heroine who not only acts as a subject of desire but becomes the object of violent male desire. The narrative itself is spare, but replete with language of seeking, gazing, and longing; the narrative construction seems to evince a "dynamic temporality"[20] that mimics the movements and displacements of desire.

The story's plot depends also on female and maternal figures, including Theocleia, who sends Thecla to her first attempted execution, and Tryphaena, who shelters her from aggressive eros. For these dimensions of the narrative, Julia Kristeva offers strands of a discourse of maternal desire.[21] In an exchange of published letters with essayist and novelist Catherine Clément, she reflects: "The serenity of maternal love is a deferred eros, desire in waiting. . . . Love-tenderness takes the place of erotic love: the 'object' of satisfaction is transformed into an 'other'—to care for, to nourish. . . . I like to think that, in our human adventure, we can encounter 'the other'—sometimes, rarely—if, and only if, we, men and women, are capable of that maternal experience, which defers eroticism into tenderness and makes an 'object' an 'other me.'"[22] More acerbically, Kristeva notes she only half believes the serene image: "the mother is never short on the tendency to annex the cherished other, to project herself onto it, to monopolize it, to dominate it, to suffocate it."[23] A few lines of a theory of maternal desire are sketched—a deferral of eroticism in love, and the ambivalent capacity either to nourish or dominate.

Close-paced narrative analysis, attentive not only to the text's two major divisions, but also to its frame stories, suggests that the *Acts of Paul and Thecla* offers a subject who is transformed in the arousal and the displacement of her own desire and in response to the desire of others. Before turning to such a reading, however, we do well to consider some key comparative texts.

COMPARING TALES OF DESIRE: NOVELS AND THE APOCRYPHAL ACTS

Erotic elements in not only *The Acts of Paul and Thecla* but all five of the *Apocryphal Acts of the Apostles* that have been considered early continue to invite comparison with the five ideal Greek romances with which they are roughly contemporary and with which they share a range of motifs—*Chaereas and Callirhoe*, *An Ephesian Tale*, *Leucippe and Clitophon*, *Daphnis and Chloe*, and an *Ethiopian Story*.[24] Well-rehearsed as such comparisons now are, they do provide context for a close analysis of the Thecla narrative.

Both groups of texts are marked by episodes of travel, adventure, imprisonment, and other mishaps, as well as by injuries, healings, apparent deaths and restorations to life. Both depict conflicts within households and cities. And both groups of texts make virginity, chastity, and fidelity key concerns—with stock figures such as predators on virginity, faithful spouses, and rejected lovers, along with heightened sexual innuendo and lingering depictions of desire. At the same time, the narrative outcomes differ markedly: the *Apocryphal Acts* narrate the works of the apostles (including attracting disciples) culminating in their deaths while the novels depict couples who fall in love, are separated by fortune and calamity, and are eventually reunited for a happy—that is, married—ending.

For more than a century, scholars have debated whether shared motifs suggest a literary relationship. Rosa Söder in 1928 concluded there was no direct literary relationship between the *Apocryphal Acts* and the novels, but that the Acts were the "literarily fixed witnesses" of ancient folk stories.[25] The possible folklore origins of the *Apocryphal Acts* received more extensive analysis through the 1980s by scholars such as Stevan L. Davies, Dennis R. MacDonald, and Virginia Burrus, each of whom also explored the possibility that women were the primary hearers and indeed tellers of these tales.[26] Most recent readings of the *Acts*, however, assume or argue for the value of more direct literary comparison to the ideal romances. Jan Bremmer, for instance, holds that the authors of at least the Acts of John, Peter, and Paul must have known the ancient romances, or others quite like them—that the narrative echoes and shared motifs cannot be coincidental.[27] Christine Thomas raises perceptive cautions about ways the *Apocryphal Acts* are in fact ill-suited to comparison with the romances, yet admits their comparative value, noting (in a now oft-quoted line), "Though motifs do not a genre make, the ideal romances and the Acts are speaking the same narrative language."[28]

Astute cultural and ideological analyses of how the *Apocryphal Acts* not only share but also invert literary motifs of the Greek romances have been offered by both Judith Perkins and Kate Cooper. Perkins persuasively attributes a socially confirming function to the novels: "These romances filled with travel, adventure, and final union idealized social unity. They offered through their trope of the loving couple a dream of a social union able to endure and overcome every eventuality of fate or fortune."[29] The *Acts*, in contrast, are in their outcome socially disruptive:

The apocryphal Acts embody an anti-social message. Through their rejection of the marriage union and the future of ongoing society such unions imply, they call for an end to contemporary society as it exists. The apocryphal Acts are able to invest their narrative with its radical significance through their intertextual reversal of the depiction of marriage and chastity in the romance.[30]

Similarly, but with greater attention to constructions of gender, Kate Cooper argues that the motifs of displacement, risk, celebration of sexuality, and threat to fidelity and chastity that mark the ideal Greek romances, that make them seem challenging to convention at a certain level, are, in the end, fundamentally conservative—celebrating the restoration of household and city: "Love, here, is not in tension with the social order; rather, the celebration of desire is a celebration of the social order's replenishment."[31] In contrast, the *Acts* depict conflicts with household and political authority instigated by an apostle claiming a new and disruptive form of social authority. Displacement, risk, inversions of sexuality, insistence on chastity—these are real challenges to established social order. Against those who see the *Apocryphal Acts* as liberatory for women, however, Cooper asserts, "The challenge by the apostle to the householder is the urgent message of these narratives, and it is essentially a conflict *between men*."[32] In their complexity of analysis, Cooper and Perkins move well beyond comparisons of motifs or discussions of genre to argue for the complex social functions of the intertextual relations among the two corpora.[33]

The influential analyses of both Cooper and Perkins continue to guide scholars of both the novels and the *Apocryphal Acts*, though at times with nuanced critique. For instance, on characterizing the novels as socially conservative given their endings in marriage, Morales observes: "It is broadly speaking true that most of the Greek novels ultimately 'valorise the civic ideal,' *if* the reader reads for the happy ending, and not the sexual adventures along the way. . . . Much of the pleasure in the narratives comes from the *tension* between the destructive, willful *eros*, and the cohesive, social bonds of marriage."[34] Others analyze how the novels themselves engage in criticism and subversion of the social order, and find the *Apocryphal Acts* less an *inversion* of the novels' ideology and more an alternate point on a cultural continuum.[35] Burrus suggests, "Indeed, it may be that the less-than-subtle subversions of the Apocryphal Acts, when read comparatively, do not so much invert as simplify and intensify certain aspects of the pagan romances' already ambivalent views of *eros* and *gamos*, city and empire—or, conversely, that the pagan romances complicate and render more ambiguous the strident social critique already conveyed by the Apocryphal Acts."[36]

Broad characterizations of *corpora*, however perceptive and helpful, at times can tend to level differences among texts, and, therefore, they invite the counterweight of closer paced readings. For instance, whether the ancient novels' depictions of desire work more to confirm or to disrupt the social order varies with the novel, and whether its ending in marriage seems climactic or anticlimactic, decisive or tenuous. To offer just one brief contrast, in Longus's pastoral novel *Daphnis and Chloe*, desire is artfully constructed as thoroughly "natural."[37] The shepherd girl and shepherd boy, abandoned children of nobility, move through slow, titillating stages of gazing, bathing, kissing, attempting unsuccessfully to mate as the sheep do. Narrator and reader share a sophisticated vantage point of amusement at their naiveté. Union, when it comes, is attended by discovery of true parentage, by social banqueting, by the arrival of the "city folk" into the country. Yet, however "natural" its impulses in this novel, sexual consummation is firmly located in social structures. In Achilles Tatius's *Leucippe and Clitophon*, however, desire is audacious and disruptive in ways that push even expected novelistic conventions. At the novel's opening, for instance, love at first sight is not reciprocal.[38] Clitophon is smitten, but Leucippe must be seduced—or almost. Much of the rest of the novel, then, tests her fidelity to him, and his to her—particularly in the episodes where he, believing Leucippe dead (having seen a convincing enactment of her decapitation) weds another woman, Melite, but delays having intercourse with her. The narrative suspense builds: Will Clitophon discover that Leucippe is alive in time to maintain his fidelity to her? Through many plot twists he does; then, just as the suspense seems relieved, Clitophon jumps over the brink, and for supposedly therapeutic reasons, has sex with Melite after all.[39] After playing outrageously throughout with desire as brinkmanship, the novel draws to a surprisingly understated conclusion—the narrator's report that Leucippe and Clitophon return home and celebrate their marriage. The "social restoration" of marriage is muted in comparison to the novel's sustained depiction of risk-taking sexuality, making any claim to "social conservatism" tenuous. Clearly, the cultural and ideological insights afforded by comparative studies also invite nuanced, particular analyses of individual narratives.[40]

The rendering of desire and of sexual renunciation in the individual *Apocryphal Acts of the Apostles* is also distinctive, even given similarities in erotic motifs and in narrative outcome. One characteristic motif of disciples who abandon spouses, fiancés, or lovers for the sake of the apostle's preaching appears in both *The Acts of Peter* and *The Acts of Andrew*. In the concluding section devoted to Peter's martyrdom, four concubines of the prefect Agrippa hear "the preaching of purity and all the words of the Lord" and make a pact with one another to renounce intercourse with the prefect (33[4]). Matters worsen, then, when a particularly beautiful woman separates from her husband, a friend of Caesar's, and when many other men and women renounce sexuality within marriage, "since they wished to worship God in sobriety and purity (διὰ τὸ σεμνῶς καὶ ἁγνῶς θέλειν αὐτοὺς θεοσεβεῖν). So there was the greatest disquiet in Rome, and Albinus put his case to Agrippa . . ." (34 [4–5]).[41] Yet the erotic substitution is not Peter but "the doctrine of purity" in place of the rejected man (or woman). The refusals and redirections of desire are treated in somewhat cursory fashion. Nevertheless, the city has been disrupted by the apostle's effects on households and the way is paved for Peter's martyrdom. This brief episode shares the motif with others of the *Apocryphal Acts*, but the *Acts of Peter* as a whole can hardly be said to participate in the inverted or re-aligned eroticism that is sometimes claimed to be a central characteristic of the *Acts* generally.

The *Acts of Andrew*, in contrast, may be the most thoroughly eroticized of the five Apocryphal Acts that have been considered early. Maximilla—the most prominent female disciple in the story—has a strong attachment to Andrew that prompts Aegeates, her spurned and jealous husband, to threaten and persecute the apostle (4).[42] She explicitly declares her experience of "erotic substitution": "I love, Aegeates, I love (φιλῶ, Αἰγεάτα, φιλῶ). And what I love is nothing of the things of this world, so as to become manifest to you; and night and day it kindles and enflames me with love for itself (ἐξάπτει καὶ φλέγει τῇ πρὸς αὐτό στοργῇ), which you yourself could not see, for it is difficult, nor could you separate me from it, for that is impossible. Leave me then to consort with it, and to find my rest in it alone."[43] Maximilla greets Andrew with gestures of intimacy: "But Maximilla went again at the usual time with Iphidamia to Andrew; and laying his hands on her face she kissed them and began to tell him in full of the demand of Aegeates" (5). Later, she follows the polymorphous Lord, "going before her in the form of Andrew" to an assignation in the prison

(14). Cooper's analysis of how desire for the apostle disrupts marriage, household, and city seems apt here, as it is for Thecla:"The substitution of apostle for marriage partner in the heroine's affections means that the persuasive force of desire is being put to a new purpose."[44] Yet the *Acts of Andrew* is characterized by a reciprocity of desire between the apostle and his disciples that is nowhere evident in *The Acts of Paul and Thecla*. Andrew, throughout the *Acts*, gives long speeches, which dominate the narrative both stylistically and theologically, for the apostle's words are shown to be uniquely salvific.[45] In one much-discussed passage, Andrew urges Maximilla not to return to her marriage bed but to remain in mutual fidelity with him. He likens her to Eve and himself to Adam—the primal couple whose suffering, ignorance, and imperfection are recapitulated and resolved in the repentance of Maximilla and the ongoing conversion of Andrew (5).[46] The relationship between Andrew and his male disciple Stratocles is also cast in eroticized language. Andrew speaks of impregnating Stratocles with the word; Stratocles responds by celebrating the fiery reception of Andrew's penetrating words.[47] Careful analyses of Andrew's language of desire have explored the theological and philosophical underpinnings of the text.[48] For purposes of contrast to *The Acts of Paul and Thecla*, however, we may simply note that the latter's spare narrative, focused more on plot than on dialogue, precludes either Thecla or Paul from offering any discursive elaboration on the transformative possibilities of desire. Moreover, whereas images of unity, procreation, and new creation shape the construction of desire in *The Acts of Andrew*, desire as displacement, lure, and final irresolution shape Thecla's story. To say the Apocryphal Acts share motifs of inverted sexuality and erotic substitution is to take only a small step toward characterizing how each works in its literary particularity.

As a prelude to examining Thecla as not only subject but object of desire, two other episodes from *The Acts of Peter* merit a brief look, both concerning virgins and their susceptibility to violation. In reconstructions of the text, both are usually placed near the beginning of the narrative, the first provided by a Coptic fragment, the other by the Pseudo-Titus epistle.[49] In the first, a crowd that is gathered to request healing from Peter asks sharply why, with his miracle-working capabilities, he neglects his beautiful, believing, virgin daughter, who lies paralyzed.[50] To demonstrate that the issue is not God's powerlessness, Peter heals her, and the crowd rejoices; then Peter returns her to paralysis, and the crowd laments. Peter explains that at her birth, "the Lord said to me, 'Peter, today there is born for you a great trial; for this (daughter) will do harm to many souls if her body remains healthy.'" Peter goes on to explain that by the age of ten, the girl had become "a temptation to many." Clearly, the story depends on a strong sense of the dangerous, erotic power of beautiful virgins. Being a believer and the daughter of the apostle Peter is not sufficient to neutralize the danger of beauty and virginity paired. Moreover, the divine warning is not that the virgin will be harmed, but that she will harm others—indeed, many others. She is culpable for the tendency of men to prey upon her.[51] A wealthy man, Ptolemaeus, having seen the girl bathing with her mother, attempts to marry her, then apparently abducts her (the text is corrupt at this point). The daughter is protected, then, not by active resistance to the predatory suitor, but by paralysis. Ptolemaeus' servants return the daughter, infirm but unviolated, to the door of her parents' home, and her parents praise the Lord for protecting her "from uncleanness and shame and . . ."[52] Throughout these events, Peter's daughter remains entirely passive. Mary Foskett remarks, "The virgin bears no name, demonstrates no action, and utters no speech. She is a body, an object of concern and an object upon whom both mortals and the deity stake a claim."[53] Through a series of divine actions, Ptolemaeus is converted, then eventually dies, yet the daughter remains paralyzed. The point seems not that men are a threat to the virgin, but that beautiful virginity threatens men.[54]

The second episode with a virgin daughter is thought to be a multiform in the fluid textual tradition of the *Acts of Peter*: that is, a narrative unit with similar function that has been recast, with characters changed.[55] In this variation, the irony is compressed. A peasant with a virgin daughter asks Peter to pray for her. The apostle promises the father that the Lord will bestow what is expedient for her soul. What is expedient, however, is instant death.[56] The "distrustful" gardener then asks Peter to raise his only daughter from the dead. Within days, the virgin is seduced by a man posing as a believer, "and the two of them never appeared again."[57] If this episode recasts that of Peter's daughter, its direction of change is to compress and exaggerate. Here the message is not merely "better paralyzed than violated," but "better dead than seduced." The passivity of the virgins in these two episodes of the *Acts of Peter* makes a striking contrast with Thecla.

We do well, then, to recall advice given by François Bovon and Eric Junod urging study of each of the *Acts* in its singularity, arguing that there was an "initial methodological bet to be made on the originality and particularity of the texts under their different aspects (literary, cultural, social, and theological)."[58] In the analysis that follows, I hope to hold together two kinds of reading of *The Acts of Paul and Thecla*, as described succinctly by an interpreter of the ancient novel, Massimo Fusillo: "an ingenuous one, following the cognitive paths of the text even if the outcome is already well-known; and a conscious one, a kind of 'metareading' analyzing the construction of meaning,"[59] in particular, the construction of desire.

MARRIED HOUSEHOLDER AND ASCETIC APOSTLE

The two-part structure of *The Acts of Paul and Thecla* is obvious and much commented upon: first in Iconium, then in Antioch, Thecla's behavior prompts conflict with a high status male and with civic authorities who attempt to execute her in the arena but instead witness her divine deliverance. Some have argued the two episodes represent originally separate stories: an earlier Antioch narrative, with a vocal, active Thecla and largely absent Paul, later being connected by an editor with the Iconium story, creating a more passive heroine, a dependence upon Paul, and a place within the larger *Acts of Paul*.[60] Yet in the final form of the text that survives, attested by many manuscripts, intricate parallels and inversions between the two episodes invite reading them as a coherent tale of a protagonist whose identity is transformed.[61] The framing and bridge episodes in the narrative also invite attention, each of which depicts the household of the Christian Onesiphorus. The tale of a virgin who renounces marriage and faces rejection by family and city is framed by the representation of a married householder with children, one who epitomizes hospitality.[62] The opening episode also invites the reader to begin discriminating among kinds of love or affection. Paul's hypocritical traveling companions, Demas and Hermogenes,[63] are said to flatter Paul ὡς ἀγαπῶντες αὐτόν, "as if they loved him," whereas Paul ἔστεργεν αὐτοὺς σφόδρα, "felt exceeding affection for them."[64] The measure of Paul's affection is that he shares the words of the Lord with them. The opening scene also introduces a key motif that runs throughout the tale: the pattern of gazing or looking for Paul. Onesiphorus stands at roadside with his children and wife—all named at the story's outset—waiting eagerly to see Paul, inspecting all passersby until one meets the description Titus has given him: short, bald, crooked legs, good body, somewhat hooked nose, knitted brow, and face full of friendliness (3). Studies of how these features would have been construed according to ancient physiognomy have reached interesting though divergent conclusions, from the suggestion that Paul here represents an ideal general like that described by Archilochus,[65] to the claim that Paul appears as a kind of Christian Heracles,[66] to the suggestion that these physical features recall negative character traits with which opponents such as those in 2 Corinthians charge Paul.[67] One other reader suggests that the point of the description is simply to make clear that Paul is not physically attractive, and therefore Thecla's subsequent fascination must have another source,[68] whereas another points to "the erotic lure of the 'ugly' philosopher."[69] Certainly, Paul is far from the beautiful adolescent male typical of the romance novel. The narrator also, however, hints that mundane physiognomic analyses will not suffice for this protagonist: ποτὲ μὲν γὰρ ἐφαίνετο ὡς ἄνθρωπος, ποτὲ δὲ ἀγγέλου πρόσωπον εἶχεν, "for at some times he appeared like a human, and at others he had the face of an angel" (3).[70]

The introductory scene, then, contrasts false and true forms of Christian affection, emphasizes looking for Paul, and offers the image of a hospitable Christian householder, with wife and children. It climaxes with Paul's preaching. Welcomed into Onesiphorus' home, Paul shares the word of God περὶ ἐγκρατείας καὶ ἀναστάσεως, concerning self-restraint and resurrection[71]—a twofold emphasis that anticipates both the renunciation and the deliverance from death of the plot to come. The beatitudes that follow—a speech form associated more with Jesus than with Paul in other early Christian writings—merge dominical with Pauline sayings, but with an encratic twist characteristic of the *Apocryphal Acts*. The first five present a particularly tightly woven progression in renunciation, moving from purity of heart (μακάριοι οἱ καθαροὶ τῇ καρδίᾳ; citing Matt 5:8) to that of flesh (μακάριοι οἱ ἁγνὴν τὴν σάρκα τηρήσαντες); from self-control (μακάριοι οἱ ἐγκρατεῖς), to worldly renunciation (μακάριοι οἱ ἀποταξάμενοι τῷ κόσμῳ τούτῳ), to the specific case of renunciation within marriage (μακάριοι οἱ ἔχοντες γυναῖκας ὡς μὴ ἔχοντες; echoing 1 Cor 7:29). The next beatitudes extol pious characteristics such as reverential awe, wisdom, and understanding, leading up to another direct citation of a Jesus saying: "Blessed are the merciful, for they shall obtain mercy . . ." (Matt 5:7). The final blessing again strikes a more distinctive note as it effects the transition from the frame story to the tale of Thecla:

μακάρια τὰ σώματα τῶν παρθένων, ὅτι αὐτὰ εὐαρεστήσουσιν τῷ θεῷ καὶ οὐκ ἀπολέσουσιν τὸν μισθὸν τῆς ἁγνείας αὐτῶν· ὅτι ὁ λόγος τοῦ πατρὸς ἔργον αὐτοῖς γενήσεται σωτηρίας εἰς ἡμέραν τοῦ υἱοῦ αὐτοῦ, καὶ ἀνάπαυσιν ἕξουσιν εἰς αἰῶνα αἰῶνος.

Blessed are the bodies of the virgins, for those bodies shall be well-pleasing to God and shall not lose the reward of their purity; for the word of the Father shall be for them a work of salvation in the day of his Son, and they shall have rest forever and ever. (6)

In a fascinating analysis of scribal modifications to the Thecla tale, Haines-Eitzen shows that this striking affirmation of the bodies of virgins caught the attention of later scribes, some of whom added "spirits/souls" (τὸ πνεύματα) to temper the blessing of the body.[72] Yet the unaltered blessing, well attested in the best manuscripts, prepares the reader for the story that follows, one that moves from a virgin's body guarded by social convention, to a desiring and desired body exposed to shame, public view, danger, and death, to a vindicated body shielded first by maternal protection, then by divine protective fire, and finally by a manly traveling cloak. Thecla's story provides one instance of a kind of narrative that Brooks has described: "Along with the semioticization of the body goes what we might call the somaticization of story: the implicit claim that the body is a key sign in narrative and a central nexus of narrative meanings."[73]

FAITHFUL HEARING OR INFATUATED GAZE?

The narrative shifts from Paul's preaching to its effects on a nearby eavesdropper: Θέκλα τις παρθένος, a certain virgin named Thecla, identified immediately by her position as daughter and fiancée. Initially, two distinct voices describe how and why Thecla is dislocated by this preaching from her social and familial identity: first, the narrator, then her mother, Theocleia. The narrator's account emphasizes the sense of hearing, with the window as access point for the word Paul speaks. Thecla's attention is caught by τὸν περὶ ἁγνείας λόγον λεγόμενον ὑπὸ τοῦ Παύλου, "the word

X

concerning purity spoken by Paul" (7). Though motionless by the window, Thecla is drawn into a sort of psychic motion: τῇ πίστει ἐπήγετο ὑπερευφραινομένη, "being led on in the faith, with extreme gladness" (Rordorf offers the intriguing translation, "elle était subjuguée par la foi").[74] Though Paul himself is not visible to Thecla, she does see many women and virgins going in to Paul, so that ἐπεπόθει, she longs intensely, to be worthy to stand in Paul's presence and hear the word of Christ. Unless that single verb of desire is construed to evoke erotic associations, the narrator's description of Paul's effect on Thecla is, in fact, rendered in rather chaste diction. When Theocleia speaks to Thamyris, however, her account of Thecla's distraction is heavily eroticized. Theocleia emphasizes Thecla's gaze and her devotion to an ἀνδρὶ ξένῳ, "a strange man." It is she, not the narrator, who suggests that Thecla is compromising herself as παρθένος (8). It is she who claims her daughter is κρατεῖται ἐπιθυμίᾳ καινῇ καὶ πάθει δεινῷ, "held by a new desire and strange passion," and concludes ἑάλωται ἡ παρθένος, "the virgin is taken captive" (9), thus fueling Thamyris's jealous concern. Is Theocleia, the reader might wonder, a reliable interpreter? Initially, the narrative seems to offer a choice of how to construe the disruptive attractions of Paul's message—as glad response to word, or as erotic infatuation with a stranger. In either case, Roland Barthes' reflections on *ravissement* and its conversionary possibilities seem apt: "Love at first sight is a hypnosis: I am fascinated by an image: at first shaken, electrified, stunned, 'paralyzed' as Menon was by Socrates, the model of loved objects, of captivating images, or again converted by an apparition, nothing distinguishing the path of enamoration from the Road to Damascus; subsequently ensnared, held fast, immobilized, nose stuck to the image (the mirror)" (or in Thecla's case, the window). He adds: "Is the scene always visual? It can be aural, the frame can be linguistic: I can fall in love with *a sentence spoken to me:* and not only because it says something which manages to touch my desire, but because of its syntactical turn (framing), which will inhabit me *like a memory*."[75] A triangulation has occurred, to which Thamyris reacts, approaching Thecla and questioning her about the πάθος that holds her ἔκπληκτον. Unresponsive to him, to her mother, and to the confusion of wailing that spreads through the household, Thecla remains ἀτενίζουσα τῷ λόγῳ Παύλου, "attending to the word of Paul"—or in Barthes' words, "in love with a sentence spoken," which does seem to inhabit her "like a memory." Her voice we do not yet hear.

WHO IS HE AND WHOSE IS SHE?

As is true in others of the *Apocryphal Acts*, Thamyris, the rejected male with a prior claim, is presented as having genuine affection for Thecla, loving her, wishing to marry her, and, therefore, now seeking to rid himself of his rival. When he encounters Paul's hypocritical traveling companions, Demas and Hermogenes first deny knowledge of who Paul is, but then claim Paul teaches that resurrection is contingent on sexual renunciation (12)—a seeming distortion.[76] In Thamyris's home for a sumptuous banquet, then, they generalize from his distress that οὕτως φιλεῖ τὸν ξένον καί ἀποστεροῦμαι γάμου, "she so loves the stranger, and I am deprived of my marriage," to a claim that Paul's effect on whole crowds is a form of seduction (14).[77]

The dialogue continues a verbal pattern of referring to Thecla as belonging to Thamyris, an uncontroversial patriarchal assumption. Thamyris's first arrival at Theocleia's house is marked by a question with the possessive pronoun made emphatic by word order and rhyme: Ποῦ μού ἐστιν ἡ θέκλα; "Where is my Thecla?" (8); Theocleia refers to τὴν σὴν Θέκλαν, "your Thecla" (9); now Demas and Hermogenes refer to τήν γυναῖκα σου Θέκλαν, "your woman Thecla" (14). The growing narrative tension, then, is in part construed as a question of ownership: Whose will Thecla be if she refuses Thamyris? As Paul is subsequently hauled by Thamyris before the governor and becomes orator again, however, the apostle says nothing of Thecla (whom he has, after all, not yet met), or of his effect on women, virgins, or marriage, but emphasizes what it is that ἐγκράτεια and ἀνάστασις draw humans away from: πάσης ἡδονῆς καὶ θανάτου, "all pleasure and death" (17).

ACTIVITY AND PASSIVITY, AGENCY AND ABJECTION

In the subsequent scene, the silent, motionless Thecla becomes active. With Paul imprisoned, the virgin whose access to public space has to this point been through a window now acts boldly:

Ἡ δὲ Θέκλα νυκτὸς περιελομένη τὰ ψέλια ἔδωκεν τῷ πυλωρῷ, καὶ ἀνοιγείσης αὐτῇ τῆς θύρας ἀπῆλθεν εἰς τὴν φυλακήν· καὶ δοῦσα τῷ δεσμοφύλακι κάτοπτρον ἀργυροῦν εἰσῆλθεν πρὸς τὸν

Παῦλον, καὶ καθίσασα παρὰ τοὺς πόδας αὐτοῦ ἤκουσεν τὰ μεγαλεῖα τοῦ θεοῦ.

But during the night, Thecla took off her bracelets and gave them to the doorkeeper and, the door being opened for her, went off to the prison. And giving the jailer her silver mirror, she went in to Paul, and sitting at his feet, heard the great things of God. (18)

The virgin trades markers of her social identity for access to Paul, with whom she is apparently alone in this midnight assignation. This new level of activity and agency, however, is tempered by elements of continuing passivity. At this point in the tale, Thecla still has not spoken.[78] Moreover, unlike the opening scene of Thecla at the window, suggestions of Thecla's chaste progress in faith are no longer kept distinct from suggestions that she is being overtaken by desire. Indeed, the narrator seems both to deny and to evoke suggestions of erotic crisis: καὶ οὐδὲν ἐδεδοίκει ὁ Παῦλος, ἀλλὰ τῇ τοῦ Θεοῦ παρρησίᾳ ἐνεπολιτεύετο· κἀκείνης ηὔξανεν ἡ πίστις, καταφιλούσης τὰ δεσμὰ αὐτου, "And Paul feared nothing, but conducted himself with the frankness of God; and her faith also increased, as she was kissing his bonds" (18). Mary Foskett notes perceptively that the narrative here and elsewhere "strains to qualify its erotic overtones."[79] One might also argue in the other direction, that the narrative works to subvert its own assertions of control. For instance, Thamyris and "her own people" then find Thecla in the prison, τρόπον τινὰ συνδεδεμένην τῇ στοργῇ, "bound with him, in a manner of speaking, in affection" (19). στέργω has already been used in the narrative to describe Paul's benevolent care for his two false friends (1), and both verb and noun convey familial or other affectionate love, usually without sexual connotations.[80] But the repeated kissing of his bonds, with the echoes of Theocleia's charge that Thecla has been captivated by Paul, load the phrase and the scene more generally with erotic overtones. Haines-Eitzen again documents scribal alterations to the sentence, attempting to manage its erotic overtones: one Greek scribe omits altogether the phrase "bound with him"; Latin versions have Thecla sitting, listening, or joining in Paul's desire of Christ, rather than bound with Paul; Syriac and Armenian versions place others in the prison with Paul and Thecla, restoring some propriety.[81] In the best attested Greek text, however, the erotic overtones continue; as Paul is taken off to the governor, Thecla's desire becomes vivid self-abasement: ἡ δὲ Θέκλα ἐκυλίετο ἐπὶ τοῦ τόπου οὗ ἐδίδασκεν ὁ Παῦλος καθήμενος ἐν τῇ φυλακῇ; "But Thecla rolled herself upon the place where, sitting in the prison, Paul had taught" (20). Agency gives way to abjection. The calculating, active subject, obtaining means to satisfy her desire to be in Paul's presence, is now subjected to his absence and to her own desire.

Assumptions about gender and desire necessarily shape a reading of this scene. The image of a young virgin violating social protocols trades off cultural stereotypes of female desire, and particularly of virgins' desire, as excessive and transgressive. Anne Carson describes ancient Greek assumptions, which persisted widely through Greco-Roman antiquity, that women were particularly lacking in control of their own boundaries and were subject to excessive erotic desire.[82] Yet Thecla is not simply depicted as transgressive "stalker" of the apostle. Her deliberate risk-taking activity seems to disrupt gender stereotypes as much as or more than to confirm them. Melissa Aubin, for instance, with nice attention to particular descriptive details, reads the scene as marking gender transformation, perhaps for both characters:

> Thus, Thecla's physical access to Paul involves revoking her traditional gender signifiers, and indeed, in the case of the mirror, a possible signifier of her former identity (3:18). Whereas shackles bind Paul's wrists in the prison, Thecla's rebellion involves the removal of the bracelets from her own wrists. This reversal, which uses the same image to connote Thecla's 'liberation' and Paul's bondage, is our first clue to the emergence of Thecla as a figure who supercedes Paul in authority and masculine license. Indeed, from this point on, Paul repeatedly appears impotent in comparison.[83]

Here again, however, the reading invites further complication, for Thecla's rolling in the dirt seems not to fit well with suggestions of "authority and masculine license." Konstan's analysis of how loss of self-control is rendered in the Greek novels may be apropos. Konstan argues that the novels differ from other ancient literary and philosophic treatments of the struggle of the soul in the face of desire: "The soul of the protagonists in the Greek novels is not the scene of this kind of struggle. The lover's helplessness is not a loss of self-control. The only moral weakness that the novel recognizes in the hero or heroine is the failure to keep faith with the beloved . . ."[84] Perhaps for Thecla, as for the couples in the novels, desire, even abject desire, becomes the precursor to and motive for fidelity; abjection may be pathway to self-control. Yet unlike the novels, in the *Acts of Paul and Thecla*, desire is asymmetrical, located only in Thecla. This scene, then, seems to disrupt both cultural conventions of male activity/female passivity and novelistic depictions of an equilibrium of desire. In the prison scene, both the activity and the passivity of desire are manifested in Thecla. Desire has dislocated Thecla from her former identity, but at this stage in the narrative, her new identity seems ambiguous or provisional. That Thamyris and her own people seek for her as for one lost seems apt (19). Activity and passivity, satisfaction and resistance, presence and absence—all are evoked and unresolved in this scene.

THE URGENCY OF THE GAZE

The pattern whereby the lack or absence of Paul fuels Thecla's desire is repeated and heightened in the next scenes. Facing judgment, Paul allows the governor to hear him gladly; Thecla, however, remains silent. Her steady, silent attention (again, the verb ἀτενίζω) to Paul is now visual, not auditory, and as she ignores the question of why she will not marry Thamyris, her gaze confirms that Paul is his rival. Nevertheless, it is not the rejected male but the volatile mother who utters the harsh cry for her daughter's execution: Κατάκαιε τὴν ἄνομον, κατάκαιε τὴν ἄνυμφον . . . , "burn the lawless one, burn the one who is no bride . . ." (20).[85] To refuse marriage is to be lawless, according to Theocleia. Horn works to make Theocleia's outcry more explicable: "That a mother who feels responsible for the proper education and conduct of her daughter, a mother who fears that her daughter's misconduct would bring shame on the family, would agree to and even promote her daugher's death instead of being willing to endure such shame is not an unreasonable explanation for Theocleia's behaviour."[86] Yet within this story, Theocleia's perspective is at odds with the narrator's, as Horn grants as she terms her "primary persecutor." The virgin who refuses her proper social role as wife evidently disrupts the household and the city more than the itinerant apostle, who is scourged and expelled from the city, whereas she is condemned to be burned.

At this potentially final separation from Paul, the acutely vulnerable Thecla, desperate for Paul, witnesses a peculiar christophany. The

pile-up of varied verbs of seeing, seeking, and attending here inten-
sifies the urgency of the gaze—Thecla wants not only to see Paul but
to be seen, but the apparent satisfaction of her desire proves ambiguous
and fleeting:

ἡ δὲ Θέκλα ὡς ἀμνὸς ἐν ἐρήμῳ περισκοπεῖ τὸν ποιμένα οὕτως
ἐκείνη τὸν Παῦλον ἐζήτει. καὶ ἐμβλέψασα εἰς τὸν ὄχλον εἶδεν
τὸν κύριον καθήμενον ὡς Παῦλον, καὶ εἶπεν Ὡς ἀνυπομονήτου
μου οὔσης ἦλθεν Παῦλος θεάσασθαί με. Καὶ προσεῖχεν αὐτῷ
ἀτενίζουσα. ο δέ εἰς οὐρανοὺς ἀπίει. (21)

But as a lamb in the wilderness looks around for the shepherd,
Thecla sought Paul. And looking intently at the crowd, she saw the
Lord seated in the likeness of Paul, and she said, "Thinking that I
am not able to endure, Paul has come to behold me." And fixing
her attention, she concentrated on him. But he went away into
heaven. (21)

For the first time, Thecla speaks, though the words seem internally
addressed.[87] Thecla's aim is to hold Paul's gaze with her own; she is drawn
by the lure of reflexivity. As Lacan remarks, "the first object of desire is to
be recognized by the other."[88] Yet Paul has been displaced; a Paul who
could earlier speak in the speech genres of Christ now is mirrored by a
Christ who can appear in the form of Paul. The earlier triangulation of
Thamyris, Paul, and Thecla is now supplanted by a new triangulation,
though with Christ mediating Paul rather than Paul mediating Christ.[89]
The aim of Thecla's gaze, of her desire, is therefore at once satisfied and
displaced. And this Christo-Pauline presence, itself a deferral, proves as
transient as the apostle himself has been. Paul's distance or retreat from
Thecla, both earlier in the narrative and in scenes to follow, here seems to
have divine endorsement.

ESCAPING MARTYRDOM AND SEEKING PAUL

In the passage immediately following, the attempted martyrdom itself is
narrated extremely briefly, almost anticlimactically. Thecla, making the
sign of the cross, is silent and then stationary. Though her own gaze has
been interrupted, her naked body becomes the object of the governor's
gaze, yet the narrative does not linger there. God quenches the fires with

a miraculous downpour, yet neither the narrator nor any character in the story comments on her deliverance, her endurance, its effect upon onlookers, or her departure from the stadium or the city.

The narrative instead shifts abruptly forward many days to Paul in a cave outside the city, reunited with the hospitable but now impoverished Onesiphorus and his family, and then to Thecla, apparently wandering in a market. Here, more than half way through the story, Thecla, now the survivor of martyrdom with a proven right to testify,[90] at last speaks to another character, voicing her continuing quest for Paul. To a child of Onesiphorus, she says: Παῦλον διώκω, ἐκ πυρὸς σωθεῖσα, "I am pursuing Paul, for I was saved from the fire" (23). The reunion scene, marked first by an alternation of prayers by Paul and Thecla, then by the only dialogue between them that lasts more than two lines, presents an ambivalent picture of the apostle. As Thecla arrives, she stands behind Paul as he prays rather ineffectually after-the-fact that the father of Christ will deliver her from the fire, she prays in response, and then, with potentially comic effect, Paul thanks the father of the Lord for so speedily answering his prayer. Paul's initial prayer adds a new element to the play of possessive pronouns regarding Thecla that has run through the narrative: Paul prays for her deliverance ὅτι σή ἐστιν, "because she is yours." Thecla's own prayer, in contrast, begins with expected piety, then takes a twist at its purpose clause: Thecla gives thanks for her deliverance ἵνα Παῦλον ἴδω, "that I might see Paul" (24). The tension between belonging to Christ and pursuing Paul is evident, though unresolved.

A reunion celebration marked by ἀγάπη πολλή is then followed by the brief direct dialogue between Paul and Thecla:

καὶ εἶπεν Θέκλα τῷ Παύλῳ Περικαροῦμαι καὶ ἀκολουθήσω σοι ὅπου δὰν πορεύῃ. Ὁ δὲ εἶπεν Ὁ καιρὸς αἰσχρός, καὶ σὺ εὔμορφος· μὴ ἄλλος σε πειρασμὸς λήψεται χείρων τοῦ πρώτου, καὶ οὐχ ὑπομείνῃς ἄλλα δειλανδρήσῃς. καὶ εἶπεν Θέκλα Μόνον δός μοι τὴν ἐν Χριστῷ σφραγῖδα, καὶ οὐχ ἄψεταί μοι πειρασμός. καὶ εἶπεν Παῦλος Θέκλα μακροθύμησον, καὶ λήψῃ τὸ ὕδωρ.

And Thecla said to Paul, "I will shear my hair and follow you wherever you might go." But he said, "The season is ill-favored, and you are beautiful. May no other temptation seize you worse than the first, and you not endure, but act cowardly." And Thecla

> said, "Only give me the seal in Christ, and temptation shall not
> touch me." And Paul said, "Be patient, Thecla, and you shall receive
> the water."(25)

Thecla's offer is commonly read as an act of self-masculinization as a means to becoming Paul's traveling companion. Her ἀκολουθήσω σοι ὅπου δᾶν πορεύῃ echoes the phrasing of a would-be disciple from the Jesus traditions (ἀκολουθήσω σοι ὅπου ἐὰν ἀπέρχῃ, Mt. 8:19, Lk 9:57), whom Jesus discourages with warnings of the hardships of itinerant life.[91] Paul's discouraging reply emphasizes not itinerancy but suspicions related to gender—he counters her offer with an insistence on her beauty and the perhaps paradoxical fear that δειλανδρήσῃς, "you will play the cowardly man." Paul's use of πειράσμος is ambiguous. If the temptation is to prove unmanly when faced with martyrdom, Thecla has proved and will prove Paul wrong. If the "worse temptation" that soon "seizes" her is a man's lustful embrace, does Paul equates a woman's victimization with her temptation? Or might the erotic connotations of Thecla's pursuit of Paul represent some form of temptation that may worsen? Paul goes on to defer her request for the seal of baptism, and the story that follows both confirms what he says (she is baptized, but must do it herself) and disconfirms it (she succumbs to no temptations, despite being deprived of the "seal"). Streete comments, "The entire exchange is fraught with gender irony and perhaps even satire in that Paul is supposed to be the one whose manly self-control would make him impervious to temptation and whose recognized authority might quell any advances on Thecla's part. . . ."[92] If Thecla's attachment to Paul itself requires a remedy, his ambiguous speech and conduct may assist the detachment.

DESIRE RESISTED, DESIRE DISPLACED

Paul's deferrals and resistances turn to betrayal and abandonment at the outset of the Antioch episode, a decisive turn, not only in the plot, but also in the characterization of both Paul and Thecla. Though briefly rendered, this scene of sexualized violence also has strong echoes in the ancient novels. Helen Morales remarks, "One striking aspect of the Greek novels is the sheer relentlessness with which women are threatened with rape . . ."[93] Another "first man of the city" out in the street asserts male prerogative over Thecla, though Alexander's lustful violence is more abrupt and unjustified than Thamyris's earlier jealous response. Paul responds to Alexander's money and gifts with: Οὐκ οἶδα τὴν γυναῖκα ἥν λέγεις, οὐδέ ἔστιν ἐμή, "I do not know the woman of whom you speak; nor is she mine" (26). Given the recurrent question in the tale of *whose Thecla is*, one might strain to excuse Paul's οὐδὲ ἔστιν ἐμή—she is, after all, God's according to Paul. But the denial of knowing her, together with Paul's complete disappearance from the Antioch narrative, exposes the preacher of blessed virginity to be no protector of virgins' bodies.[94] Subjected to Alexander's forceful embrace, Thecla seeks (ἐζήτει) for Paul for the last time in Antioch, but now her visual effort is accompanied by forceful resistance and a shout of self-defense and self-identification: μὴ βιάσῃ τὴν ξένην, μὴ βιάσῃ τὴν τοῦ θεοῦ δούλην, "Do not do violence to the stranger, do not do violence to the slave of God" (26).[95] From this point and throughout the subsequent scenes in Antioch, Thecla is a vocal, active defender of her own purity, identifying herself repeatedly not as Paul's pursuer but as God's female slave.[96]

The episode in Antioch in many ways parallels that in Iconium, with a spurned high-status male, a sympathetic yet condemning governor, a mother figure, an attempted execution in the arena. Other key narrative elements, however, are not so much repeated with variation as inverted or significantly redeployed. In Iconium, the narrative lingers over the series of precipitating incidents leading to Thecla's interrogation, then swiftly relates her near martyrdom. In Antioch, the precipitating incident and judgment are brief, whereas the attempted execution and associated events are prolonged and multistaged. In Iconium, fire is the means of attempted execution; in Antioch, fire becomes divine, protective enclosure and means of escape, preventing beasts from destroying her and onlookers from viewing her nakedness.

The charge against Thecla has also changed. In Iconium, the παρθένος is condemned for refusing to marry; by being defiantly ἄνυμφον she makes herself ἄνομον. In Antioch, she is not once referred to as παρθένος or ἄνυμφος but is condemned on a charge of being Ἱερόσυλος, a sacrilegious person, a disruptor of civic piety. The charge arises abruptly from her resistance to Alexander's sexual aggression, tearing his mantle, removing his crown or wreath, making him appear scandalized or conquered. To help explain the accusation, Dennis MacDonald draws from the Armenian version of the Thecla tale, which adds that she "tore off the golden crown of the figure of Caesar, which he had on his head, and dashed it to the ground." MacDonald comments, "This variant, even if secondary, captures the intent of the original, for Alexander does not accuse her of assault but of sacrilege (AP 3:28). She had mocked the cult of the Augustus by violating the imperial numen associated with the wreath."[97] Making the charge more understandable, however, may lessen its effect. For at the stark level of the Greek text, the charge of Ἱερόσυλος indicates that the city equates an assault on male honor and resistance to an elite male's eros with an assault on a temple or resistance to civic piety. Issues of gender and desire are from this point reconfigured. Whereas Thecla in Iconium is presented as desirous subject in search of Paul, Thecla in Antioch is resistant object of male sexual aggression, her purity protected by her own agency, by female allies, and by God. Indeed, male and female characters in Antioch are strikingly polarized. In Iconium, antagonists and supporters do not divide by gender: Some women and virgins are adherents of Paul's teaching, while Theocleia is the chief antagonist; Demas, Hermogenes, and Thamyris are also antagonists, but Onesiphorus is an adherent; a mixture of οἱ παῖδες καὶ αἱ παρθένοι, youths and virgins, bring the fuel for Thecla's execution in the earlier episode (22). In Antioch, however, the women of the city, functioning as a collective character, are immediately, indeed inexplicably, Thecla's supporters, repeatedly objecting that the city and the judgment against Thecla are impious. They shout, Κακὴ κρίσις, ἀνοσία κρίσις, "An evil judgment, an impious judgment" (27), and pray, Ὦ Θεέ, ἀνοσία κρίσις γίνεται ἐν τῇ πόλει ταύτῃ, "Oh God, an impious judgment has occurred in this city" (28). These are vocal women, as Thecla now is a vocal woman, whose public utterances seem to function as McInerney describes:

> The reactions of the women in the audience suggest something more than sympathy, however. They function as a *conclamatio*, an acclamation, which was in the Roman world of late antiquity a very specific form of public speech with definite religious and civic implications. . . . Public acclamations were often recorded by stenographers and appended to records of legislative proceedings, or inscribed on monuments or milestones. Acclamation is constituted by voices speaking in unison, often in ritual and repetitive language, and indicated in description or transcription by phrases such as *mia phone*, "in one voice."[98]

The women's vocal defense of Thecla is matched by the fierce lioness, who shows solidarity in the pregames processional (28), then fights to the death against male beasts attacking Thecla during the games themselves (33).

Male characters, however, are uniformly unhelpful if not aggressive. Paul's disappearance (26), the governor's ineffectual sympathy (34), and Alexander's sustained aggression are all motivated by their perception of Thecla as a beautiful and desirable woman. Lions, bears, and seals are unable to kill τὴν θηριομάχον, "the female fighter with beasts" (30). When "other more terrible beasts" are let loose, Thecla's chorus of female supporters throws such an abundance of perfumes into the arena that the animals are drugged into sleep. Alexander's last resort conveys graphically the male erotic threat to Thecla: Καὶ ἔδησαν αὐτὴν ἐκ τῶν ποδῶν μέσον τῶν ταύρων, καὶ ὑπὸ τὰ ἀναγκαῖα αὐτῶν πεπυρωμένα σίδηρα ὑπέθηκαν, ἵνα πλείονα ταραχθέντες ἀποκτείνωσιν αὐτήν, "And they bound her by the feet between two bulls, and they placed flaming hot irons under their necessary parts, so that being deranged, they would kill her" (35). Had the reader missed the threat of male sexual aggression to this point, burning heat under the genitals of bulls positioned to tear the woman up the middle makes it inescapable. Yet divine fire bests sexual fire: the "cloud of fire" that has encompassed Thecla's body since she baptized herself burns through the ropes tying her to the bulls, and she is freed. Erotic desire in the Antioch episode of the tale is located in male beasts and humans, not in Thecla herself; it is a threat from without rather than a destabilizing force from within. Gender polarization seems part of the resistance to aggressive male desire.

Next to Thecla, the character in Antioch who is most in narrative focus, and whose perspective is most frequently provided is Tryphaena, relative of the emperor, female head of elite household, who becomes a replacement mother: taking Thecla "under her protection" (εἰς τήρησιν) and receiving her as a consolation (εἰς παραμυθίαν)" for her deceased daughter, Falconilla (27). In Kristeva's words, in maternal desire, "the 'object' of satisfaction is transformed into an 'other'—to care for, to nourish. . . ."[99] In part, Tryphaena certainly serves as a patron to Thecla, in a relationship that is voluntary and asymmetrical, yet personalized and reciprocal.[100] Yet maternal language predominates: Tryphaena calls her, τέκνον μου δεύτερον Θέκλα, "my second daughter, Thecla" (29). Her dreams, prayers, and thoughts regarding Thecla are all reported by the narrator, and she functions as the inverse of Theocleia, Thecla's birth mother. Whereas Theocleia insisted on marriage, Tryphaena protects purity understood as sexual renunciation. Whereas Theocleia was the one who cried out (ἀνέκραγεν) for Thecla's execution in Antioch (20), Tryphaena cries loudly (ἀνέκραξεν) and puts Alexander to flight when he arrives to take Thecla to the games, deferring the destructive threat of male eros (30). After Thecla's final miraculous deliverance from the arena, Tryphaena assigns to her τὰ ἐμὰ πάντα, "all that is mine" (39). The conversion of Tryphaena's household, including τῶν παιδισκῶν τὰς πλείονας, "most of the female servants," and marked by μεγάλην χαράν, "great joy" (39) redresses the earlier terrible wailing of Theocleia's household, including her παιδίσκαι, over the loss of Thecla (10).

Yet Tryphaena supplants more than Theocleia's role; she also provides for Thecla what Paul and his absences repeatedly withhold or deny. The same verb of benevolent affection that has been used for Paul and Thecla is also used for Tryphaena's maternal affection for Thecla, but strengthened: στέργουσα ἐμπόνως, "loving her intensely" (29). Whereas Paul was nowhere to be found when Thecla sought him ὡς ἀμνὸς ἐν ἐρήμῳ, "as a lamb in the desert" (21), Tryphaena protects τήν ξένην τήν ἔρημον Θεκλάν, "the desolate stranger, Thecla" (Falconilla's words at 28). Whereas Paul disappeared as Alexander molested Thecla, Thecla honors Tryphaena, καὶ ὅτι με ἀγνὴν ἐτήρησεν, "because she preserved me pure" (31). Whereas Paul was nowhere to be found at Thecla's first execution, and an apparition of the Lord had to sub in, Tryphaena follows her during the exhibition of the beasts (28), stays close to Thecla (ἡ δὲ Τρύφαινα οὐκ ἀπέστη, "but Tryphaena did not stand aloof") and holds her hand on the way to the arena (31). Finally, with a gendered irony, Tryphaena's timely, feminine fainting stops the games (36). That moment also provides a key turn in the various claims about threats to the city: while Theocleia has said Paul will destroy Iconium (9), and Thamyris repeats the charge (15–16), the women of Antioch say the charge against Thecla will destroy Antioch (32), and now Alexander urges the governor to stop the games or the presumed death of the emperor's relative will destroy the city (36). Paul, the preacher of ἐγκράτεια and ανάστασις, is outdone by the maternal figure who actively protects ἐγκράτεια and concludes, Νῦν πιστεύω ὅτι νεκροὶ ἐγείρονται, "Now I believe that the dead are raised" (39).

Yet in the series of narrative reversals and replacements Paul is supplanted not only by Tryphaena but by God. As Alexander comes to take Thecla to the games and Tryphaena laments, οὐδεὶς ὁ βοηθῶν, "There is no-one to help," it is Paul's absence as helper that is most notable. She pleads, ὁ θεὸς Θέκλης τοῦ τέκνου μου. Βοήθησον Θέκλη; "O God of Thecla my child, help Thecla" (30). The shift from Paul to God is most evident in the characterization of Thecla. Her image as seeker after Paul gives way to her activity as preacher, confessor, and slave of God. The verbs of seeing and seeking that dominate descriptions of Thecla in the Iconium episode are replaced by speeches and prayers in Antioch. She vocally protests Alexander's assault; she petitions for protection of her purity; she prays at least three times, interceding for others as well as petitioning for her own deliverance.[101] And she not only speaks but acts: most notably, baptizing herself. The fast-paced narrative deviates from its usual spare quality as it reiterates the statement about Thecla's autobaptism:

Τότε εἰσβάλλουσιν πολλὰ θηρία, ἑστώσης αὐτῆς καὶ ἐκτετακυί-
ας τὰς χεῖρας καὶ προσευχομένης. ὡς δὲ ἐτέλεσεν τὴν
προσευχήν, ἐστράφη καὶ εἶδεν ὄρυγμα μέγα πλῆρες ὕδατος, καὶ
εἶπεν Νῦν καιρὸς λούσασθαί με. καὶ ἔβαλεν ἑαυτὴν λέγουσα Ἐν
τῷ ὀνόματι Ἰησοῦ Χριστοῦ ὑστέρᾳ ἡμέρᾳ βαπτίζομαι. Καὶ
ἰδοῦσαι αἱ γυναῖκες καὶ πᾶς ὁ ὄχλος ἔκλαυσαν λέγοντες Μὴ
βάλῃς ἑαυτὴν εἰς τὸ ὕδωρ, ὥστε καὶ τὸν ἡγεμόνα δακρῦσαι, ὅτι
τοιοῦτον κάλλος φῶκαι ἔμελλον ἐσθίειν. ἡ μὲν οὖν ἔβαλεν ἑαυτὴν
εἰς τὸ ὕδωρ ἐν τῷ ὀνόματι Ἰησοῦ Χριστοῦ . . .

Then they cast in many beasts, as she stood and stretched out her hands and prayed. But when she finished the prayer, she turned and saw a great pit full of water, and she said, "Now is the time for me to wash myself." And she cast herself in saying, "In the name of Jesus Christ on the last day I baptize myself." And as they saw it, the women and the whole crowd wept, saying, "Do not cast yourself in the water!" So that even the governor cried that such beauty was about to be eaten by seals. So, then, she threw herself into the water in the name of Jesus Christ . . . (34)

Both the narrator and God vindicate Thecla's desperate act, performed in an apparent conviction that this is to be her last day. The story first puts her self-pronounced baptismal formula "in the name of Jesus Christ" in direct speech, then the narrator repeats it, as though to emphasize that she did the ritual properly. God responds with the enveloping fire that prevents beasts from touching her or her naked body from being seen.

After her attempted execution, the Governor's question is not *whose* Thecla is, but *who* she is: τίς εἶ σύ; Thecla responds, Ἐγὼ μέν εἰμι Θεοῦ τοῦ ζῶντος δούλη, "I am a female slave of the living God," then offers a speech about who God is, full of Psalmic language of shelter and refuge (37). Whereas in the Iconium arena, the Lord appeared in the place of Paul, in Antioch, Paul is supplanted by the single God. The Governor overturns the accusation that Thecla is Ἱερόσυλος by pronouncing her τὴν τοῦ θεοῦ δούλην τὴν θεοσεβῆ, the pious slave of God (38). As the whole city of Iconium was previously shaken by Paul (πόλιν ἀνασείει, 9), now the whole city of Antioch is shaken by the sound of women's praise (σεισθῆναι πᾶσαν τὴν πόλιν, 38).

REVERBERATION

Yet the resolution of desire is not so tidy. The final section of *The Acts of Paul and Thecla* offers what Barthes calls *retentissement*, a reverberation—a return to the unresolved tension of desire.[102] Ἡ δὲ Θέκλα Παῦλον ἐπεπόθει καὶ ἐζήτει αὐτὸν περιπέμπουσα πανταχοῦ; "But Thecla yearned for Paul and sought after him, sending in every direction" (40). The verb of desire, ἐπιποθέω, is the same one used the first time Thecla yearns to be worthy to stand in Paul's presence (8). The first and last expressions of desire for Paul are the same. Learning that Paul is at Myra, Thecla travels with a group of young men and maidservants to meet him (a seeming end to the gender polarization in Antioch), dressed in a mantle she has sewn into a cloak after the fashion of men. Paul is amazed, and still fretting incorrectly about πειρασμός, temptation. Yet though her quest for Paul has re-emerged, Thecla is a reconstituted self, no longer gazing silently. She initiates direct speech; she announces her baptism. Indeed, it is Paul who is initially silent, whose astonishment is reported by the narrator and discerned by Thecla. After hearing her full account, and her intention to return to Iconium, Paul does speak, with remarkable words commissioning her as a female apostle: "Go and teach the word of God!"[103] Yet, like his earlier prayer for her deliverance, the words seem belated, ineffectual. Through Tryphaena's means, Thecla becomes benefactor to Paul, providing clothing and gold for Paul's service to the poor (41).

What, then, does one make of her final return to Iconium?

Αὐτὴ δὲ ἀπῆλθεν εἰς Ἰκόνιον. καὶ εἰσέρχεται εἰς τὸν Ὀνησιφόρου
οἶκον, καὶ ἔπεσεν εἰς τὸ ἔδαφος ὅπου Παῦλος καθεζόμενος
ἐδίδασκεν τὰ λόγια τοῦ Θεοῦ, καὶ ἔκλαιεν λέγουσα Ὁ Θεός μου
καὶ τοῦ οἴκου τούτου, ὅπου μοι τὸ φῶς ἔλαμψεν, Χριστὲ Ἰησοῦ ὁ
υἱὸς τοῦ Θεοῦ, ὁ ἐμοὶ βοηθὸς ἐν φυλακῇ, βοηθὸς ἐπὶ ἡγεμόνων,
βοηθὸς ἐν πυρί, βοηθὸς ἐν θηρίοις, αὐτὸς εἶ θεός, καὶ σοὶ ἡ δόξα
εἰς τοὺς αἰῶνας, ἀμήν.

But she went away to Iconium. She entered the house of Onesiphorus and threw herself onto the floor where Paul, sitting, had
taught the words of God, and she cried, saying, "O God of mine
and of this house, where the light shone to me, Christ Jesus the son
of God, my helper in prison, my helper before governors, my
helper in the fire, my helper among beasts, you are God, and to you
be glory forever, Amen." (42)

Thecla's action and posture echo her earlier abjection in the prison when
Paul was taken from her; here, however, she throws herself down but does
not "roll." Her prayer, moreover, does not mention Paul, but recapitulates
the plot, resolutely expressing praise of God and of Christ Jesus as her
helper (βοηθὸς) at each stage of what she has endured. The slight reprise
of the motif of longing and desire, therefore, does not return Thecla to the
earlier stage of insistent, infatuated seeking for Paul, though it does suggest
that desire leaves an unresolved and destabilizing residue. With the narrator's brief comment that Thamyris is dead, the final scene becomes an
appeal to the mother who rejected her, an unanswered question about
maternal desire: "Mother Theocleia (Θεοκλεία μῆτηρ), can you believe
that the Lord lives in heaven? For if you desire money (εἴτε χρήματα
ποθεῖς) the Lord will give it to you through me; or if your child (εἴτε τὸ
τέκνον), behold, I am standing beside you" (43). The tale closes by men-
tioning Thecla's long ministry in Seleucia, followed by death.[104]

REREADING/REWRITING THECLA AND DESIRE

The elements of desire in *The Acts of Paul and Thecla* leave some readers
uneasy, though for differing reasons. Some see the emphasis on Thecla's
emotional attachment to and longing for Paul as inconsistent with her
autonomy and agency, a possible consequence of embedding a previously
independent *Acts of Thecla* within the *Acts of Paul*, thereby subordinating

the transgressive female minister to the apostle.[105] In antiquity, also, Thecla's manifestations of desire were apparently an interpretive sticking point
for some readers. The author of the fourth-century *Life and Miracles of the
Holy Apostle and Martyr of Christ Thecla*, retells and expands the *Acts of
Thecla*, adding a second book of stories about such wonders as Thecla's
healings of various illnesses, her interventions on behalf of marriage, and
her protection of her own cultic sanctuary.[106] Scott Fitzgerald Johnson
offers a recent literary study of the *Life*, and Elizabeth Castelli also analyzes
it as "compelling testimony to the role of collective memory in generating
a useable past for Christians out of a story that incorporates compelling
episodes of innocent suffering and eventual vindication."[107] Gilbert Dagron's earlier commentary on the *Life* shows how its elaborations and omis-
sions serve to diminish criticism of Paul (gone, for example, is Paul's denial
that he knows "the woman") and to minimize or explain potentially scan-
dalous conduct in Thecla, particularly conduct that might inspire women
to preach or baptize.[108]

How, then, does this later author rewrite elements of desire in Thecla's
tale? In key places, the author minimizes depictions of Thecla as subject of
desire. In the scene of Thecla at her window transfixed by Paul's words, the
Life spreads the symptoms of desire among more auditors; whether they
are men or women, Paul inspires $εἰς$ $πολλὴν$ $καὶ$ $ἄπειρον$ $ἐπιθυμίαν$ $τῶν$
$ὑπερ$ $τῆς$ $εὐσεβείας$ $λόγων$ $ἐνάγειν$ (3.3–4), "a great and boundless desire
to attend to words of piety." Thecla's own symptoms are retained but
explained: her motionlessness is due to her modesty, her age, and custom
(3.11–12); her self-neglect is not love-sickness but the beginning of self-
restrained refusals of food, primping, perfumes (3.19–24). Her desire is
named but carefully qualified by an adjective: $τὴν$ $καλὴν$ $ἐπιθυμίαν$,
"good" or "honorable desire" (3.12–13). In the prison scene, her bold
action in coming to Paul is acknowledged to be shocking behavior for a
maiden, but is hedged by the narrator's offering three alternate social perspectives for reading her actions: "she conceived and carried out a deed
very rash for a young girl, very courageous for an older woman, and even
very zealous for a Christian initiate" (8.15–17).[109] Again, rather than
leaving a reader to speculate that desire motivates her, the narrator names
her desire, and insists on its sanctity: $ὁ$ $γὰρ$ $περὶ$ $τὴν$ $εὐσέβειαν$ $ἔρως$ $ἤδη$
$καὶ$ $εἰς$ $τολμηροτέρας$ $αὐτὴν$ $ἐνῆγεν$ $ἐνθυμήσεις$ $καὶ$ $πρόξεις$; "For the
eros concerning piety already had led her even to extreme audacity of
thought and action" (8.21–22). Paul himself carefully directs Thecla's erotic

intention, offering a long speech to the explicit end that she might be both betrothed and escorted like a bride to Christ (8.43–44). When Thecla is condemned in Iconium, and Christ appears in the form of Paul, the appearance is not preceded by any emphasis on Thecla's gaze and does not conclude with an ambiguous disappearance (12.33–48). Thecla's desire, then, is variously safeguarded, diffused, or diverted by the narrator's lengthy interventions throughout the Iconium sequence. Yet in a different turn, the tendency is reversed in the closing episode in which Thecla again seeks Paul, with the *Life* heightening Thecla's desire and rooting it in dependence: "The martyr was in awe (ἐτεθήπει) of Paul, and now had no other words but 'Paul,' and 'Where's Paul?,' and 'Who can point me to this one, whom Christ gave as a guide to me and a teacher in his way of life and faith?' For, though she had become widely known and famous from her miracles, she was not now disdainful of her teacher."[110] At the reunion in Iconium, the narrator elaborates the scene, adding new details, such as Thecla kissing the place where Paul once sat (27.5–7). Her prayer, which in the second-century *Acts* is only directed to God and Christ and does not mention Paul, in the *Life* explicitly articulates her dependence upon Paul and her gratitude that she was worthy to find Paul again and receive strength from his words (27.8–15). Whereas the early *Acts of Thecla* shows desire as a destabilizing force that fuels Thecla's movement out of household and city and into itinerant ministry but attenuates the final reverberation of desire, the later *Life of Thecla* diminishes the conversionary possibilities of desire, but heightens its subordinating effects at the close of Thecla's story.

Thecla as *object* of aggressive male desire is elaborated strikingly in the *Life*. At the opening of the Antioch scene, Alexander's raging desire is heightened and exaggerated (15.8–16).[111] In an explanation of Alexander's irresistible passion, the narrator makes clear that ἔρως begins with the eyes. Not surprisingly, then, Thecla, in this telling of her story, does not look around desperately for Paul; the gaze belongs only to Alexander. The heightening of Alexander's violent derangement has the effect of exonerating Paul, who attempts to deter him, but cannot (15.34–38). Thecla tears Alexander's cloak, and, as Castelli notes, "a relic of the garment, the author interjects, is preserved as a souvenir (μνήμη) in Thecla's temple so that people can see."[112]

Other late ancient treatments of Thecla depict her desire as love for and betrothal to Christ. Pseudo-Chrysostom's "Panegyric to Thecla," probably dating to the fifth or sixth century, describes Thecla crying for a heavenly bridegroom, and weaves more Pauline texts into her story to extend the image:

> Her flattering relatives kept flowing around her, but she saw Paul appear affirming her, "I betrothed you to Christ to present you as a pure bride to her one husband" (2 Cor 11:2). Her domestic servants beseeched her with tears, but she looked erotically at the Bridegroom. "Who shall separate you from the love of Christ?" (Rom 8:35).[113]

When recent scholars suggest that Thecla in the *Acts* moves from being a bride for Thamyris to being a bride of Christ,[114] or when they trace a progressive platonic elevation of Thecla's desire from Thamyris to Paul to God,[115] they are, to some extent, recapitulating old interpretations. They are also making simple and schematic something that the spare second-century narrative itself leaves more opaque. The appearances, diversions, and reappearances of desire in the *Acts of Thecla* better invite a reading of desire as displacement, as a chain of substitutions. To identify the displacements in this tale as a straightforward series (Thamyris to Paul to Christ/God) is to deny the extent to which the aims of desire remain cloaked, to disregard the possibility that the aim and trajectory of desire may be other than it appears to the subject,[116] and to minimize the paradoxes of a passionate quest for ἐγκράτεια. More simply, Thecla's devotion to God is not expressed at any point as a form of ἐπιθυμία or πάθος. She characterizes herself consistently as God's slave, not God's bride. Although the story is structured so that Paul is supplanted in the second half, not merely by Tryphaena, but more emphatically by God, the narrative offers no corresponding redirection of the manifestations of desire.

Desire, however, initiates the transformation in Thecla's identity. Again, Butler offers a helpful restatement of Lacan: "Lacan's formulation that 'desire is for the desire of the Other' works in at least two ways: the desire for the Other's desire, to be its object, but also to mime its ways and, in miming, to assume an identity other than one's own."[117] Desire subverts Thecla's socially constructed self and reverses her intention. Just as in many of the ancient novels, infatuation or lovesickness becomes a mechanism of detachment from previous social identity, an impetus that disrupts prior social relations and launches a new allegiance. As interpreters such as Fusillo and Konstan have made plain, for the couples in the Greek romances, the instabilities of desire both precede and propel subsequent fidelity and chastity.[118] For Thecla, desire brings about a disintegration and reconstitution of her social self, as infatuation gives way to fidelity, as voice takes precedence over gaze, as ἐγκράτεια supplants marriage.[119]

What, then, might attention to the interplay of desire and self-restraint contribute to the discussion of gender construction in *The Acts of Paul and Thecla*? Thecla's transformation from cloistered virgin to gladiator, from passive listener to bold preacher, from pursuer of Paul to intercessor for others can indeed be read as progressive masculinization.[120] Her agency and activity through the latter half of the story transgress the usual cultural codes for femininity. Yet elite writers such as Plutarch and Musonius Rufus both argued that manliness or courage in women is admirable precisely when it is necessary to protect chastity.[121] If we remain attentive to the vulnerability of Thecla's body and her purity to aggressive male desire— then it seems the story offers a kind of gender bending that requires gender polarization as well. If this is masculinization, it is a form only a woman could experience, and requires the agency of other women and the protection of maternal desire. Transvestitism seems the better term.[122] Moreover, an easy characterization of Thecla's own transformation as a move from feminine desire to masculine control belies the complexity of how desire and restraint function in the narrative. Desire takes destructive forms in certain characters, and Thecla is never so autonomous as to be unaffected. Yet desire is destabilizing in ways that propel conversion— social re-identification, ritual act, changes in language, changes in the self. ἐγκρατεία with its companion value ἀνάστασις are not the antidotes to Thecla's new desire and strange passion, but the objects and structuring principles. The final scene—with the woman's body in a man's cloak, the autonomous confessor who one last time seeks Paul, then offers herself again as child that her mother might desire—closes a tale that effects paradoxical conversion, not merely of the protagonist, but of complex cultural codes.

FOUR

Aseneth and the Sublime Turn

THE ANCIENT GREEK LITERARY CRITIC CALLED "LONGINUS" in his treatise *On Sublimity* (περὶ ὕψους), written some-time between the first and third centuries CE,[1] preserves an ode of Sappho, an exemplary treatment, he says, of "the passions involved in the madness of love":

> That one seems to me to be like the gods, the man whosoever sits facing you and listens nearby to your sweet speech and desir-able laughter—which surely terrifies the heart in my chest; for as I look briefly at you, so can I no longer speak at all, my tongue is silent, broken, a silken fire suddenly has spread beneath my skin, with my eyes I see nothing, my hearing hums, a cold sweat grips me, a trembling seizes me entire, more pale than grass am I, I seem to myself to be little short of dead. But everything is to be endured . . . (10.2)[2]

That the poem expresses woman-centered desire in both object and subject goes unremarked by Longinus. His response, however, is intense: "Do you not marvel at the way she pursues, all at once, her soul and body, her hearing and tongue, her vision and complexion, all lost to her as though not hers at all? She is cold and hot, mad and sane, frightened and near death, all by turns. The result is that we see in her not a single emo-tion, but a complex of emotions" (10.3).[3] The gaze of desire renders the speaker speechless, overtaken by conflict and contradiction, approaching passionate self-dissolution and in pursuit of herself. Longinus notes that the disintegrative effect of passion is common, even conventional. Yet Sappho is extraordinary: "Lovers experience all this; Sappho's excellence . . . lies in her adoption and combination of the most striking details" (10.3). That is, the poet's control of language, her keen articulation of her body's disarticulation, her concentrated eloquence about speechlessness, make the poem an instance of the Longinian sublime—what Neil Hertz has termed a movement of disintegration and figurative reconstitution that may be called "the sublime turn."[4]

Sublimity, ὕψος, is not just the key term in Longinus, but a slippery one.[5] The sublime is at once (or variously) a quality of literary excellence, a social category, an ethical achievement, and perhaps most consistently and evocatively, an ecstatic state, or response, or effect on a reader, surpassing either literary pleasure or rhetorical persuasion: "For grandeur produces ecstasy rather than persuasion in the hearer; and the combination of wonder and astonishment always proves superior to the merely persuasive and pleasant" (4). Sublimity is also, throughout Longinus's text, performed or enacted or demonstrated by the critic himself. Readers become *voyeurs* as we watch this critic's enactment of sublime responses to a range of literary and rhetorical citations. In Alexander Pope's words, Longinus "is himself the great Sublime he draws."[6] As Hertz made clear in his seminal essay on Longinus, the texts this critic cites, and the analyses he offers of them, show that, for him, sublimity is not simply "greatness of thought or style"—it is found, rather, in complex passages that often bring together the threat of a dissociation of sensibility, or of personal or cultural loss, with a sublime, recuperative turn expressed literarily or rhetorically.[7]

What might we notice if we move from Sappho's poetic delineation and Longinus's response to another ancient text depicting a woman's desire and sublime turn: the story of Aseneth? The protagonist in the novella *Joseph and Aseneth*, a text known in some early manuscripts as simply *Aseneth* or *The Prayer and Conversion of Aseneth*, is an Egyptian virgin, beautiful but, at the story's outset, emphatically pagan. The story imaginatively fills gaps in a terse, single verse from Genesis: "Pharoah gave Joseph the name Zaphenath-paneah; and he gave him Asenath daughter of Potiphera, priest of On, as his wife. Thus Joseph gained authority over the land of Egypt" (41:45 NRSV). Brief and enigmatic, the note in Genesis nevertheless joins an Egyptian to the Israelite patriarch and links marriage and cultural power. Part One, the longest part of the story, offers one answer to the question of how the honored Hebrew patriarch known for his sexual self-restraint was married by Pharoah to the daughter of an Egyptian priest. Part Two, then, might be seen as a long elaboration of "Thus Joseph gained authority"—offering a story that shows *in what way* Joseph's marriage increased his sweeping power in Egypt. The protagonist, however, is not Joseph, but Aseneth. Like Thecla, she is high-born, stunningly beautiful, and much desired by elite males. Furthermore, this story, like the *Apocryphal Acts*, has affinities with the ancient Greek romances, and seems both to imitate and to subvert some of the novels' conventions and ideologies. The text shares with *The Shepherd of Hermas* some interestingly similar elements of cosmology and a crucial emphasis on a heavenly figure who personifies *Metanoia*. It shares with both the Thecla and Hermas narratives an intricate interplay of images of purity and self-restraint, motifs of desire, and the transformed identity of its central figure. Early in the tale, the arrogance and sense of identity of the beautiful virgin Aseneth suddenly disintegrates at the sight of Joseph. Faced with the adamant "ethnic separatism" of this desirable "alien virgin,"[8] she abruptly repudiates her Egyptian deities, and through lingering stages of inner and outer transformation becomes a fittingly radiant bride for Joseph and a paradigmatic convert to Israel's God. As Aseneth's personal and cultural identity become malleable, then newly stabilized, Joseph and Joseph's God gain authority within Egypt.

Similar motifs notwithstanding, the narrative texture of *Joseph and Aseneth* differs strikingly from both *The Acts of Paul and Thecla* and *The Shepherd of Hermas*. Aseneth's tale is characterized by minimal external action in its first and most extended section. Rather than action, the narrative is dominated by detailed and vivid descriptions of settings, of clothing, and of bodies as well as by soliloquies, prayers, and dialogue with a striking figure who appears from heaven. Its language is densely figurative and allusive, with symbols that prompt varied interpretations. Strictly allegorical readings of the text seem unconvincing, but its narrative texture, extravagant language, and extremes of emotion and experience repeatedly suggest surpluses of meaning that reach well beyond the literal. Longinus, then, may offer ways to enhance a close reading of the ancient tale of *Joseph and Aseneth*, not just through the resonance of Sappho's ode and his extensive critical lexicon. Longinus's literary-rhetorical exploration of ecstasy, passion, threat, moral and cultural transformation, and the sublime may selectively be brought alongside Aseneth's story to see what reciprocal insights may be generated. As Peter Brooks has remarked of his own readings, the goal is not to lay a theory over a text as an interpretive grid, but "to think in terms of an interference of two systems, where you start from two different places, one in the literary text, the other in theoretical considerations, and try to see what their merger looks like, and what happens as they start to contaminate one another, as you create a sort of effect of superimposition of one on the other (and vice versa). . . ."[9] Such a reading benefits, however, from a selective overview of elements in the scholarly discussion of this intriguing text.

UNCERTAINTIES ABOUT *ASENETH:*
TEXT AND CONTEXT

With *Joseph and Aseneth*, as with many other texts classed as "Old Testament Pseudepigrapha," the level of controversy about basic questions of text, date, provenance, and authorship is high—higher than for *The Shepherd of Hermas* and the other Apostolic Fathers or for *The Acts of Paul and Thecla* and the other Apocryphal Acts, and higher now than a decade ago.[10] Scholars continue to debate whether a longer or shorter recension of the text is more likely to be original. The debate stems from significant textual studies undertaken in the 1960s by Marc Philonenko and Christoph Burchard.[11] Both scholars agreed that the sixteen surviving Greek texts of *Joseph and Aseneth* could be grouped into four text families, *a, b, c,* and *d,* and that of these, *a* and *c* showed signs of being late revisions of an earlier version. Of the two remaining text families, Philonenko argued that the earliest was *d,* a shorter version of the tale that is without, among other things, significant sections of Aseneth's private revelatory experience. Burchard preferred *b,* arguing that *d* was a later truncation of the more original longer tale. Burchard's argument appeared to persuade most scholars at least until the 1990s, and the longer version of Aseneth became the basis of many scholarly studies.[12]

In the last decade, however, the preference for the longer text has been challenged. The text-critical discussion has also shifted toward comparison of the two text families as distinctive literary works (or reworkings) in their own right, each with somewhat different ideological investments in representing the female protagonist. Angela Standhartinger analyzes both

Philonenko's and Burchard's reconstructed texts, arguing that priority
goes to the shorter text, and that many of the redactional interventions of
the longer text are gender related. The shorter text is less sexualized and
less androcentric, she claims, whereas the longer makes Aseneth more
dependent on male figures for her transformation.[13] Ross Kraemer devotes
a chapter in her extensive study of *Aseneth* to how "traditional elements,"
including "underlying biblical and parabiblical paradigms," are enhanced
in the longer reconstruction.[14] Overall, Kraemer concludes that the differences are more explicable if one assumes a movement from the shorter
text to the longer. She, too, finds a perceptible difference in gender construction in the longer text.[15] Edith Humphrey, generally unpersuaded by
these arguments, takes up many details of both Standhartinger's and Kraemer's analyses and suggests alternate explanations and readings. Humphrey
also offers a careful literary analysis to support her preference for the
longer text, arguing that its structure and development evince a greater
narrative integrity than does the shorter text.[16] Burchard has recently
reviewed afresh the text-critical evidence, responded to Standhartinger
and Kraemer, and offered a refined argument for the longer text.[17] For the
kind of analysis I here propose, the longer recension's more ample motifs,
together with its greater development of Aseneth's elevated, revelatory
experience recommend it. I rely, therefore, on Burchard's reconstruction,
available in his recently published eclectic text, without arguing it is necessarily the earlier or more original.[18]

Scholars have tended to treat as interconnected the questions of provenance, dating, and authorial identity. Many have taken the story's setting
in Egypt as a reliable indication of its provenance (though some note that
Egypt might simply provide an exotic locale for a novella). Most have
concluded or assumed the author is Jewish, concerned with maintaining
Jewish identity, and perhaps with the status of proselytes within Judaism.
In style and content, *Joseph and Aseneth* seems to presuppose knowledge of
the Septuagint. In its depiction of Egypt, the text may assume or advocate
a level of social tolerance toward Jews. Many scholars, then, use these
interconnected considerations to date the text between approximately 110
BCE and 115 CE.[19]

A multifaceted and erudite challenge to that set of linked assumptions
has come from Ross Kraemer. She argues that a prudent agnosticism
may be the most reasonable stance to the question of the religious self-
understanding of the author, who she suggests could have been either a

Christian or a non-Christian Jew, and to questions of provenance, suggesting that "Aseneth could have been composed virtually anywhere in the Greek-speaking world in the late Roman period."[20] About dating, however, Kraemer offers not agnosticism but a strong counterproposal to the prior consensus, arguing that *Aseneth* is a late-ancient tale, "more likely to have been composed no earlier than the third century CE."[21] This conclusion partly derives from the extensive work Kraemer does to trace similarities between *Joseph and Aseneth* and other forms of late antique religion: from solar imagery, to magical adjurations of angels, to Neoplatonic and Jewish mystical speculation, especially Hekhalot texts. Kraemer also notes that all the direct witnesses to the text are late and that there are no secure allusions to the text in the Hellenistic or early Roman periods.[22] Specialists have expressed skepticism about some aspects of Kraemer's analysis (including the late-ancient dating) but appreciation for the complexity and nuance of her study.[23] Answers to questions of provenance, authorial identity, and date can no longer be assumed secure, but are being newly argued. Collins, for example, makes a fresh case for the previous consensus position—composition in Egypt by a Jewish author between roughly 100 BCE and 100 CE. He underscores the story's focus on the problem of religious intermarriage—a concern "ubiquitous in ancient Jewish literature" and relatively less prominent in Christian texts—and suggests the story's second part would have been particularly resonant for Jews in Egypt in the last century of Ptolemaic rule.[24]

LITERARY BACKGROUNDS FOR A CHAMELEON-LIKE TALE

At the close of her wide-ranging study, adducing multiple history-of-religions parallels to *Aseneth*, Kraemer acknowledges candidly, "Like the ancient image of the chameleon, [*Aseneth*'s] texts tend to resemble whatever we lay them against . . ."[25] The question of where best to find comparative texts, however, remains pressing. Pervo phrased the question pointedly several decades ago: "what works should we read against Jos. and As. in order to clarify our understanding of its purpose and function?"[26] To begin, one must, I think, lay *Joseph and Aseneth* alongside the biblical texts to which the story clearly refers or which it markedly resembles. Burchard's extensive footnotes in his *Old Testament Pseudepigrapha* translation and Kraemer's rich study of biblical and parabiblical elements in

Aseneth make these parallels readily available. At the most straightforward level, *Joseph and Aseneth* is said to function as "rewritten Bible."[27] It presupposes the Genesis Joseph traditions (the reader, for instance, must supply prior knowledge of seven years of plenty, seven of famine, as well as of Joseph's prior escapades with a predatory woman and jealous brothers), yet answers questions left begging by Genesis's brevity. The allusive range of the story, however, goes well beyond Genesis to a complex play of relationships with other biblical and extrabiblical texts. Sapiential treatments of Woman Wisdom and her counterpart, the Strange Woman, are echoed in descriptions of Aseneth's transformation.[28] The story also draws from the Song of Songs with depictions of the lover's posture, gaze, and body along with images of walled gardens of delight. Prophetic imagery is evoked, such as Zion as the daughter of God, as the walled city of refuge, and as the divine bride. Other features of *Joseph and Aseneth* recall apocalyptic texts, with their heavens wrenched open, startling epiphanies, and enigmatic, polyvalent symbolism.[29] These intertextual elements are incorporated in the tale, not as transparent citations, but in varying permutations, oppositions, and degrees of indefiniteness. That is, the story does not so much cite the rich range of biblical intertexts as transpose them from their original significations to the new signifying system of *Joseph and Aseneth*.[30]

Other scholars lay *Joseph and Aseneth* beside ancient texts that speak of conversion of pagans to Judaism. That is, the story about how an Egyptian girl becomes a fitting wife for a Hebrew patriarch is sometimes examined for what it might say about whether Judaism was a missionary religion, what rituals or processes might accompany conversion to Judaism, what the status of proselytes within Judaism might be, or more broadly, how relations between Jews and Gentiles might be construed. Though some have argued that the text supports or provides evidence for proselytizing activity, the balanced treatment of Randall Chesnutt more convincingly concludes that *Joseph and Aseneth* is not a missionary work, but does intend to elevate the status of proselytes within the Jewish community.[31] The text's symbolism offers little evidence of historical conversion rituals, but a high view of the full incorporation of converts into Jewish community, and therewith a reminder to Jews of their privileges and responsibilities.[32]

The set of texts among which the chameleon-like *Joseph and Aseneth* seems particularly at home is that of the ancient novel in its varied forms. Like the ideal Greek romances, *Joseph and Aseneth* features a pair of high-born, extraordinarily beautiful lovers both committed first to virginity, then to chastity; a divinely ordained marriage that faces obstacles that must be overcome; language of initiation and death linked to proving oneself worthy of marriage; and the approximation of the lovers to divinities in their appearance and their social function.[33] Like the Greek romances, *Joseph and Aseneth* is working with cultural constructions of marriage, gender, desire, and transformation. Like certain other Jewish novellas, particularly Susanna, Greek Esther, and Judith, *Joseph and Aseneth* features a female heroine, who, as Wills remarks, "is much more than a new stock figure in the repertoire of characters; she is the medium through which certain obsessions of the author and audience are expressed."[34] Aseneth shares with these stories scenes of self-abasement, including undressing and dressing and extended prayers, that convey some form of change in identity. Across these stories, the woman's body is a locus of interest and often an object of desire by male characters—desire that motivates the plot. It is men's desire for women that Esther and Judith strategically activate and that Susanna must defend against, like Aseneth in part two of her story, thus becoming heroes who save the Jewish people and exemplify the resourcefulness and cultural superiority by which the Jewish people resist domination.[35] Nevertheless, none of the other stories, in my reading, offers a woman whose own erotic desire compels her. As comparative texts for Aseneth, they offer no parallel to her disintegrative experiences of desire, her mystical and ecstatic experience of divine transformation, or her paradigmatic role as proselyte.

To account for the mystical or esoteric elements of *Joseph and Aseneth*, the "something more" of this text, scholars have looked elsewhere. Philonenko's commentary discussed three types of novel he thought were identifiable in the text: *roman missionaire*, with Aseneth as a model of repentance and conversion; *roman à clef*, with Aseneth portrayed in a way that corresponds "trait pour trait" with the Egyptian goddess Neith; and *roman mistique*, complete with astrological imagery, a gnostic mythological drama similar to Sophia's redemption through union with divine Logos, and a sacramental ritual reminiscent of mystery cult initiations and feasts.[36] Edith Humphrey argues that the whole epiphany and revelation sequence "compares aptly to the genre 'apocalypse' in mode, structure, content, and function." She concludes that the tale may be seen fruitfully as a "romance with a difference," a difference that must be illuminated by reference to works that are neither romantic nor novelistic."[37] Pervo, in an analysis that

predates that of Wills, accounts differently for the combination of revelatory and romance elements in Aseneth's story, arguing that it belongs to a
tradition of ancient Jewish sapiential novels like Tobit, *Ahikar*, and the first
six chapters of Daniel, in which a traditional popular story has been
enriched by (and possibly subordinated to) edifying wisdom material.
Though Pervo explores ways the ancient erotic romances also influence
Joseph and Aseneth, he holds that "the love story obviously serves as a scant
frame for a religious message . . ."[38]

Pervo's remark in no way summarizes his several complex and lively
readings of the tale, but it asks to be tested.[39] What is it that makes *Joseph
and Aseneth* at once a love story and a story of spiritual change? Is one
aspect of Aseneth's identity transformation subordinate to another? How
are the connections drawn between Aseneth's transformation from virgin to bride, from stranger to kin, from idolater to venerator of the most
high God? A reading of *Joseph and Aseneth* framed by such questions
should attend closely to the range of textual markers of Aseneth's identity and its malleability. Her status as "virgin" proves especially resonant
throughout the text—particularly ambivalent and conducive to transformation—as she seeks union with the virgin Joseph.[40] Furthermore, this
highly visual tale, which has both characters and readers frequently
gazing at various bodies, uses moments when bodies might or do touch
one another as key junctures for issues of piety, kinship, and cultural
identity. I propose, then, a sequential analysis of the story that will attend
closely to the interplay of desire and restraint encoded in virginity and in
male-female contact, and that will explore how conversion functions as
cultural passage that changes the vectors of political authority. I read
Joseph and Aseneth alongside selections from Longinus's *On Sublimity*,
showing that this ancient critic's account of the literary and rhetorical
strategies suited to convey, represent, and perhaps even induce ecstasy
and sublime transformation has some explanatory power for this story. In
offering a literary and rhetorical interpretation, I benefit from Edith
Humphrey's analysis of the text's subsections according to time, space,
and action; characters and imagery; discourse and tone; plot and structure.[41] Humphrey is attentive to both parts of *Joseph and Aseneth*, and
astute about its structure—tracing the presence of chiastic arrangements
and recurrent triads that give particular emphasis to certain features of
the text. My reading is less oriented to structure, attending more to
localized but recurrent figures of speech and textures of language, and

more to the question of how pious restraint, passionate transformation, and cultural power merge in Aseneth's story.

THE VIRGIN ENCLOSED

Joseph and Aseneth opens in Biblical style (Septuagintal, to be precise), with the same words used to begin the books of Joshua, Judges, Ruth, and 2 Samuel: καὶ ἐγένετο, "And it happened . . ." The narrator presupposes the reader's familiarity with Joseph and Pharoah, who are named but not described. Amidst a plentiful harvest, Joseph is on the grain-gathering circuit. Two characters not recognizable from Genesis are then introduced at slower pace. Descriptors of social role and status, of wealth and of particular virtues precede the naming of Pentephres,[42] priest of Heliopolis. He is, πλούσιος σφόδρα καὶ φρόνιμος καὶ ἐπιεικὴς,[43] "exceedingly wealthy and prudent and gentle" (1.3)—admirable qualities in this narrative world. The next character, then, is introduced by familial and sexual status, rather than by virtues: καὶ ἦν θυγάτηρ αὐτῷ παρθένος, "he had a daughter, a virgin . . . ," then by her age—eighteen—and her surpassing beauty (1.4). This beauty, the narrator emphasizes, recalls three generations of Hebrew matriarchs leading to Joseph.

> καὶ αὕτη οὐδὲν εἶχεν ὅμοιον τῶν παρθένων τῶν Αἰγυπτίων ἀλλὰ
> ἦν κατὰ πάντα ὁμοία ταῖς θυγατράσι τῶν Ἑβραίων καὶ ἦν
> μεγάλη ὡς Σάρρα καὶ ὡραία ὡς Ῥεβέκκα καὶ καλὴ ὡς Ῥαχήλ.
> καὶ ἦν τὸ ὄνομα τῆς παρθένου ἐκείνης Ἀσενέθ.

And she was in no way similar to the virgins of the Egyptians but was in every way similar to the daughters of the Hebrews; and she was tall like Sarah and ripe like Rebecca and beautiful like Rachel. And the name of that virgin was Aseneth. (1.5)

The boundaries between Hebrews and Egyptians seem permeable in the opening section: The virtue of an Egyptian priest is admirable; the superlative beauty of the Egyptian virgin daughter is assimilable to that of Joseph's foremothers. So, too, the status of the virgin seems poised for change. At eighteen, it is time to marry, truly to resemble matriarchs. Emphasizing Aseneth's liminality, one more cluster of characters is introduced: high status Egyptian males for whom Aseneth's beauty and desirability cause strife, and one in particular—Pharoah's son, whose request for Aseneth is denied by Pharoah for reasons of social status. The brief opening passage, then, introduces key characters, describing males in terms of virtue, wealth, social function, relations of power, and desire for a beautiful woman, and describing the female protagonist as a virgin ripe in harvest season. Hints of social conflict are located not between Hebrews and Egyptians, but among Egyptians, prompted, in good romance fashion, by the exceptional beauty of the virgin. The action is now motivated: which man will succeed in marrying this virgin who looks like Joseph's foremothers? And when will Joseph's harvesting activities bring him in contact with Aseneth and her worthy father?

The next section begins with a stark characterization of Aseneth's attitude toward men, indeed toward everyone: Καὶ ἦν Ἀσενὲθ ἐξουθενοῦσα καὶ καταπτύουσα πάντα ἄνδρα καὶ ἦν ἀλαζὼν καὶ ὑπερήφανος πρὸς πάντα ἄνθρωπον, "And Aseneth was despising and acting with contempt toward every man, and she was boastful and arrogant toward every person" (2.1). With the tantalizing detail that no man had ever seen her (so strife among suitors is based on hearsay?), the narrative shifts to vividly descriptive passages that serve to explain both Aseneth's arrogance and her inaccessibility. Literary theorist Mieke Bal remarks that within narrative, "Description is a privileged site of focalization, and as such it has great impact on the ideological and aesthetic effect of the text."[44] So, too, Longinus strongly urges *visualization*, or φαντασία, or "image-production," as a strategy "extremely productive of grandeur, magnificence, and urgency" (15.1). The description of Aseneth's tower— an exaggerated cloister—is the first of the story's many elaborated descriptions. Using the palette of purple, violet, white, gold, and silver that recurs throughout the tale, the architecture and adornments are given particularly elaborate treatment. The amplification of detail, its quantity and superfluity,[45] makes Aseneth seem "the archetypical protected maiden."[46] Yet that same superfluity creates a sense of excess and instability. The tower protects not only her virginity, but her piety. The first chamber, with its floor of purple stones, walls of precious stones, ceiling of gold, serves as sanctuary:

καὶ ἦσαν ἐντὸς τοῦ θαλάμου ἐκείνου εἰς τοὺς τοίχους πεπηγμένοι
οἱ θεοὶ τῶν Αἰγυπτίων ὧν οὐκ ἦν ἀριθμὸς χρυσοῖ καὶ ἀργυροῖ.
καὶ πάντας ἐκείνους ἐσέβετο Ἀσενέθ καί ἐφοβεῖτο αὐτοὺς καὶ
θυσίας αὐτοῖς ἐπετέλει καθ᾽ ἡμέραν.

And within that chamber there were attached to the walls gods of the Egyptians, gold and silver and innumerable. And Aseneth worshipped them all and feared them and performed sacrifices to them every day. (2.3)

Pious devotion is juxtaposed with feminine adornment, as the second chamber houses Aseneth's chests, filled with clothing interwoven with gold, silver, costly stones, and "all the ornaments of her virginity" (2.4). Her third chamber houses "all the good things of the earth."[47] Then come the chambers for her companion virgins, all beautiful as the stars, all untainted by contact with men. Aseneth's regard for the seven differs markedly from her contempt for all men: καί ἠγάπα αὐτὰς πάνυ, "and she loved them very much" (2.6). The structure and function of the tower make it templelike, designed to protect both sexual status and piety, with the "holy of holies" being Aseneth's large chamber, ὅπου ἡ παρθενία αὐτῆς ἐτρέφετο, "where her virginity was being nurtured" (2.7). Her bed, then, is presented climactically as untainted sanctuary:

καὶ ἦν κλίνη χρυσῆ ἑστῶσα ἐν τῷ θαλάμῳ ἀποβλέπουσα πρὸς τὴν θυρίδα κατὰ ἀνατολὰς καὶ ἦν ἡ κλίνη ἐστρωμένη πορφυρᾶ χρυσοϋφῆ ἐξ ὑακίνθου καὶ πορφύρας καὶ βύσσου καθυφασμένη. καὶ ἐν ταύτῃ τῇ κλίνῃ ἐκάθευδεν Ἀσενὲθ μόνη καὶ ἀνὴρ ἢ γυνὴ ἑτέρα οὐδέποτε ἐκάθισεν ἐπ' αὐτῇ πλὴν τῆς Ἀσενὲθ μόνης.

And there was a golden bed standing in the chamber, looking toward the window toward the east and the bed was covered with gold-woven purple, interwoven with purple and violet. And in this bed, Aseneth slept alone, and no man or other woman had ever sat upon it, only Aseneth alone. (2.8–9)

The repetition of *alone* reinforces Aseneth's devotion to virginity, with conflicting associations—admirable and cherished, yet associated with utter contempt for men and extreme devotion to Egyptian deities. The focalization shifts, then, from the interior chambers to the courtyard around the house—with its high wall, four gates, eighteen powerful armed young men at each gate.[48] Throughout the description, the striking insistence first on interior space then on an enclosing wall is a sharp contrast to the itineracy of Joseph: the architecture separates insider and outsider.

The opulent imagery conveys at once both impressive abundance and untenable excess, and thereby generates ambivalence. Pentephres's exceptional wealth marks high status, but the extremes of its use for the protection of one arrogant girl seem excessive. Aseneth's piety and the regularity and thoroughness of her religious devotion seem admirable, yet Aseneth has too many gods, and the wrong ones. Most tellingly, the vivid descriptive passage conveys ambivalence about virginity. What is one to think when the sexual restraint of virginity understood as preparatory to marriage turns to arrogant repudiation of men? When does virginity itself admit of excess?[49] The very amplification and vividness of detail, the descriptive hyperbole, generates a kind of suspense. The hyperprotection of this archetypal virgin and her pagan piety waits to be penetrated, complicated, dissolved, or confounded.

The sense of erotic suspense seems heightened by the intertextual play of the passage. Already relying on Genesis as its underlying story, the narrative here also echoes the Song of Songs. Such moments of literary *mimesis*—a phenomenon much discussed by ancient literary and rhetorical analysts—link the text with a literary past that is also a cultural past somehow being appropriated or complicated in the present.[50] For Longinus, *mimesis* shifts the identity of the author or reader in ways that resemble "possession" or "inspiration": *mimesis*, he says, is another "road to sublimity" by which "Many are possessed by a spirit not their own" (13.1). As the Pythia at Delphi is inspired by a divine vapor, so imitators of the ancients receive inspiring "effluences" (13.2). Aseneth's courtyard, full of fruitful trees and an abundant water source, combined with its purpose of protecting the virgin, both draws upon and transposes a memorable image from the Song of Songs:

> A garden locked is my sister, my bride,
> a garden locked, a fountain sealed.
> Your channel is an orchard of pomegranates with all choicest
>   fruits,
> henna with nard, nard and saffron, calamus and cinnamon,
> with all trees of frankincense,
> myrrh and aloes, with all chief spices—
> a garden fountain, a well of living water,
> and flowing streams from Lebanon. (4:12–15 NRSV)

The intertextual resonances are "effluences" of the biblically shaped cultural identity into which Aseneth will be incorporated. More immediately, they also reinforce the latent eroticism: a garden locked asks to be unlocked.

With a repetition of καὶ ἐγένετο, "And it happened . . ." the action of the tale begins (3.1), as the itinerant Joseph sends ahead a message concerning his arrival in Heliopolis, and his intention to refresh himself "under the shadow" of Pentephres's house. Aseneth, unaware of Joseph's approach, prepares to greet her parents returning from their country estate, where they have been, the narrator reminds the reader, "for it was the time of harvest" (3.5). Her characteristic preparatory action, to be oft-repeated, is to dress herself in fine fabrics and vivid colors—purple, violet, white, gold—and with emblems of her piety:

κaί ἦσαν τὸ ὀνόματα τῶν θεῶν τῶν Αἰγυπτίων ἐγκεκολαμμένα πανταχοῦ ἐπί τε τοῖς ψελίοις καὶ τοῖς λίθοις καὶ τὰ πρόσωπα τῶν εἰδώλων πάντων ἦσαν ἐκτετυπωμένα ἐν αὐτοῖς.

And there were names of the Egyptian gods engraved everywhere on the bracelets and the stones, and the faces of all the idols were carved on them. (3.6)

The reader (who, of course, knows Genesis) rightly anticipates conflict with Joseph's monotheism. Yet throughout the tale, Aseneth's emphatically plural gods are also in tension with the tendency of the other Egyptian characters to speak of a singular God. Pentephres, preparing to welcome his guest, ascribes to Joseph the epithet, Ἰωσὴφ δυνατὸς τοῦ θεοῦ, "Joseph, the powerful one of God" (3.4). And Aseneth's parents both rejoice at her approach διότι ἑώρων αὐτὴν κεκοσμημένην ὡς νύμφην θεοῦ, "because they saw her adorned like a bride of God" (4.1). Their words provide a heavy narrative anticipation of Aseneth's impending transformation, and another sign that to be an idolatrous virgin is a transitional state.

The familial interaction that follows begins tenderly, with much emphasis on the physical contact that belongs to kinship: kissing, gift-giving, sitting close. The intimacy is disrupted, then, as the Egyptian priest commends the piety, restrained sexual status, and political stature of Joseph, and announces an intended marriage for his emphatically pagan and virgin daughter:

καὶ ἔστιν Ἰωσὴφ ἀνὴρ θεοσεβὴς καὶ σώφρων καὶ παρθένος ὡς σὺ σήμερον καὶ ἔστιν Ἰωσὴφ ἀνὴρ δυνατὸς ἐν σοφίᾳ καὶ ἐπιστήμη καὶ πνεῦμα θεοῦ ἐστιν ἐπ᾽ αὐτῷ καὶ χάρις κυρίου μετ᾽ αὐτοῦ. δεῦρο δὴ τέκνον μου καὶ παραδώσω σε αὐτῷ εἰς γυναῖκα καὶ ἔσῃ αὐτῷ νύμφη καὶ αὐτὸς ἔσται σου νυμφίος εἰς τὸν αἰῶνα χρόνον.

And Joseph is a man who worships God, and is self-controlled, and a virgin like you today, and Joseph is a man powerful in wisdom and experience, and the spirit of God is upon him, and the grace of God is with him. Come, my child, and I will hand you over to him for his wife, and you will be a bride to him, and he will be your bridegroom for ever. (4.7–8)

As the Egyptian priest recommends the God-venerating Hebrew, religious intermarriage seems unproblematic from the Egyptian perspective. Aseneth's refusal is so furious that a new color enters the palette of her costume: red sweat. Offering a suspicious reading of the Genesis accounts of Joseph's adventures, she rejects him as beneath her status, as an alien, and as sexually compromised. Virginity continues as a form of disdain; for her, virgin and bride seem antitheses.[51]

THE ENCLOSURE BREACHED

Joseph's arrival unlocks the garden. Greeted by the entire household, save Aseneth who has fled to watch from her tower window, Joseph makes a spectacular entrance on Pharoah's golden chariot drawn by four white horses. His clothing echoes Aseneth's "bride of God" attire in color and fabric, visually making him a match for her, yet with a crucial difference: in place of her stones engraved with the names and images of innumerable Egyptian deities, his crown is set with "twelve chosen stones, and twelve golden rays"—properly symbolic for a son of Israel. In this narrative world, however, this difference does not make Joseph a "stranger." Although Aseneth has complained that he is an alien and fugitive (ἀλλοφύλῳ καὶ φυγάδι, 4.9), one brief but emphatic detail in this episode implies otherwise. After Joseph enters, the gates of Pentephres's enclave are closed and locked behind him to keep out πᾶς ἀνὴρ καὶ γυνὴ ἀλλότριοι, "every strange man and woman." The narrator then repeats, καὶ ἐξεκλείσθησαν πάντες οἱ ἀλλότριοι, "and all the strangers were shut out" (5:6). Joseph becomes an insider.

The single sentence that renders Joseph's effect on Aseneth is star-tlingly brief. Aseneth suffers love at first sight, but this is no lingering lovesickness characterized by passivity or lethargy or melancholia, but a sharp, sudden attack conveyed by forceful verbs. The optics of infatuation receive no emphasis. The story presupposes the literary conventions of lovesickness represented by Sappho, or Thecla, or lovers from the Greek romances, yet strikingly compresses them:

Καὶ εἶδεν Ἀσενὲθ τὸν Ἰωσὴφ ἐπί τοῦ ἅρματος καὶ κατενύγη ἰσχυρῶς καὶ παρεκλάσθη ἡ ψυχὴ αὐτῆς καὶ παρείθη τὰ γόνατα αὐτῆς καὶ ἐτρόμαξεν ὅλον τὸ σῶμα αὐτῆς καὶ ἐφοβήθη φόβον μέγαν.

And Aseneth saw Joseph upon the chariot, and she was strongly cut, and her soul was crushed, and her knees were paralyzed, and her whole body trembled, and she was greatly fearful. (6.1)

The narrative effect is the inverse of that in the amplified description of her rooms. Instead of being deluged with details, the reader is struck, like Aseneth, with the abruptness and threat of violent emotion.[52]

Though the narrator is terse, Aseneth finds poetic language to voice, albeit silently, the reversals she is experiencing. Her internal soliloquy is structured partly by a series of rhetorical questions: What shall I do now . . . ? Who among men . . . ? Where shall I go . . . ? Where shall I flee. . . ? The syntax conveys immediacy and, according to Longinus, the effect of both speaker and hearer being "carried away": "What are we to say of inquiries and questions? . . . For emotion carries us away more easily when it seems to be generated by the occasion rather than deliberately assumed by the speaker, and the self-directed question and its answer represent precisely this momentary quality of emotion" (18.2). Aseneth corrects her prior ignorance of Joseph's true identity, rejecting her earlier ῥήματα πονηρά, "evil words": he is not a son of a shepherd, but a son of God. Much as gold dominated the narrator's previous description of Joseph, Aseneth now describes him with language infused with a meta-phorics of light. Rich studies have been undertaken of the Helios and other astrological imagery, both here and in the subsequent revelatory sequence.[53] Aseneth takes Joseph's beauty and light as evidence that he is a son of God, then dwells on the ways that Joseph's light-generating capacity will give him vision that she cannot evade. Her language echoes

several Psalms, including 139:"Where can I go from your spirit? Or where
can I flee from your presence? . . . If I say, 'Surely the darkness shall cover
me, and the light around me become night,' even the darkness is not dark
to you; the night is as bright as the day, for darkness is as light to you" (139:
7, 11–12 NRSV). Joseph's radiance and his capacity to see and find her
associate him with the divine.[54] Aseneth's soliloquy voices the beginning
of transformation. Still adorned with idols, she addresses a first prayer to
Joseph's God. Still secluded in her tower, she expresses the beginnings of
self-abnegation. No longer too proud to be Joseph's bride forever, she
prays to be given to Joseph, εἰς παιδίσκην καὶ εἰς δούλην καὶ δουλεύσω
αὐτῷ εἰς τὸν αἰῶνα χρόνον,"as a female servant and slave and I will serve
him forever" (6.8).

EYES, MOUTHS, HANDS, BREASTS

The scene that follows is infused with two interconnected questions.
What kind of bodily interaction with others is proper for a man (or
woman) who worships God? And, who constitutes a stranger—one
from whom the body must be withheld? As Joseph and Aseneth meet,
their encounter is charged with the possibilities and limits of contact,
and key parts of their bodies become metonymic of answers to these
questions: in particular, mouths, but also eyes, hands, and breasts. Joseph's
careful separation for eating stresses the boundaried body and meals as a
crucial identity marker: "because Joseph never ate with the Egyptians,
for this was an abomination to him" (7.1). His eyes, however, have just
the penetrating power that Aseneth has feared, since he evidently sees
her leaning through a window[55] despite his being inside Pentephres's
house. Assuming that she, like all other wives and daughters, is suffering
from his beauty and will molest him, Joseph demands that the much-
cherished virgin be the one to leave the house. Pentephres invokes
Aseneth's identity as daughter—member of this hospitable household—
and as a "virgin hating every man." However much misandry conveys
contempt, it also functions as reassurance of nonpredatory purity. Her
sexual self-restraint gives her a shared identity with Joseph (7.7). On the
basis of household identity and sexual identity, Pentephres recommends
Aseneth to Joseph as "sister," an ambiguous term evoking both familial
relationship and potential sister-bride connections.[56] Joseph accepts: εἰ

θυγάτηρ ὑμῶν ἐστι καὶ παρθένος ὑπάρχει ἡκέτω ὅτι ἀδελφή μού ἐστι καὶ ἀγαπῶ αὐτὴν ἀπὸ τῆς σήμερον ὡς ἀδελφήν μου; "If she is your daughter and a virgin, permit her to come, for she is my sister and I will love her from this day as my sister"(7.8).[57] The problem of "strangers" is sharpened, however, when Aseneth arrives and Pentephres urges her to kiss Joseph. Penn remarks, "In asking Aseneth to kiss Joseph, her 'brother,' Pentephres suggests an action that will overcome markers of difference and establish a familial connection between Aseneth and Joseph."[58] Joseph, however, rejects the connection as he repels Aseneth's kiss and her desire, suggestively represented:

καὶ ὡς προσῆλθεν Ἀσενὲθ φιλῆσαι τὸν Ἰωσὴφ ἐξέτεινεν Ἰωσὴφ τὴν χεῖρα αὐτοῦ τὴν δεξιὰν καὶ ἔθηκε πρός τὸ στῆθος αὐτῆς ἀνάμεσον τῶν δύο μασθῶν αὐτης καὶ ἦσαν οἱ μασθοὶ αὐτῆς ἤδη ἑστῶτες ὥσπερ μῆλα ὡραῖα.

And as Aseneth approached to kiss Joseph, Joseph stretched out his right hand and placed it on her chest between her two breasts and her breasts were already standing like ripe apples. (8.5)

The Song of Songs may here be echoed again, a passage associating breasts with the apple-like scent of the mouth, with kisses, and with reciprocal desire (Song of Songs 7:8–10). Yet Aseneth's desire is starkly unreciprocated. In Joseph's proprieties of piety, the boundaries of and for eating, drinking and anointing also constitute the boundaries for kissing:[59]

καὶ εἶπεν Ἰωσήφ· οὐκ ἔστι προσῆκον ἀνδρὶ θεοσεβεῖ ὅς εὐλογεῖ τῷ στόματι αὐτοῦ τὸν θεὸν τὸν ζῶντα καὶ ἐσθίει ἄρτον εὐλογημ-ένον ζωῆς καὶ πίνει ποτήριον εὐλογημένον ἀθανασίας καὶ χρίεται χρίσματι εὐλογημένῳ ἀφθαρσίας φιλῆσαι γυναῖκα ἀλλοτρίαν ἥτις εὐλογεῖ τῷ στόματι αὐτῆς εἴδωλα νεκρὰ καὶ κωφὰ καὶ ἐσθίει ἐκ τῆς τραπέζης αὐτῶν ἄρτον ἀγχόνης καὶ πίνει ἐκ τῆς σπονδῆς αὐτῶν ποτήριον ἐνέδρας καὶ χρίεται χρίσματι ἀπωλείας.

And Joseph said, "It is not proper for a God-venerating man who blesses the living God with his mouth and eats the blessed bread of life and drinks from the blessed cup of immortality and anoints himself with the blessed ointment of incorruptibility to kiss a strange woman who blesses with her mouth dead and dumb idols and eats from their table bread of strangulation and drinks a cup of ambush from their libation and anoints her self with the anointing of destruction. (8.5)

The triad of bread, cup, and ointment recurs throughout *Joseph and Aseneth*—six times in the longer text—sometimes modulating to bread, cup, and inclusion among God's people. With its eucharistic overtones or other sacred-meal suggestions, the triad has sometimes been interpreted as reflecting a particular ritual, but the linked symbols seem rather to function both as definitive boundary markers—indicators of "ethnic and religious particularism"—and as signs of the privileged life and immortality of those within the community of believers.[60] That which can overcome the foreignness or strangeness of a woman (or man) is defined, then, not just as shared sexual self-restraint, but as a necessary combination of kinship and the proper veneration of God.

ἀλλ᾽ ἀνὴρ θεοσεβὴς φιλήσει τὴν μητέρα αὐτοῦ καὶ τὴν ἀδελφὴν τὴν ἐκ τῆς μητρὸς αὐτοῦ καὶ τὴν ἀδελφὴν τὴν ἐκ τῆς φυλῆς καὶ τῆς συγγενείας αὐτοῦ καὶ τὴν γυναῖκα τὴν σύγκοιτον αὐτοῦ αἵτινες εὐλογοῦσι τῷ στόματι αὐτῶν τὸν θεὸν τὸν ζῶντα. ὁμοίως καὶ γυναικὶ θεοσεβεῖ οὐκ ἔστι προσῆκον φιλῆσαι ἄνδρα ἀλλότριον διότι βδέλυγμά ἐστι τοῦτο ἐνώπιον κυρίου τοῦ θεοῦ.

But a God-venerating man will kiss his mother and his sister from his mother and his sister from his clan and family and the wife of his bed who bless with their mouths the living God. In the same way, it is not proper for a God-venerating woman to kiss a strange man, because it is an abomination before the Lord God. (8.6–7)

Whatever transformation has begun in Aseneth is not sufficient to cross the boundaries to Joseph's community and Joseph's mouth. If kisses mark kinship and piety, then refused kisses sharpen boundaries.[61]

Aseneth's distress at Joseph's rejection is expressed through sighs, gaze, and tears—all recognizable symptoms of desire. She is κατενύγη ἰσχυρῶς, "cut strongly," but so, too, is Joseph κατενύγη, the narrator tells us, and because he is "meek and merciful and fearing God," he (finally) moves his right hand from between her breasts to place it on her head and utter a prayer for her conversion: partly in conventional language, that Aseneth may move from darkness to light, from error to truth, from death to life;[62] yet also in imagery distinctive to the text, that Aseneth be allowed to use her mouth eating and drinking (though at this point, not kissing) in ways appropriate to the chosen people of God (8.9).

ASENETH ALONE: CHANGES IN VOICE AND PERSON

The narrative's next section begins the central transforming episodes of the story as shifts in Aseneth's speaking voice carry shifts in her identity.[63] The story depicts Aseneth in solitude, first engaged in symbolic action, then in soliloquies. Through these new speech forms, *mimesis* becomes at once literary and cultural as the pagan heroine takes on the clothing and speech forms of the Jewish penitent. The section begins with (to borrow Longinus again), "Disconnected and yet hurried phrases [which] convey the impression of an agitation which both obstructs the reader and drives him on" (19.1). In an intense and mixed response to Joseph's rejection and intercession, Aseneth flees, rejoicing, to her upper floor and falls exhausted upon her bed. She experiences χαρὰ καὶ λύπη καὶ φόβος πολὺς καὶ τρόμος καὶ ἱδρὼς συνεχὴς, "joy and grief and great fear and trembling and continuous sweating" (9.1). Desire then becomes indistinguishable from spiritual remorse; the same physical symptoms bear both significations. As Aseneth is left alone, lovesickness is fused with *metanoia*, repentance.

> καὶ ἔκλαυσε κλαυθμῷ μεγάλῳ καὶ πικρῷ καὶ μετενόει ἀπὸ τῶν θεῶν αὐτῆς ὧν ἐσέβετο καὶ προσώχθισε τοῖς εἰδώλοις πᾶσι καὶ περιέμενε τοῦ γενέσθαι ἑσπέραν.

> And she wept with great and bitter weeping, and she repented of her gods whom she had been worshipping and spurned all the idols and waited for evening to come. (9.2)

Aseneth's week alone constitutes a preparatory period of mourning, beginning with repudiation of markers of her social identity (her clothing) and her piety (her gods and her stock of food and drink), all thrown out the appropriate window to benefit either the poor or strange dogs. The visual palette changes from purple, gold, and white to black and ash grey as she dons a mourning robe and both fills her chamber and covers her body with ashes. For seven days, Aseneth is in a liminal state, engaged in repetitive, ritualized acts of mourning (10.14–17).

On the eighth day, her mourning silence and inarticulate sighs and screams change to extended, patterned, poetic uses of language: one silent soliloquy delivered with her head in her lap; a second delivered raised on her knees and in the *orans* position; and finally a spoken confession of sin and prayer of repentance. The narrative pace is slow and the language frequently hyperbolic. Aseneth mentions Joseph seldom in the first two "speeches," other than twice to identify the God she addresses as "God of the powerful Joseph." There is no language of erotic desire, though *virgin* gains new associations. In her first soliloquy, Aseneth declares herself abandoned and hated by her family. *Virgin* here acquires connotations of forsakenness, as she refers to herself as ἐγὼ ἡ παρθένος καὶ ὀρφανὴ καὶ ἔρημος καὶ ἐγκαταλελειμμένη καὶ μεμισημένη; "I the virgin and orphan and deserted one and abandoned and hated" (11.3). This claim of familial repudiation and disinheritance (11.5) is nowhere confirmed in the story. Nor, of course, is her claim that her hatred of men has earned her universal hatred by men (11.6). As Pervo remarks, "In part this dissonance stems from her role as typical and representative proselyte, one who experiences as the model and patron of other converts the sufferings and alienation a change of religion may bring."[64] The culminating estrangement, however, is God's hatred because of her idolatry. Nevertheless, Aseneth resolves to turn to God as refuge, father, and protector (11.11–14). Her second soliloquy attempts to summon courage to utter God's name, even if risking God's anger (11.16–18).

When Aseneth at last speaks, her confession and prayer is long and repetitious, both formulaic and extravagant by turns.[65] She articulates her position poised between old divinities and new, between old kinship and new, and between virginity and some other state yet to be defined. In an opening long series of relative clauses, she celebrates God as creator of all things.[66] Aseneth's cosmology envisions creation founded on waters and stones, an obedient cosmos created by fiat, and ultimately a living cosmos.[67] She moves, then, to an elaboration of her penitence, and offers a tender image of God as the father who snatches a little child to his breast protectively (12.8). The threat from which God must rescue her comes from the wild old lion, chief of the Egyptian gods. Aseneth utters an extraordinary sequence of images of natural wildness and threat: the lion will throw her into flame, which will throw her into hurricane, which will throw her into darkness, which will throw her into the deep of the sea, where the sea monster from eternity will swallow and destroy her

(12.9–11). The amplification and hyperbole gives extreme expression to the danger she perceives on the threshold between gods. So, too, positioned between familial identities, having envisioned God as embracing father, she petitions God to take Pentephres's place (12.15) and recapitulates her renunciatory actions of the past week (13.1–12).

Throughout the prayer, *virgin* as self-reference carries varied associations. Aseneth acknowledges her previous arrogance by calling herself "virgin and queen" (12.5). As in the soliloquy, she conveys her vulnerability by linking *virgin* with *orphan* (12.14). She, also, for the first time associates virginity with ignorance, an ignorance that led her unwittingly into the error of blasphemy against "my lord Joseph" (13.13).[68] At the prayer's close, then, she returns to her desire for Joseph—in emphatic, final position. Her language echoes the brief soliloquy and prayer she uttered after her first shattering sight of Joseph, rehearsing her error in not recognizing the all-beautiful Joseph as God's son.

> κύριε παρατίθημί σοι αὐτὸν ὅτι ἐγὼ ἀγαπῶ αὐτὸν ὑπὲρ τὴν ψυχήν μου.
> διατήρησον αὐτὸν ἐν τῇ σοφίᾳ τῆς χάριτός σου.
> καὶ σὺ κύριε παράθου με αὐτῷ εἰς παιδίσκην καὶ δούλην.
> κἀγὼ στρώσω τὴν κλίνην αὐτοῦ καὶ νίψω τοὺς πόδας αὐτοῦ καὶ διακονήσω αὐτῷ.
> καὶ ἔσομαι αὐτῷ δούλη καὶ δουλεύσω αὐτῷ εἰς τὸν αἰῶνα χρόνον.

Lord, I commit him to you, because I love him more than my own self.
Preserve him in the wisdom of your grace.
And you, Lord, commit me to him as a female servant and slave.
And I will make his bed and wash his feet and minister to him.
And I will be to him a slave, and I will minister to him for ever.
(13.15)

The prayer in part conveys complexities of interreligious, intercultural negotiation, as the elite Egyptian virgin prays to be enslaved to the formerly enslaved Hebrew. Yet Wills captures well another reading of Aseneth's seven-day mourning: "[it] has moved to suspend the reader in a position of utmost vulnerability and precariousness, an experience not of Jewish triumphalism (as in the base narrative) but of extreme ambivalence and personal anxiety. . . ."[69]

THE ANTHROPOS FROM HEAVEN

Aseneth's prayer ends, the morning star gently rises, then the heavens split apart and an unspeakably great light appears (14.2).[70] An *anthropos* or man from heaven addresses Aseneth with a twofold repetition of her name reminiscent of Biblical call stories, and so begins the story's climactic scene of revelation and transformation. The concentration of figurative language through this revelatory episode is intense. Heavenly figures, virgins, brides, a woman as city, heavenly books of life, honeycombs, bees, crosses, paradisal gardens, a heaven-bound chariot—the proliferation is audacious, an excess that works to suspend the ordinary and expected. As the text reaches toward sublimity, understood as ecstasy, as exalted reality, and as moral transformation, Longinus becomes a particularly apt counterpoint to the story's literary strategies. Unlike other ancient rhetoricians such as Aristotle and Theophrastus, who recommend that a writer or speaker should only use two or three metaphors close together, Longinus urges daring use of figures to generate sublimity. Given the intrinsic and sublimity-producing alliance between passion and figures, the right occasions for a proliferation of metaphor, Longinus says, "are when emotions come flooding in and bring the multiplication of metaphors with them as a necessary accompaniment" (32.1). Yet it is not just that figures may assist the depiction of passion and generate sublimity. Sublimity also provides a kind of protective cover for figures. In his discussion of *phantasia*, Longinus argues that the vividness of rhetorical or literary visualization aids sublimity by distracting the hearer from the facts before him. *Phantasia* generates a kind of "brilliance" against which the lesser colors of merely factual arguments fade. The result is exciting and ecstatic, but also coercive: the hearer is forcibly captured by the figure and the sublimity it generates (15.6). About metaphor and other figures, he similarly argues "that strong and appropriate emotions and genuine sublimity are a specific palliative for multiplied or daring metaphors, because their nature is to sweep and drive all these other things along with the surging tide of their movement. Indeed it might be truer to say that they *demand* the hazardous. They never allow the hearer leisure to count the metaphors, because he too shares the speaker's enthusiasm" (32.4). For Aseneth, and perhaps for her readers, the figurative concentration of the experiences mediated by the *anthropos* from heaven are presented as all-absorbing, overwhelming, irresistible, and productive of ecstasy.

Identifying himself as the commander of God's hosts, the *anthropos from heaven*—with his complete resemblance to Joseph overlaid by extreme manifestations of fire and light—guides Aseneth through a series of experiences performing or announcing her thoroughgoing identity transformation. First, he requires her to change her clothing. As instructed, Aseneth removes her mourning attire, dresses in a new and distinguished linen robe, wraps one girdle around her waist, and another around her breast. Uninstructed, however, she also covers her head with a veil, previously untouched, made of the same fabric as her robe—a garment that earns her correction from the heavenly visitor:

Καὶ ἦλθε πρὸς τὸν ἄνθρωπον εἰς τὸν θάλαμον αὐτῆς τὸν πρῶτον καὶ ἔστη ἐνώπιον αὐτοῦ. καὶ εἶπεν αὐτῇ ὁ ἄνθρωπος· ἀπόστειλον δὴ τὸ θέριστρον ἀπὸ τῆς κεφαλῆς σου καὶ ἵνα τί σὺ τοῦτο πεποίηκας; διότι σὺ εἶ παρθένος ἁγνὴ σήμερον καὶ ἡ κεφαλή σού ἐστιν ὡς ἀνδρὸς νεανίσκου.

And she went to the man in her first chamber and stood before him. And the man said to her, "Remove indeed the veil from your head. And why did you do this? For you are today a pure virgin and your head is like a young man's. (15.1)

However ambiguous Aseneth's virginity has been to this point in the story—representing worthy sexual self-restraint, but also arrogance, disdain, youthful ignorance, and vulnerability—at this moment she is a παρθένος ἁγνή, a pure or holy or chaste virgin, the first time the qualifier has been used. Unadorned, and doubly girded, in this state, brief though it will be, she needs no veil. Her head's being like a young man may imply either a temporary masculinity or a temporary androgyny, either of which, as Philonenko and Kraemer note, can characterize initiates in many religious traditions.[71] Her veil removed, Aseneth now receives words of acceptance and of promise from the anthropos, structured by a threefold repetition of θάρσει Ἀσενὲθ ἡ παρθένος ἁγνή, "Courage, Aseneth, pure virgin." He pronounces, first, the acceptability of her seven days of self-affliction; second, her name written in the heavenly book of life and her ability to partake of the threefold blessing of bread-cup-anointing; third, that she has been given to Joseph as bride, and that Joseph will be her bridegroom for ever (15.3–6). Her state as παρθένος ἁγνή, therefore, is liminal.

With transformation of identity marked by change of clothing, change
in her character as παρθένος, and some kind of temporary gender transformation, the man from heaven then announces a change of name, yet
also connects that new name with another figure whom Aseneth strongly
resembles: the feminine personification of Metanoia.

καὶ τὸ ὄνομά σου οὐκέτι κληθήσεται Ἀσενὲθ ἀλλ᾽ἔσται τὸ ὄνομά
σου πόλις καταφυγῆς διότι ἐν σοὶ καταφεύξονται ἔθνη πολλὰ ἐπὶ
κύριον τὸν θεὸν τὸν ὕψιστον καὶ ὑπὸ τὰς πτέρυγάς σου
σκεπασθήσονται λαοὶ πολλοὶ πεποιθότες ἐπὶ κυρίῳ τῷ θεῷ καὶ
ἐν τῷ τείχει σου διαφυλαχθήσονται οἱ προσκείμενοι τῷ θεῷ τῷ
ὑψίστῳ ἐν ὀνόματι τῆς μετανοίας.

And your name shall no longer be Aseneth but your name shall be
city of refuge, because in you many nations will take refuge with
the Lord God Most High. And under your wings will be sheltered
many people trusting in the Lord God, and behind your walls will
be guarded those who are attached to the Most High God in the
name of Metanoia. (15.7)

As virgin, Aseneth has been sheltered in a walled edifice. As bride or
matron, she will *become* the protective edifice, not οἶκος but πόλις, in
whom many will be sheltered.[72] Moreover, she who first rejected Joseph
as φυγάδι, fugitive, will now become πόλις καταφυγῆς, city of refuge.
Those she will guard, however, will be attached to God through the figure
of Metanoia, whom the heavenly man goes on to describe more fully, in
terms that reflect God's character but that also correspond repeatedly with
Aseneth. Aseneth has been presented in the story as daughter, albeit at
times a rebellious one, yet Metanoia is an exceedingly beautiful and good
daughter of the Most High (15.7). Continuously interceding with God on
behalf of all who repent, she is particularly attached to virgins and is herself a virgin, though not arrogant and scornful as Aseneth was: καὶ ἔστιν ἡ
μετάνοια καλὴ σφόδρα παρθένος καθαρὰ καὶ γελῶσα πάντοτε καὶ ἔστιν
ἐπιεικὴς καὶ πραεῖα; "And Metanoia is an exceedingly beautiful virgin
and always laughing and is gentle and meek" (15.8). As Aseneth was greeted
as sister (in a qualified sense) to Joseph, so Metanoia is sister to this heavenly man who thoroughly resembles Joseph, though surpassing him in
glory. The *anthropos* concludes his description of her, with an echo of how
Aseneth loves her own seven companion virgins: καὶ καθότι ὑμᾶς τὰς

παρθένους ἀγαπᾷ κἀγὼ ὑμᾶς ἀγαπῶ; "And because she loves you virgins, I love you also" (15.8). In this fascinating interweaving of the soon-to-be-married City of Refuge with the virginal Metanoia, the παρθένος ἀγνή that Aseneth has become at this point in the story represents both. That is, in her bare-headed, white-robed, androgynous or masculinized liminal state, Aseneth is malleable, analogous to the fundamental identity change that is Metanoia, repentance or change of mind. *Virgin* now seems to represent not only self-restraint or preparatory purity, but mutability of identity.

The anthropos immediately instructs another change of clothes; Aseneth is to don a mysterious wedding robe, τὴν στολὴν τὴν ἀρχαίαν καὶ πρώτην τὴν ἀποκειμένην ἐν τῷ θαλάμῳ σου ἀπ᾽ ἀρχῆς, "the ancient and first robe laid in your chamber from the beginning" (15.10). The pure virgin is to become good bride, and Joseph is on his way. Aseneth herself, however, slows the action, complicates her own transformation with a question, then a suggestion, perhaps trying to delay the heavenly man's departure. She first asks the name of the *anthropos* from heaven, but is denied, since his name is ineffable (15.11–12)—an emphatic rendering of the tale's motif of nonrecognition of identity. With surprisingly erotic overtones, the virgin who previously refused Joseph's kiss puts her hand on the heavenly visitor's knees and urges him to sit on her bed, that innermost holy place of her cloister-as-sanctuary, on which no man or woman has previously sat. She whose mouth has been unworthy of life-giving bread and cup asks the man from heaven to allow her to bring bread and wine for him.

The suggestiveness continues in the mysterious symbolic episode of the honeycomb, which renews the story's emphasis on mouths: what comes from them, what purifies them, what they may give and receive. The honeycomb Aseneth mysteriously finds in her storeroom has an exhalation like that from the mouth of the heavenly man (16.11–12). The comb is full, the man tells her, of the spirit of life, made from roses of life in the paradise of God. "And all the angels of God eat of it and all the chosen of God and all the sons of the Most High, because this is a comb of life, and everyone who eats of it will not die for ever and ever" (16.15).

In a particularly enigmatic symbolic action, the heavenly man draws a red cross shape on the edge of the honeycomb, causing bees to emerge, in the colors that have been characteristic through the story–purple, violet, scarlet, gold-woven linen cloaks, golden diadems. The bees build a second comb directly on Aseneth's lips, then are commanded to fly away. Some go directly to heaven. Others who want to injure Aseneth fall dead, are resurrected by the *anthropos*, and seek shelter on fruit-bearing trees. The explanations of the scene range from the specific allegorical reading by Gideon Bohak, to the suggestions of both wisdom literature and neoplatonic parallels by Ross Kraemer.[73] In a perceptive note, Humphrey remarks on the persistent difficulty of interpreting the passage: "Perhaps the resistance is inherent in the text, and not simply due to the denseness of critics. That is, it may well be that the passage is for mystification, not for interpretation."[74] Yet certain interpretations seem available. When Aseneth has eaten of the honeycomb, the angel tells her she has received the bread-cup-anointment triad, so central a symbol of acceptance by God (16.16).[75] Aseneth's eating of the honeycomb makes her participant in the sweetness of God's mercy.[76] And with the tingling sensory vividness of the passage—vision, scent, taste, touch—the eating of the honeycomb as a transferral of angelic breath serves as a substitute kiss, both satisfying of desire and anticipatory of a further satisfaction.[77]

As fire consumes the comb, and fragrance fills the chamber, Aseneth performs the first act of her new sheltering role, seeking a blessing for her seven companion virgins, who will become seven pillars of the city of refuge (17.4). As Joseph had earlier arrived in a chariot drawn by four horses, so the *anthropos* departs in a more glorious version. Aseneth, who earlier confessed herself unable to recognize Joseph as son of God, now admits herself ignorant that "a god came to me." Whereas she earlier prayed to become *Joseph's* servant, she now refers to herself as *the Lord's* slave and female servant (17.9). Throughout this climactic episode, revelation has unfolded, not by reference to standards of moderation and decorum, but through hyperbole. And yet, Longinus suggests that even hyperbole has its standard, even linguistic overreaching may be assessed as credible or not: "for we form the impression that the hyperbole is a reasonable product of the situation, not that the situation has been chosen for the sake of the hyperbole. As I keep saying, acts and emotions which approach ecstasy provide a justification for, and an antidote to, any linguistic audacity" (38.4). To grant reasonableness to the linguistic audacity of *Joseph and Aseneth* in its epiphanic sequence and throughout would require granting credibility to the ultimate realities in which the story is invested. To do that, however, might be to risk that a mysterious encounter with a representative of the divine may be transformative, irresistibly so.

TRANSFORMATION AND UNION: EYES, MOUTHS, HANDS, BREASTS

The heightened language modulates in the next scenes, moving from Aseneth's preparations for Joseph's arrival to their marriage. Aseneth converses with a new character—her foster-father—whose lifelong involvement with this "virgin who has never been seen by a man" obliquely conveys that men who are part of the household do not count as threats to virgins. She undertakes one last clothing change, now into the white and gold of her wedding attire, marked by a violet stone, and a veil properly covering her head "like a bride." In distress over her "fallen" face, she turns, then, to wash her face in pure water, and sees in her reflection a divine change of appearance that surpasses any of the clothing changes she has performed, and any of the pronouncements the heavenly visitor has made. Joseph's radiance and the heavenly visitor's radiance are now answered by the radiance of Aseneth's face:

καὶ ἦν ὡς ὁ ἥλιος καὶ οἱ ὀφθαλμοὶ αὐτῆς ὡς ἑωσφόρος ἀνατέλλων
καὶ αἱ παρειαὶ αὐτῆς ὡς ἄρουραι τοῦ ὑψίστου καὶ ἐν ταῖς παρειαῖς
ἐρυθρὸς ὡς αἷμα υἱοῦ ἀνθρώπου και τὰ χείλη αὐτῆς ὡς ῥόδον
ζωῆς ἐξερχόμενον ἐκ τῆς κάλυκος αὐτοῦ καὶ οἱ ὀδόντες αὐτῆς ὡς
πολεμισταὶ συντεταγμένοι εἰς πόλεμον καὶ αἱ τρίχες τῆς κεφαλῆς
αὐτῆς ὡς ἄμπελος ἐν τῷ παραδείσῳ τοῦ θεοῦ εὐθηνοῦσα ἐν τοῖς
καρποῖς αὐτῆς καὶ ὁ τράχηλος αὐτῆς ὡς κυπάρισσος παμποίκι-
λος καὶ οἱ μασθοὶ αὐτῆς ὡς τὰ ὄρη τοῦ θεοῦ τοῦ ὑψίστου.

And it was like the sun, and her eyes were like a rising morning star, and her cheeks like fields of the Most High, and on her cheeks there was red like a blood of a son of man, and her lips were like a rose of life coming out of its leaves, and her teeth like fighting men arranged for battle, and the hair of her head was like a vine in the paradise of God thriving in its fruits, and her neck like a completely diverse cypress, and her breasts were like the mountains of the Most High God. (18.9)

The *blazon* of the woman's body has many biblical and nonbiblical parallels, including several lingering passages in Song of Songs.[78] It continues the concentrated use of tropes from the episode with the heavenly visitor, and provides the culmination of the identity-transforming experiences so far narrated.[79]

As Joseph enters the household (again, with the narrator's note that all strangers remain outside), it is now Aseneth who has become unrecognizable because of her association with divinity, causing Joseph to ask, τίς εἶ σὺ ταχέως ἀνάγγειλόν μοι; "Who are you? Tell me quickly" (19.4). Aseneth briefly rehearses her experiences. Joseph pronounces her a woman-building blessed by God, then urges the pure virgin to come to him. The same parts of the body that earlier were used to reinforce otherness, distance and rejection now are intimately joined—hands, eyes, breasts, and mouths, in particular, kissing mouths:

Καὶ ἐξέτεινε τὰς χεῖρας αὐτοῦ Ἰωσὴφ καὶ ἐκάλεσε τὴν Ἀσενὲθ ἐν νεύματι τῶν ὀφθαλμῶν αὐτοῦ. καὶ ἐξέτεινε καὶ Ἀσενὲθ τὰς χεῖρας αὐτῆς καὶ ἔδραμε πρὸς Ἰωσὴφ καὶ ἔπεσεν ἐπὶ τὸ στῆθος αὐτοῦ. καὶ ἐνηγκαλίσατο αὐτὴν ὁ Ἰωσὴφ καὶ ἡ Ἀσενὲθ τὸν Ἰωσὴφ καὶ ἠσπάσαντο ἀλλήλους ἐπιπολὺ καὶ ἀνέζησαν ἀμφότεροι τῷ πνεύματι αὐτῶν. καὶ κατεφίλησεν ὁ Ἰωσὴφ τὴν Ἀσενὲθ καὶ ἔδωκεν αὐτῇ πνεῦμα ζωῆς καὶ κατεφίλησεν αὐτὴν τὸ δεύτερον καὶ ἔδωκεν αὐτῇ πνεῦμα σοφίας καὶ κατεφίλησεν αὐτὴν τὸ τρίτον καὶ ἔδωκεν αὐτῇ πνεῦμα ἀληθείας. καὶ περιεπλάκησαν ἀλλήλοις ἐπιπολὺ καὶ ἔσφιγξαν τὰ δεσμὰ τῶν χειρῶν αὐτῶν.

And Joseph reached out his hands and called Aseneth by a wink of his eyes. And Aseneth also reached out her hands and ran to Joseph and fell on his breast. And Joseph put his arms around her, and Aseneth put hers around Joseph, and they kissed each other for a long time and both came to life in their spirit. And Joseph kissed Aseneth and gave her spirit of life, and he kissed her a second time and gave her spirit of wisdom, and he kissed her a third time and gave her spirit of truth. And they embraced one another for a long time and intertwined their hands like bonds. (19.10–20.1)

That kisses are an exchange of spirit is a well-known convention, but by this point in the text, the imparting of spirits also has heavenly association. Indeed, Joseph's kiss recapitulates what the honeycomb has already done for Aseneth, reiterating transformation, and linking its religious and erotic manifestations.[80] Joseph and Aseneth's physical interconnections continue as she washes his feet, he kisses her hand, she kisses his head, and she insists that his feet, hands, and soul are now hers, and no other virgin or woman will wash them (20.4). With an enigmatic simile, Joseph takes particular note of her hands, "and they were like hands of life, and her fingers fine like fingers of a fast-writing scribe" (20.5). Perhaps the simile links here to the previous book-of-life imagery, where she is the first inscribed, and is given a role in sheltering others who will receive life (15:4; 15:12).

In the wedding scene, it is noteworthy that Egyptians who have undergone no identifiable conversion nevertheless use devout language for God, as was true in the opening episode. Aseneth's foster-father exclaims, "At last the Lord God of heaven has chosen you as a bride for his firstborn son, Joseph!" (18.11). Her parents give glory to "God who gives life to the dead" (20.7). And Pharoah, as he performs their wedding, speaks blessings in the name of "the Lord God the Most High" (21.6). Even at this climactic turn in a story of a virgin's repentance and identity transformation, the broader boundaries of piety between Hebrews and Egyptians seem fluid.

The culmination of Pharoah's actions is to arrange for one more kiss between Aseneth and Joseph:

> καὶ περιέστρεψεν αὐτοὺς Φαραὼ πρὸς ἀλλήλους ἐπὶ τὰ πρόσωπα αὐτῶν καὶ προσήγαγεν αὐτοὺς ἐπὶ τὸ στόμα αὐτῶν καὶ ἦρσεν αὐτοὺς ἐπὶ τὰ χείλη αὐτῶν καὶ κατεφίλησαν ἀλλήλους.

> And Pharoah turned them around toward each other face to face and brought them mouth to mouth and joined them by their lips, and they kissed each other." (21.7)

Michael Penn offers categories for the kinds of kissing that appear in the tale so far:

> The work's 'kissing scenes' can be placed into three, occasionally overlapping, categories: kissing that excludes Aseneth (e.g. Joseph's refusal to kiss her), kissing that transforms Aseneth (e.g. the angelic honeycomb and Joseph's three kisses), and kissing that includes her within Judaism (e.g. Joseph's three kisses, kisses of hands and head and their marriage kiss). The kiss both sets up the opening dilemma and produces its resolution.[81]

A seven-day marriage feast balances the seven days of Aseneth's repentance, and the action concludes with an understated reference (with no mention of a bed) to the conception of Manasseh and Ephraim (Gen 41:50–52). Burrus remarks perceptively: "The kiss is all the erotic consummation that this novel text yields. . . .Virgins make the best lovers, where the teasing suspense of deferral is recognized as the key to erotic (as well as novelistic) art."[82]

Yet Aseneth still has the last word, as the long version of the tale concludes Part One with a Psalm in her voice—she is now fully *mimetic* of the Psalmic language of Israel. In ritualized, liturgical language of confession, the first nine stanzas retell the early part of her story and emphasize negative dimensions of the kind of virgin she once was and the kind of piety she once practiced. The turning point of the Psalm comes with the declaration, "But I will be the bride of the great king's firstborn son."[83] The final stanza then, makes Joseph the forceful agent of Aseneth's transformation—pulling her down from dominance, humbling her arrogance, catching or capturing her like a fish on a hook with his beauty, wisdom, and spirit. Joseph, then, is said by his power to have brought her to the God of the ages, with the result that she could eat, drink, and become his bride. The Psalm is a surprising and revealing close to the story of Aseneth's identity transformation. Making Joseph the agent of her transformation belies Aseneth's considerable autonomy, manifested throughout the story.[84] Yet the Psalm also emphasizes the strong connection between her erotic desire and her transformed religious identity.[85] The Psalm, however, suggests an inverse characterization: that the irresistible, even dominating, attractions of Joseph have made her acceptance by the Most High God possible. The Psalm has at least one further effect. In its retelling, Aseneth's Psalm erases both Aseneth's solitary experience and the *anthropos* from heaven and thereby mutes the epiphanic/mysterious element in the story, returning the reader to a more mundane narrative horizon. Perhaps the Psalm thus helps the transition to the last section of the tale—in which although there will be magically disintegrating swords and evidence of unnatural beauty and prowess, there are no heavens torn apart, no heavenly chariots, no mysterious epiphanies.

CONVERSION AND THE STABILIZATION OF CULTURE, OR, ASENETH AND HER MEN

In the intriguing final section to Longinus's treatise "On the Sublime," he discusses the political and cultural contexts for and consequences of the sublime. However coercive the figurative operations of sublimity may be, Longinus argues that the sublime functions to protect the civic order from those of "enslaved" character. Too's analysis of Longinus shows how he reaches back to Greek literary models and thereby shows the power of the Greek past against a defective Roman present. Sublimity is not merely aesthetic and personal; the transporting dislocation of the subject has civic, freeing, ennobling implications.[86] The final section of *Joseph and Aseneth* narrates the civic implications of Aseneth's transformation: the pagan converted to Judaism—through a process marked by overpowering tropical and figurative density and shifts in the speaking voice—now becomes the restrained, walled city of safety for the Jewish community. The plot, still touched by magical and mystical elements, is narrated in a more spare style, oriented more toward plot than descriptive or metaphorical extravagance or dense intertextual echoes. Aseneth's conversion now becomes salvific for the community: no longer "stranger" or "other" herself, she becomes an agent through whom the threat of both hostile Egyptians and treacherous Israelites may be thwarted and the power of Joseph extended.

With a repetition of καὶ ἐγένετο, "And it happened . . . ," the second part of *Joseph and Aseneth* begins, now set during the seven years of famine. If the first part of the tale offered an explanation of how Pharoah gave Aseneth, the daughter of an Egyptian priest, to Joseph as his wife, the second part may serve to explain the other half of the brief verse in Genesis: "Thus Joseph gained authority over the land of Egypt" (41:45b NRSV). Jacob and his sons have come to Goshen, the narrator reports briefly, and Joseph will be busy in this sequel with grain giving rather than grain gathering. In the opening domestic scene, Aseneth initiates a visit to Jacob. The episode echoes and inverts Part One's episode with Aseneth and her Egyptian parents, and incorporates her into the new structure of kinship and piety through the familiar markers of bodily intimacy and kiss:

καὶ ἐκάλεσεν αὐτὴν Ἰακὼβ πρὸς ἑαυτὸν καὶ εὐλόγησεν αὐτὴν καὶ κατεφίλησεν αὐτήν. καὶ ἐξέτεινεν Ἀσενὲθ τὰς χεῖρας αὐτῆς καὶ ἐκράτησε τοῦ αὐχένος Ἰακὼβ καὶ ἐκρεμάσθη ἐπὶ τὸν τράχηλον τοῦ πατρὸς αὐτῆς καθὼς κρέματαί τις ἐπὶ τὸν τράχηλον τοῦ πατρὸς αὐτοῦ ὅταν ἐκ πολέμου ἐπανέλθῃ εἰς τὸν οἶκον αὐτοῦ καὶ κατεφίλησεν αὐτόν. καὶ μετὰ ταῦτα ἔφαγον καὶ ἔπιον.

And Jacob called her to him and blessed her and kissed her. And Aseneth reached out her hands and grasped Jacob's neck and hung

upon the neck of her father just as someone hangs upon the neck
of his father when he returns to his house from battle, and she
kissed him. And after these things they ate and drank. (22.9–10)

The image of the child around the father's neck directly repeats imagery
from Aseneth's earlier long confession and prayer (12.8), while the addition of a battle helps foreshadow the plot to come. Given the tale's sustained emphasis on whom one may and may not touch or kiss, Aseneth's
intimacy with Jacob confirms that she has been transformed from the
liminality of virginity to the safety of married woman, from stranger to
kin, from idolater to God-venerator. So, too, with Joseph's brothers
Simeon and Levi, particularly Levi. As they ride home, with Joseph on
Aseneth's left and Levi on her right, Aseneth grasps Levi's hand and loves
him exceedingly, as he in turn loves her very much (22.12–13), a reciprocal affection founded, the narrator insists, on their shared mystical
experience.[87] Aseneth loves him for his prophetic power, he her for
her identity as city of refuge.[88] Both familial and mystical identities denature desire, sanctify male-female contact, and prepare for the conflicts
that ensue.

Yet not all desire is nonthreatening. The action of Part Two is fueled
by the jealous romance-novel plot of Pharoah's son: fueled by lovesickness for Aseneth—he is κατενύγη, "cut" because of her beauty, as Aseneth
herself was earlier at the sight of Joseph. Yet the political and cultural
conflicts are complex and do not reduce to Egyptians against Israelites.
Pharoah's son has murderous designs on his father. Joseph's brothers are
divided (a division with roots in the problematic place of children of
slaves within a kinship structure). Pharoah's son attempts to recruit allies
from Joseph's brothers. With Levi and Simeon, he fails, as Levi models an
anger-free, meek response conveniently enforced by a show of flaming
swords. With the sons of Bilhah and Zilpah, he succeeds, Dan and Gad
proving particularly treacherous. The plot is to murder Pharoah, have
Joseph's brothers murder Joseph, and ambush Aseneth. Aseneth, no longer
cloistered, travels outside her home, though guarded by Joseph's interces-
sory prayer and an armed guard. The ambush proceeds; Levi and the sons
of Leah come to the rescue; Benjamin—beautiful and strong at the prom-
ising age of eighteen—wounds Pharoah's son and kills his troops with
stones. The sons of Bilhah and Zilpah attempt to kill Aseneth, but the
woman whose ability to pray at length has been well established in Part

One, prays a surprisingly brief prayer for deliverance, and their swords disintegrate into ashes.

In the climax of this episode, Aseneth fulfills her role as city or source of refuge, as she intercedes for the treacherous brothers and preaches non-retaliation within Joseph's family. As she counters Simeon's insistence on executing those who plotted against Israel and Joseph, kissing and touching now convey not just membership in family but conciliatory intimacy:

καὶ ἐξέτεινεν Ἀσενὲθ τὴν δεξιὰν αὐτῆς χεῖρα καὶ ἥψατο τῆς γενειάδος τοῦ Συμεὼν καὶ κατεφίλησεν αὐτὸν καὶ εἶπεν· μηδαμῶς ἀδελφὲ ποιήσεις κακὸν ἀντὶ κακοῦ τῷ πλησίον σου. τῷ κυρίῳ δώσεις ἐκδικήσειν τὴν ὕβριν αὐτῶν. καὶ αὐτοὶ ἀδελφοὶ ὑμῶν εἰσι καὶ γένος τοῦ πατρὸς ὑμῶν Ἰσραὴλ καὶ ἔφυγον μηκόθεν ἀπὸ προσώπου ὑμῶν.

And Aseneth reached out her right hand and touched Simeon's beard and kissed him and said, "By no means, brother, will you do evil for evil to your neighbor. You will give to the Lord the judgment of their hubris. And they are your brothers and the offspring of your father Israel, and they fled far from your presence. (28.14)

Certainly, the episode might belong to Penn's category of "kisses that mark inclusion within family and people of God," but it could be taken as a different sort: kisses that encourage refuge, clemency, resolution of conflict. Levi, who perceives Aseneth's desire to save the traitorous brothers, marks his understanding by kissing her hand (28.15).

With that kiss, Aseneth recedes from the narrative, leaving Levi to save Pharoah's son (who nonetheless dies soon after) and Joseph to rule all of Egypt for forty-eight years after Pharoah's death; then he carefully turns power over to Pharoah's grandson, having acted as a father to him (29). *Thus*, we learn, through Aseneth's divine function as city of refuge within Egypt and within Joseph's clan, "Joseph gained authority over the land of Egypt" (41:45b, NRSV).

THE DIMENSIONS OF SUBLIME TRANSFORMATION

Throughout *Joseph and Aseneth*, the key locus for issues of boundaries and of passion, of restraint and of excess, is the virgin Aseneth. Joseph, too, is a virgin, but for the male character, the status is rather less ambiguous, a straightforward (though not always appealing) marker of piety and morality. Joseph's virginity means he resists (frequently) predatory female sexuality, sets strict boundaries about contact with foreign women, and remains chaste until marriage. Aseneth as virgin, however, is polyvalent. Her virginity signifies worthy sexual purity and is accompanied by expected social confinement and inevitable discussions about suitors. She, like her seven star-like companion virgins, represents an esteemed status for young women. But virginity in the tale also acquires, as we have seen, associations of misandry, generalized arrogance and defiance, youthful ignorance, and even abandonment and vulnerability. The virgin encodes not just restraint, but excess, including excessive and misplaced piety. Those who study *Joseph and Aseneth* for evidence of missionizing or broad issues of Jew-Gentile relations do well to notice that male Egyptians are not characterized as ridiculously excessive idolaters; they are in fact capable of using unqualified pious language about the most-high God. Aseneth's gender and sexual status make her a particularly labile symbol of urgently needed change. In the crucial scene in which she becomes "pure virgin," unveiled, with a head like a young man, she represents *Metanoia*—repentance, transformability, mutability, mobility. Unlike in *The Acts of Thecla* and other ancient asceticizing literature, female virginity in *Joseph and Aseneth* is not a sustainable state, but a state of profound liminality, uniquely capable of representing transformation. In striking contrast, the imagery for Aseneth as walled-city and place of refuge is insistently fixed, stable, immobile, and safe.[89]

In the many scenes in which the eyes, hands, breasts, necks, and especially mouths of characters are emphasized, and whereever bodily contact between Aseneth and various men is either prevented or described, we see that erotic motifs connect all the modes of transformation in the story—from virgin to bride, stranger to kin, idolater to God venerator. Desire obviously informs Aseneth's first deflected attempt to kiss Joseph, as well as their post-transformation lingering kiss. Indeed, before turning to the particular kinds of spirit that Joseph unilaterally imparts to Aseneth, the reunion scene offers a brief moment of mutuality: "and they kissed each other for a long time, and they both came to life in their spirits" (19.10). Yet even the scenes where Aseneth's touch or kiss is not construed as erotic—her filial embrace with Jacob, her mystically charged communion with Levi, her pure-virgin-on-a-pure-bed touch to the knees of the heavenly *anthropos*—all depend on the potential eroticism of a woman's touch, even as they refuse it. That is, in order to denature desire the tale must activate it. Such scenes suggest that the love story is no mere frame on which to stretch the story of religious transformation. So, too, in other scenes, the author merges two registers of language for the self-dissolution that precedes identity transformation: Erotic language for the disintegrative experiences of desire blends with religious language for the suffering and alienation associated with penitence. Love sickness and spiritual remorse have shared physical symptoms, shared dissociative man-ifestations, and, throughout Aseneth's story, the language is blended so that it is both the love of God that makes romantic passion possible and romantic passion that makes the love of God possible. At some level, Aseneth's Psalm gets it right—her transformation *is* all about Joseph's desirability even when it is about something more or other than Joseph's desirability.

Throughout this analysis the several turns to Longinus imply not that *Joseph and Aseneth* would necessarily have passed the ancient critic's discriminating literary standards, but that the tale's operations of language share some assumptions with the author of *On Sublimity*. Through its intense concentrations of figures of speech, its superfluity of detail, its vivid image production, its proliferation of tropes, *Joseph and Aseneth* offers language that exceeds and transgresses the ordinary and expected, that violates restraint in order to transport not merely the central char-acter but the reader into a transformed and elevated reality. And yet, sublimity, with its ecstasy and extravagant passion, also presupposes restraint, "needs the curb as well as the spur" (2.2). Longinus is emphatic that the sublime is no indicator of literary or moral decadence. Rather, the cultivation of sublimity depends upon success in "the unlimited war which lays hold on our desires, and all the passions which beset and ravage our modern life" (44.6). So, too, *Joseph and Aseneth* offers itself, not just as a discharge of imagination, but as a source of moral and spir-itual elevation, its extravagances of plot, description, and style predicated upon restraint. Longinus remarks, "Other literary qualities prove their users to be human; sublimity raises us towards the spiritual greatness of god" (36.1). Aseneth, the exemplar of the mutability of *metanoia*, becomes the city of refuge—the space within which godly virtues of clemency, self-control, and civic service not only advance Israelite authority but create complex interconnections and transactions between Israelite and

Egyptian identity.[90] Though elements of her story suggest the coercive aspects of sublimity—the ways she is acted upon, perhaps irresistibly, by male figures and a male deity—in her long soliloquies, prayers, and dialogues, Aseneth, like Sappho, gives voice to her own disintegrative experience and to a sublime, recuperative turn, a recuperation not only of the self, but of culture.

FIVE

Conclusion

The Narrativity of Desire, Restraint, and Conversion

THE *SHEPHERD OF HERMAS, THE ACTS OF PAUL AND Thecla*, and *Joseph and Aseneth* are aptly termed "conversion tales" because each narrates the transformation of a protagonist's piety and identity, both personal and social. Their strikingly different narrative textures generate discrete reading experiences of *how* conversion takes place. *The Shepherd* suggests that identity transformation issues from the discursive disciplines of self-scrutiny, from dreams and visions that mediate divine perspective, and from interpretive decoding of reality, and that such a process is prolonged, repetitive, and erratic. For Hermas and for readers, the ongoing process of deciphering desire seems never quite completed, but is nevertheless marked by change, which is not merely personal but has an insistently social dimension. The challenges to Hermas merge continuously into challenges to his household and to the church, and he becomes a converted prophet of conversion. In *The Acts of Paul and Thecla*, the driving of plot and the movement in social space, with little access to the interiority of any character, evokes conversion as a consequence of the pressure of drive, lure, and test. Thecla's narrative consists of a succession of displacements from one setting to the next, propelled by the movement of desire. Thecla is changed, and may stretch the boundaries of the Pauline movement the text imagines. In *Joseph and Aseneth*, the narrative is marked by visual and visionary intensity—intensely descriptive passages, reaches of figurative intensity, even sublimity. The intertextuality of the narrative (its echoes of Genesis, Song of Songs, and penitential texts, among many others) turn literary mimesis into cultural transposition. For Aseneth, desire utterly debases and radically elevates, then moves her and her readers to a plane of restrained social relations. Aseneth not only is changed but herself changes Joseph's community—the figure of liminality becomes the refuge in which cultural renegotiation takes place. If for a moment one may risk oversimplication to claim the benefits of contrast, these three stories, respectively, exemplify ways of telling a conversion story dominated by dialogue and copiousness (*Hermas*), by plot and spareness (*Thecla*), and by visualization, mimesis, and variation in narrative pace (*Aseneth*). The experience of conversion is differentiated by its narrative modes.

As we have seen, the three tales also narrate the transformation of the protagonist's identity by a complex interweaving of gender-laden elements, in particular virginity, celibacy, masculinity, self-restraint and desire. To repeat one of Ross Kraemer's observations, "the ideal transformation narrative . . . may well be one that utilizes gender as a central component of difference."[1]

In *The Shepherd of Hermas*, manliness is construed ethically, socially, and ecclesially—as a matter of scrutinizing desires, managing households, and carrying out prophetic ministry. Masculinity is also a theological category: as with the manly nature of Christ, the spirit infuses flesh to provide strength instead of softness, rejuvenation instead of feebleness. The dangers to be avoided seem more economic than erotic, yet the intermittent appearance of female figures, including attractive virgins who ambiguously exemplify manliness, generates tension that fosters ongoing change in Hermas. The female figures enhance, by mechanisms of desire and resistance, the guidance given by Hermas's primary companion, the male angel of *metanoia*.

For Thecla, the identifier *virgin* marks her social and sexual status at the outset of the story. Conventional associations with virginity explain her susceptibility to lovesickness, the scandal of her pursuit of Paul, and her being the object of the *eros* of men. As the story proceeds, however, the category of *virgin* seems more social than sexual. Although Thecla embraces a life of perpetual celibacy, once she has survived the first attempted execution and moved out of her own household and city, the term *virgin* is no longer used to describe her. That is, once Thecla becomes an active, vocal, protector of her own purity, a baptizer of herself, a confessor of Christ, and a teacher of other women and men, neither she, nor the narrator, nor the other characters refer to her as *virgin*, but with descriptors such as "female fighter with the beasts," "female slave of God," "daughter," and, emphatically at the narrative's close, "teacher." Yet Thecla's transformation is not well described simply as masculinization, for even at her most active and vocal, her predicament and her cast of women supporters, particularly the maternal Tryphaena, make hers an insistently female experience. Transvestitism may be the better concept, since the assumption of masculine behavior keeps signaling femaleness as well. However one characterizes it, *The Acts of Paul and Thecla* narrates the conversion of a virgin changed by ἐγκράτεια and ἀνάστασις—self-restraint and rising up or resurrection. And the tale begins and moves forward as a story of desire—the desires of a young girl, of elite men, and of mothers.

In Aseneth, virginity is an ambiguous marker that carries both expected associations—purity in preparation for marriage along with strong regard for sexual and gendered boundaries—and others less expected. Before her transformation, Aseneth as virgin also represents excess of disdain and arrogance, of false devotion to false gods, of ignorance, and of vulnerability to abandonment. After her seven-day self-abasement and repentance, her soliloquies and prayers, and her encounter with the startling ἄνθρωπος from heaven, Aseneth becomes, in one brief scene, a pure virgin poised to become a bride, now with an unveiled head like a young man's. At this point of extreme liminality, between genders, between recognizable social states, Aseneth is likened to heavenly Metanoia—a beautiful, laughing, loving, pure virgin, image of divinely mediated transformation. The instability and provisional nature of virginity are here given symbolic resonance, suggesting transformability of piety and cultural identity. Aseneth ends the story, then, not as virgin but as bride and wife, not unstable and in need of change, but as walled city of refuge, exemplifying the ability to resist anger, to refuse retaliatory violence, and to model the ongoing malleability of cultural difference.

As the texts use gender as a component of difference, they also deploy desire and restraint as their modes of transformation. In each tale, the pressures toward conversion are in certain respects coercive and dislocating. Yet as their stories unfold, Hermas, Thecla, and Aseneth are neither passive nor compliant, but actors who negotiate changed places in their narrated social worlds. Each in some way renounces erotic consummation (either finally or provisionally), but also experiences the transformative possibilities of desire itself. Beyond their shared motifs, however, the dynamics of the three stories suggest that the configurations of desire, restraint, and identity operating in ancient imperial culture were diverse.

These narratives frequently skirt the canons of realism. Thecla's desire propels her into threatening arenas, but lionesses, women's perfumes, and divine fire protect her. Hermas's dalliance with the virgins is set in Arcadia—an idealized literary world where one expects a "pastoral" outcome. When the heavens rip open, Aseneth finds herself in a state in which placing a hand on the knee of a heavenly *anthropos* on her bed earns blessing, not rebuke. Yet perhaps *The Shepherd of Hermas, The Acts of Paul and Thecla*, and *Joseph and Aseneth* do propose modes of transformed identity imitable in the ancient social world. Tertullian tells us that Thecla's tale did indeed prompt some to claim the right of women to baptize—the key marker of early Christian conversion—and the vitality of the cult of Thecla over centuries suggests diverse social consequences of her story. For Aseneth, no historical evidence suggests how or to what effect her story was read, but perhaps her tale did enhance the status of proselytes within Judaism, or present a paradigm of repentance, conversion, or interethnic negotiation. Given Hermas's popularity in early Christianity, perhaps his seriousness about communal responsibility together with his cheerfully erratic self-scrutiny seemed an accessible model within church life.

What narrative analysis more securely shows, however, is that each of these stories offers an intriguing and distinctive development of the thematic of desire, restraint, and conversion. Each in the end represents desire, not as an antithesis to, but as an expressive mode of self-restraint. All three texts illustrate how the meaning making of conversion is an effect of story. Close analysis of their textual energetics suggests ways that authors and readers were and are drawn into the narrative coherence (and incoherence) of conversion. Goldhill remarks "[T]he formulation of the desiring subject is a process in which reading—with its hesitations, appropriations, fantasies, and blindnesses—plays a fundamental role."[2] In the disciplines of narrative, in the textures of story, Hermas, Thecla, and Aseneth variously involve their readers in the embrace of renunciation and the conversionary seductions of self-control.

Notes

Chapter One

1. Peter Brooks, *Reading for the Plot* (New York: Alfred A. Knopf, 1984), 37.
2. Diane Austin-Broos, "The Anthropology of Conversion: An Introduction," in *The Anthropology of Religious Conversion* (ed. Andrew Buskser and Stephen D. Glazier; Lanham, Md.: Rowman & Littlefield, 2003), 2; 1–12.
3. For example, Philo writes: "we must rejoice with them, as if, though blind at the first they had recovered their sight and had come from the deepest darkness to behold the most radiant light" (*On the Virtues* 178). Or from the New Testament: ". . . to open their eyes so that they may turn from darkness to light and from the power of Satan to God, so that they may receive forgiveness of sins and a place among those who are sanctified by faith in me" (Acts 26:18 NRSV); "Therefore we have been buried with him by baptism into death, so that, just as Christ was raised from the dead by the glory of the Father, so we too might walk in newness of life" (Rom 6:3–4 NRSV).
4. So Philo: "They are called proselytes because they have come over to a new and God-loving way of life" (*On the Special Laws* 1.51).
5. From the New Testament, for instance: "Put to death, therefore, whatever in you is earthly: fornication, impurity, passion, evil desire, and greed (which is idolatry)" (Col 3:5 NRSV). Metaphors for conversion vary widely in Jewish and Christian antiquity, of course. For the prevalence of death/life and darkness/light imagery as well as other common figures, see Paul Aubin, *Le Probléme de la Conversion* (Paris: Beauchesne et ses Fils, 1962); Beverly Gaventa, *From Darkness to Light: Conversion in the New Testament* (Philadelphia: Fortress, 1986).
6. See further discussion below.

7. See the discussion of introductory issues in Carolyn Osiek, *Shepherd of Hermas: A Commentary* (Minneapolis: Fortress, 1999) and in chapter 2, which follows.

8. See the discussion in Edgar Hennecke and Wilhelm Schneemelcher, "The Acts of Paul: Introduction," in *New Testament Apocrypha* (ed. Wilhelm Schneemelcher; trans. R. McL. Wilson; Louisville: Westminster/John Knox, 1992), 2.213–237, and in chapter 3.

9. See Edith M. Humphrey, "Issues in Reading and Interpretation," in *Joseph and Aseneth* (Sheffield.: Sheffield, 2000), 17–37; Randall D. Chesnutt, "History of Research," *From Death to Life: Conversion in Joseph and Aseneth* (JSPSS16; Sheffield.: Sheffield, 1995), 20–95. See also chapter 4.

10. Ross Shepard Kraemer, *When Aseneth Met Joseph: A Late Antique Tale of the Biblical Patriarch and His Egyptian Wife, Reconsidered* (New York: Oxford University Press, 1998), 194.

11. A. D. Nock, *Conversion: The Old and the New in Religion from Alexander the Great to Augustine of Hippo* (Oxford: Clarendon, 1933).

12. William James, "Lecture VIII," *Varieties of Religious Experience* (The Gifford Lectures; New York: Modern Library, 1902), 167.

13. James, "Lecture IX," *Varieties of Religious Experience*, 193.

14. James, "Lecture IX," *Varieties of Religious Experience*, 202–07.

15. Nock, *Conversion*, 7.

16. Nock, *Conversion*, 14.

17. So James remarks, "Even in the most voluntarily built-up sort of regeneration there are passages of partial self-surrender interposed; and in the great majority of all cases, when the will had done its uttermost toward bringing one close to the complete unification aspired after, it seems that the very last step must be left to other forces and performed without the help of its activity. In other words, self-surrender becomes then indispensable." Lecture IX, *Varieties of Religious Experience*, 204.

18. Subsequent scholarship has, of course, variously challenged, complicated, and extended such characterizations, as well as Nock's claims about "conversion" in antiquity being distinctive to Judaism and Christianity. Christian Décobert provides a revaluation of Nock on the occasion of a new edition of *Conversion*. See "La Conversion Comme Aversion," *Archives de Sciences Sociales des Religions* 104 (1998): 33–60.

19. The 1970s and 1980s saw a range of innovative social science studies of conversion, prompted at least in part by the 1960s social phenomenon of new religious movements. For useful surveys see two essays by Lewis R. Rambo, published two decades apart: "Current Research on Religious Conversion," *Religious Studies Review* 8.2 (1982): 146–59; "Anthropology and the Study of Conversion," in *The Anthropology of Religious Conversion*, 211–22.

20. J. Lofland and R. Stark, "Becoming a World Saver: A Theory of Conversion to a Deviant Perspective," *American Sociological Review* 30 (1965): 862–875. See further review of theories in Steve Bruce, "Sociology of Conversion:

The Last Twenty-Five Years," in *Paradigms, Poetics and Politics of Conversion* (ed. Jan N. Bremmer, J. van Bekkum Wout, and Arie L. Molendjik; Leuven: Peeters, 2006), 1–11.

21. Rodney Stark and Roger Finke, "Religious Choices: Conversion and Reaffiliation," in *Acts of Faith: Explaining the Human Side of Religion* (Berkeley: University of California Press, 2000), 114–138; James T. Richardson, "The Active vs. Passive Convert: Paradigm Conflict in Conversion/Recruitment Research," *Journal for the Scientific Study of Religion* 24 (1985): 119–236.

22. See, for instance, Lewis R. Rambo, *Understanding Religious Conversion* (New Haven: Yale University Press, 1993); Barbara G. Meyerhoff, Linda A. Camino, and Edith Turner, "Rites of Passage: An Overview," *Encyclopedia of Religion* 12 (New York: Macmillan, 1987), 380–7.

23. Pentecostalism and Islam are much discussed, but studies extend beyond these traditions. Recent anthologies suggest the range of studies: Jan N. Bremmer, Wout J. van Bekkum, and Arie L. Molendijk, eds., *Paradigms, Poetics and Politics of Conversion* (Leuven: Peeters, 2006); Andrew Buckser and Stephen D. Glazier, *The Anthropology of Religious Conversion* (Lanham, Md.: Rowman & Littlefield, 2003); Jan N. Bremmer, Wout J. van Bekkum, and Arie L. Molendijk, eds., *Cultures of Conversion* (Leuven: Peeters, 2006). Joel B. Green brings neurobiological research to bear on the interpretation of early Christian views of conversion in *Body, Soul, and Human Life: The Nature of Humanity in the Bible* (Grand Rapids: Baker Academic, 2008), 106–139.

24. Austin-Broos, "The Anthropology of Conversion," 2.

25. Gauri Viswanathan, *Outside the Fold: Conversion, Modernity, and Belief* (Princeton: Princeton University Press, 1998), xvi.

26. Rambo, "Anthropology and the Study of Conversion," 220, commenting on Viswanathan's *Outside the Fold*.

27. See, for instance, Thomas M. Finn, *From Death to Rebirth: Ritual and Conversion in Antiquity* (New York: Paulist Press, 1997), 17–34; Martin Goodman, *Mission and Conversion: Proselytizing in the Religious History of the Roman Empire* (Oxford: Clarendon Press, 1994); Eugene V. Gallagher, "Conversion and Community in Late Antiquity," *Journal of Religion* 73 (1993): 1–15; Scot McKnight, *Turning to Jesus: the Sociology of Conversion in the Gospels* (Louisville: Westminster John Knox, 2002).

28. Ramsey Macmullen, "Conversion: A Historian's View," *The Second Century* 5.2 (1985/1986): 67–81; and *Christianizing the Roman Empire* a.d. *100–400* (New Haven: Yale University Press, 1984); Rodney Stark, *The Rise of Christianity* (New York: HarperSanFrancisco, 1997).

29. See Shaye Cohen, *The Beginnings of Jewishness: Boundaries, Varieties, Uncertainties* (Berkeley: University of California Press, 1999); Goodman, *Mission and Conversion*, along with Louis Feldman, "Was Judaism a Missionary Religion in Ancient Times?" in *Jewish Assimilation, Acculturation and Accommodation: Past*

Traditions, Current Issues and Future Prospects (Lanham, Md.: University Press of America, 1992), 24–37. See also Shaye Cohen, "Was Judaism in Antiquity a Missionary Religion?" in Feldman, *Jewish Assimilation*, 14–23.

30. Judith Lieu surveys scholarship up to the mid 1990s and adds her own assessment in, "The 'Attraction of Women' in/To Early Judaism and Christianity: Gender and the Politics of Conversion," *Journal for the Study of the New Testament* 72 (1998): 5–22. See also Shelly Matthews, *First Converts: Rich Pagan Women and the Rhetoric of Mission in Early Judaism and Christianity* (Stanford: Stanford University Press, 2001); Ross Shepard Kraemer and Mary Rose D'Angelo, eds., *Women and Christian Origins* (New York: Oxford University Press, 1999); Carolyn Osiek and Margaret M. MacDonald, *A Woman's Place: House Churches in Earliest Christianity* (Minneapolis: Fortress, 2005).

31. Lieu, "The 'Attraction of Women' in/To Early Judaism and Christianity," 20.

32. Elizabeth A. Clark, "Engendering the Study of Religion," in *The Future of the Study of Religion: Proceedings of Congress 2000* (ed. Slavica Jakelić and Lori Pearson; Leiden: Brill, 2004), 217–42.

33. Lewis P. Hinchman and Sandra K. Hinchman, *Memory, Identity, Community: The Idea of Narrative in the Human Sciences* (New York: SUNY Press, 1997), xiv.

34. Hinchman and Hinchman, *Memory, Identity, Community*, xiv.

35. Hetty Zock, "Paradigms in Psychological Conversion Research," in *Paradigms, Poetics, and Politics of Conversion*, 41–58; 54–55. But see the critique of the literary turn in Bruce, "Sociology of Conversion," 10–11.

36. Paula Fredricksen, "Paul and Augustine: Conversion Narratives, Orthodox Traditions, and the Retrospective Self," *Journal of Theological Studies* 37 (1986): 3–34.

37. Tim Whitmarsh, *Ancient Greek Literature* (Malden, Mass.: Polity Press, 2004), 212.

38. Morales remarks, "The young men and women [in the Greek novel] do not so much choose to fall in love as are zapped into an altered state from on high, either by *Eros* himself (theomorphised in Chariton and Xenophon) or by the visual aspect of the beloved which stimulates desire." Helen Morales, "The history of sexuality," in *The Greek and Roman Novel* (ed., Tim Whitmarsh; Cambridge: Cambridge University Press, 2008), 42; 39–55.

39. Chariton, *Chaereas and Callirhoe*, I.1, in *Collected Ancient Greek Novels*, (ed. and transl., B. P. Reardon; Berkeley: University of California Press, 1989), 21; 17–124.

40. *Chaereas and Callirhoe*, I.1; Reardon, 22.

41. For further analysis, see Ryan K. Balot, "Foucault, Chariton, and the Masculine Self," *Helios* 25 (1998): 139–62.

42. *Chaereas and Callirhoe*, II.4; Reardon, 41. Whitmarsh analyzes Dionysius' self-dialogue in Tim Whitmarsh, "Dialogues in love: Bakhtin and his critics on the Greek novel," in *The Bakhtin Circle and Ancient Narrative*, (ed. R. Bracht Branham; Groningen: Barkhuis Publishing & Groningen University Library, 2005), 107–29.

43. *Chaereas and Callirhoe*,V.9; Reardon, 87.

44. Michel Foucault, *The Use of Pleasure* (*The History of Sexuality*,Vol. 2; trans. Robert Hurley; New York:Vintage Books, 1990); *The Care of the Self* (*The History of Sexuality*.Vol. 3; trans. Robert Hurley; New York:Vintage Books, 1988). Critiques of Foucault and other Foucauldians, particularly from feminist classicists, continue. See, for instance, Amy Richlin, "Zeus and Metis: Foucault, Feminism, Classics," *Helios* 18 (1991): 160–180; Marilyn Skinner, "Introduction," *Roman Sexualities* (ed. Judith Hallett and Marilyn B. Skinner; Princeton: Princeton University Press, 1997), 3–27. Stephen Moore wittily warns New Testament scholars against "tripping blithely through a battlefield" of the "sexuality wars" in classics; Stephen D. Moore,"'O Man, Who Art Thou . . . ?': Masculinity Studies and New Testament Studies," in *New Testament Masculinities* (Semeia Studies; Atlanta: Society of Biblical Literature, 2003), 1–21.

45. Pierre Hadot, *Philosophy as a Way of Life: Spiritual Exercises from Socrates to Foucault* (trans. Michael Chase; Oxford: Blackwell, 1995), 81–83. Hadot's earlier essay influenced Foucault's analysis, "Exercices spirituels," *Annuaire de la 5e Section de l'Ecole pratique des Hautes Etudes* (1975–1976). Foucault discusses the conversion to the self in Michel Foucault,"The Hermeneutic of the Subject," in *Ethics: Subjectivity and Truth* (*Essential Works of Foucault 1954–84, Vol. 1*; ed. Paul Rabinow; New York: New Press, 1997), 96; and *The Care of the Self*, 67. Throughout Greek philosophical literature, verb and noun forms derived from στρέφω, *to turn*, are used to convey philosophic conversion. Plato, for example, uses the noun μεταστροφή and the verb περιστρέφεσθαι for the turn toward the Good or Truth (although when the inhabitant of the cave turns toward the light in *Republic* 518c-d, Plato's term is περιαγωγή, rather than a form of στρέφω). See the discussion of "Paideia as Conversion" in Werner Jaeger, *Paideia: the Ideals of Greek Culture* (New York: Oxford University Press, 1943), 2.295–300. See also Martha Nussbaum, *The Therapy of Desire: Theory and Practice in Hellenistic Ethics* (Princeton: Princeton University Press, 1994).

46. See, for example, the discussion by Christopher Gill, *The Structured Self in Hellenistic and Roman Thought* (New York: Oxford University Press, 2006).

47. Epictetus, *Discourses and Enchiridion* Book III (trans. Thomas Wentworth Higginson; New York: Walter J. Black, 1944), 177–178. See discussion by Hadot, *Philosophy as a Way of Life*, 201.

48. I here rely on A.A. Long, "Epictetus on Emotions," in *From Epicurus to Epictetus: Studies in Hellenistic and Roman Philosophy* (Oxford: Clarendon Press, 2006), 381.

49. Epictetus, *Discourses*, 178.

50. For summaries of such techniques see Foucault,"The Hermeneutics of the Subject," 100–105, and "Technologies of the Self," in *Ethics*, 223–51.

51. Seneca,"On Anger," III.36.1–3, in *Moral Essays* (trans. John W. Basare; New York: Putnam's, 1928), 1.339–41.

52. Seneca, "On Tranquility of Mind" in *Moral Essays*, 2.215–37.

53. Seneca, "On Tranquility," 215.

54. See discussion by Hadot, *Philosophy As a Way of Life*, 179–205.

55. Marcus Aurelius, *The Meditations* (trans. A.S.L. Farquharson; New York: Oxford University Press, 1989), VIII.48, 76.

56. Plutarch, "On Being Aware of Moral Progress," in *Essays* (trans. Robin Waterfield; New York: Penguin, 1992), 137–145. See comment by Richard Sorabji, *Emotion and Peace of Mind: From Stoic Agitation to Christian Temptation* (The Gifford Lectures; New York: Oxford University Press, 2000), 218.

57. Gill, *The Structured Self*, 35; 95–6.

58. Bibliography on gender construction in antiquity is rich and varied. See, for instance, Maud W. Gleason, *Making Men: Sophists and Self-Presentation in Ancient Rome* (Princeton: Princeton University Press, 1995); Ralph M. Rosen & Ineke Sluiter, *Andreia: Studies in Manliness and Courage in Classical Antiquity* (Leiden: Brill, 2003); Judith Hallett and Marilyn B. Skinner, eds., *Roman Sexualities* (Princeton: Princeton University Press, 1997); Dale Martin, *The Corinthian Body* (New Haven: Yale University Press, 1995); L. Stephanie Cobb, *Dying to be Men: Gender and Language in Early Christian Martyr Texts* (New York: Columbia University Press, 2008).

59. Philo, *Questions and Answers on Genesis*, 1.8

60. Philo, *On the Virtues*, Greek text from *Philo* (LCL, Vol 8; transl., F.H. Colson; Cambridge: Harvard University Press, 1939), 1.14.

61. Philo, *On the Virtues*, 1.27.

62. Philo, *On the Virtues*, 1.21. For a perceptive analysis of Philo's gendered appeals in the treatise, see Walter T. Wilson, "Pious Soldiers, Gender Deviants, and the Ideology of Actium: Courage and Warfare in Philo's *De Fortitudine*," *Studia Philonica Annual* 17 (2005): 1–32. Wilson persuasively links Philo's rejection of aberrant gender norms with Augustan rhetoric about the defeat of Antony and Cleopatra at Actium—"the import of which was clarified by means of a system of polarized signifiers familiar from Hellenic political rhetoric." Wilson sees Philo's strategy as part of his broader political effort to show the superiority of the Jewish politeia and thereby "secure the civil rights of the Jewish community in Alexandria" (24, 31).

63. Guy Nave offers a wide survey of usages of μετάνοια and μετανοέω from classical literature through the first two centuries CE in *The Role and Function of Repentance in Luke-Acts* (Atlanta: Society of Biblical Literature, 2002), 39–144. With narrower scope, Laurel Fulkerson finds in ancient Athens rhetorical appeals to remorse and regret as proper recognition of regrettable action that has harmed others. "*Metameleia* and Friends: Remorse and Repentance in Fifth- and Fourth-Century Athenian Orators," *Phoenix* 58 (2004): 241–59. Robert A. Kaster, *Emotion, Restraint, and Community in Ancient Rome* (New York: Oxford University Press, 2005) concludes, in part, "Now, it is not at all true that being Roman meant never having to say you're sorry, and I do not suggest that the Romans

were innocent of what we think of as remorse. It is the case, however, that they almost never used the language of *paenitentia* to represent that experience. Rather, when they had occasion to express remorse, it tended to appear in the guise of shame" (82). For an influential early twentieth-century debate about pre-Christian use, see Eduard Norden, *Agnostos Theos* (Stuttgart: B.G. Teubner, 1912) and Werner Jaeger, review of Eduard Norden, *Agnostos Theos*, reprinted in *Scripta Minora* I (Rome: Edizioni di Storia e Litteratura, 1960).

64. John T. Fitzgerald and L. Michael White, eds., *The Tabula of Cebes* (Chico, Calif.: Scholars Press, 1983), 79. See further discussion in relation to *The Shepherd of Hermas* in chapter 2.

65. Cicero, *Pro Murena* 61. Cited in David Winston, "Philo's Doctrine of Repentance," in *The School of Moses: Studies in Philo and Hellenistic Religion* (ed. John Peter Kenney; Atlanta: Scholar's Press, 1995), 29; 29–40.

66. "Musonius Rufus, The Roman Socrates," introduction, texts, and transl., Cora E. Lutz, *Yale Classical Studies* 10 (1967): 143; 3–147.

67. David Konstan, "Philo's *De Virtutibus* in the Perspective of Classical Greek Philosophy," *Studia Philonica Annual* 18 (2006): 59; 59–72.

68. In the *Septuagint*, ἐπιστροφή or ἐπιστρέφειν are consistently used to translate the Hebrew word *shuv*, which has as its basic meaning *turn back* or *return*, while μετάνοια translates the Hebrew *naham: to be sorry, to regret, or to suffer grief*. In Philo's writings, however, as in the New Testament, stable distinctions between μετάνοια and ἐπιστροφή shift. The words may be used distinctly from one another, or to imply a sequence ("repent and be converted"), or interchangeably. See *Theological Dictionary of the New Testament* 4:979–984; Bailey, "*Metanoia* in the Writings of Philo Judaeus," *SBL Seminar Papers 1991* (Society of Biblical Literature Seminar Papers 28; Atlanta: Scholars Press, 1991), 135–41; J.W. Heikkinen, "Notes on 'Epistrepho' and 'Metanoeo,'" *Ecumenical Review* 19 (1967): 313–16; Nave, "Philo," in *The Role and Function of Repentance in Luke-Acts*, 85–96.

69. Philo, *On the Virtues*, 1.176.

70. Philo, *On the Virtues*, 1.179.

71. Philo, *On the Virtues*, 1.180–81.

72. Philo, *On the Virtues*, 1.177; see also *On the Special Laws* 1.51–52.

73. Philo, *On Flight and Finding*, 1.157–159; *Allegorical Interpretation*, 3.106; *Questions and Answers on Genesis*, 2.13.

74. Philo, *On the Posterity of Cain*, 1.178.

75. Jennifer Wright Knust, *Abandoned to Lust: Sexual Slander and Ancient Christianity* (New York: Columbia University Press, 2006).

76. Knust, *Abandoned to Lust*, 31, 42.

77. Knust, *Abandoned to Lust*, 28.

78. Knust, *Abandoned to Lust*, 3.

79. Whitmarsh, *Ancient Greek Literature*, 212.

80. Chariton, *Chaereas and Callirhoe*, V.8; Reardon, 85.

81. Simon Goldhill, *Foucault's Virginity: Ancient Erotic Fiction and the History of Sexuality* (Cambridge: Cambridge University Press, 1995).

82. Plutarch, "Of Moral Virtue," 471.

83. Plutarch, "On Being Aware of Moral Progress," 136.

84. Froma Zeitlin remarks that these two dialogues were much in vogue during the period of Plutarch and the novels, both of which turned Plato's perspectives into marriage-oriented arguments. Froma Zeitlin, "Religion," in *The Greek and Roman Novel* (ed. Tim Whitmarsh; Cambridge: Cambridge University Press, 2008), 102; 91–108. See Goldhill's analysis, *Foucault's Virginity*, 145–61.

85. Plutarch, *Eroticus*, 16 [759] in *Selected Essays and Dialogues* (ed. and transl. Donald Russell; New York: Oxford University Press, 1993), 264.

86. Plutarch, *Eroticus*, 19 [764], 273–74.

87. Plutarch, *Eroticus*, 21 [767], 277.

88. Virginia Burrus, "Introduction," *Toward a Theology of Eros: Transfiguring Passion at the Limits of Discipline* (ed. Virginia Burrus and Catherine Keller; New York: Fordham University Press, 2006), xiii.

89. Froma Zeitlin, "Religion," 94.

90. See the discussion of textual fluidity and ancient audiences by Christine M. Thomas, "Stories Without Texts and Without Authors: The Problem of Fluidity in Ancient Novelistic Texts and Early Christian Literature," in *Ancient Fiction and Early Christian Narrative* (Society of Biblical Literature Symposium Series; Atlanta: Scholars Press, 1998), 273–91.

91. Brooks, *Reading for the Plot*, 37.

92. Brooks, *Reading for the Plot*, 61.

93. For a view of the productive "interference" of theory with narrative analysis, see "Constructing Narrative: An Interview with Peter Brooks, Conducted by John S. Rickard and Harold Schweizer," in Peter Brooks, *Psychoanalysis and Storytelling* (Oxford: Blackwell, 1994), 105–06.

94. Foucault, *The Use of Pleasure*, 63.

95. Mieke Bal, *Narratology: Introduction to the Theory of Narrative* (2nd ed.; Toronto: University of Toronto Press, 1999), 121.

96. 'Longinus,' "On Sublimity," in *Ancient Literary Criticism: The Principal Texts in New Translations* (trans. D. A. Russell; New York: Oxford University Press, 1972), 460–503.

97. David M. Halperin, John J. Winkler, and Froma I. Zeitlin, "Introduction," in *Before Sexuality: The Construction of Erotic Experience in the Ancient Greek World* (ed. David M. Halperin, John J. Winkler, and Froma I. Zeitlin; Princeton: Princeton University Press, 1990), 5; 3–20.

98. See again Thomas, "Stories Without Texts and Without Authors," 273–91.

99. My description here is shaped by Shlomith Rimmon's contrast of "Paraphrase vs. Texture," part of a masterful summary of narratological theory in general and Gerard Genette in particular. Shlomith Rimmon, "A Comprehensive Theory of Narrative: Genette's *Figures III* and the Structuralist Study of Fiction," *Poetics and Theory of Literature* (1976): 33–62; 35–37.

100. Teresa de Lauretis, *Alice Doesn't: Feminism, Semiotics, Cinema* (Bloomington: Indiana University Press, 1984), 106.

101. Geoffrey Galt Harpham, *The Ascetic Imperative in Culture and Criticism* (Chicago: University of Chicago Press, 1987), 62.

Chapter Two

1. Robin Lane Fox, *Pagans and Christians* (New York: HarperSanFrancisco, 1986), 381.

2. Peter Brown, *The Body and Society: Men, Women and Sexual Renunciation in Early Christianity* (New York: Columbia University Press, 1988), 69.

3. J. Lawson, *A Theological and Historical Introduction to the Apostolic Fathers* (New York: MacMillan, 1961), 253. Cited along with other scholarly castigations of Hermas's shortcomings in J. Christian Wilson, *Toward a Reassessment of the Shepherd of Hermas: Its Date and Its Pneumatology* (Lewiston, Maine: Mellen, 1993), 2.

4. A. Hilhorst, "Erotic Elements in the *Shepherd* of Hermas," *Groningen Colloquia on the Novel* (Groningen: Egbert Forsten, 1998), 4.193.

5. See Carolyn Osiek's succinct and thorough summary of the manuscript tradition and citation by other early Christian writers, in *Shepherd of Hermas: A Commentary* (*Hermeneia*; Minneapolis: Fortress Press, 1999), 1–7.

6. See, for instance *Stromateis* I.29.181.1 and II.1.3.5. A full catalogue and analysis of early citations of Hermas is offered by Philippe Henne, *L'Unité du Pasteur d'Hermas* (Paris: Gabalda, 1992), 16–44.

7. Tertullian, *De pudicitia* 10 and 20; also cited in Osiek, *Shepherd of Hermas*, 4 and in Henne, *L'Unité*, 17.

8. Dating issues are discussed by Osiek, *Shepherd of Hermas*, 18–20, and Wilson, *Reassessment*, 9–61. Questions of the text's unity, whether it is the product of a single author or multiple hands, are discussed later.

9. For example, Karl Rahner, *Theological Investigations, Vol XV, Penance in the Early Church* (London: Darton, Longman & Todd, 1956), 57–113.

10. Osiek chooses to translate μετάνοια as *conversion* rather than as *repentance* in order to convey "personal and corporate transformation through the power of the good spirit, which necessitates new commitments for the future, not only the eschatological future, but the immediate historical future as well"; *Shepherd of Hermas*, 30.

11. Michel Foucault, *The Use of Pleasure* (*The History of Sexuality*, Vol. 2; trans. Robert Hurley; New York: Vintage Books, 1990), 12–13.

12. Pierre Hadot, for instance, notes, "In the view of philosophical schools, mankind's principal cause of suffering, disorder, and unconsciousness were the passions . . . Philosophy thus appears, in the first place, as a therapeutic of the passions . . ." *Philosophy as a Way of Life: Spiritual Exercises from Socrates to Foucault* (ed. Arnold I. Davidson; trans. Michael Chase; Oxford: Blackwell, 1995), 83. See also Martha Nussbaum, *The Therapy of Desire: Theory and*

Practice in Hellenistic Ethics (Princeton: Princeton University Press, 1994),
13–47; Richard Sorabji, Emotion and Peace of Mind: From Stoic Agitation to
Christian Temptation (The Gifford Lectures; New York: Oxford University
Press, 2000).

13. M. Dibelius, Der Hirt des Hermas (Tübingen: Mohr, Paul Siebeck, 1923).
Dibelius's commentary remains a valued touchstone in scholarly discussion
of Hermas.

14. Hilhorst, for instance, argues that the Shepherd's erotic elements, borrowed
from pagan literature, "are in opposition to Christian values"; "Erotic Elements," 403.

15. See W. Grundmann, "ἐγκράτεια," in Theological Dictionary of the New Testament (ed. Gerhard Kittell; trans. Geoffrey W. Bromiley; Grand Rapids:
Eeerdmans, 1967), 2.339–342.

16. Osiek, Shepherd of Hermas, 104.

17. Foucault, The Use of Pleasure, 65.

18. Helen North discusses the Aristotelean distinction between sophrosyne and
enkrateia, as well as other uses of the term in the philosophic tradition in
Sophrosyne: Self-Knowledge and Self-Restraint in Greek Literature (Ithaca: Cornell University Press, 1966), 197–203; 227–28. Foucault summarizes North's
discussion in The Use of Pleasure, 64–65.

19. The prominence of enkrateia in 4 Maccabees, its link to constructions of
masculinity, and its similarity to Hermas, are discussed by Stephen D.
Moore and Janice Capel Anderson, "Taking It Like A Man: Masculinity in
4 Maccabees," Journal of Biblical Literature 117 (1998): 249–73. See also David
C. Aune, "Mastery of the Passions: Philo, 4 Maccabees and Earliest Christianity," in Hellenization Revisited: Shaping a Christian Response within the
Greco-Roman World (ed. Wendy E. Helleman; Lanham, Md.: University Press
of America, 1994), 125–58.

20. Terms like ὄρεξις, ὁρμή, and ἔρως do not appear. ἡδονή is used five times.
Forms of ἐπιθυμέω and ἐπιθυμία, however, appear approximately 50 times,
a frequency matching that of διψυχία—a much discussed term in The
Shepherd. For discussion of an early Christian writer with a highly differentiated vocabulary for desire, see David G. Hunter, "The Language of Desire:
Clement of Alexandria's Transformation of Ascetic Discourse," Semeia 57
(1991): 95–111.

21. Foucault, The Use of Pleasure, 11.

22. See "The Oral World of Early Christianity in Rome: The Case of Hermas,"
in Judaism and Christianity in First-Century Rome (ed. Karl P. Donfried and
Peter Richardson; Grand Rapids: Eerdmans, 1998), 151–74. Henry Chadwick
offers the wry, offhand remark that the simplicity of Hermas's Greek suggests
he was "intellectually challenged." Henry Chadwick, review of Norbert
Brox, Der Hirt Des Hermas, Journal of Ecclesiastical History 47 (1996): 119.

23. Giet posits three authors: (1) one designated "Hermas" who wrote Visions
I-IV at the close of first century; (2) the "Shepherd," perhaps the brother

of Bishop Pius mentioned in the Muratorian Fragment, who composed *Similitude* IX toward the middle of the second century; and (3) the "Pseudo Shepherd," writing *Vision* V, the *Mandates*, and *Similitudes* I-VIII and X and putting the whole document together around 161 CE. Stanislas Giet, *Hermas et les Pasteurs: Les trois auteurs du Pasteur d'Hermas* (Paris: Presses universitaires du France, 1963). See also Giet,. "Les trois auteurs du Pasteur d'Hermas," *Studia Patristica* 8.2 (1966): 10–23. Others, such as Coleborne, have taken the multiple authorship hypothesis to further and less plausible extremes. W. Coleborne, "A Linguistic Approach to the Problem of Structure and Composition of the Shepherd of Hermas," *Colloquium* 3 (1967): 133–42.

24. Henne, *L'Unité;* J.C. Wilson, *Five Problems in the Interpretation of the Shepherd of Hermas* (Lewiston, Maine: Mellen, 1995).

25. For the argument of single authorship over a protracted period of composition, see Norbert Brox, *Der Hirt des Hermas* (Göttingen: Vendenhoeck and Ruprecht, 1991).

26. For oft-cited summaries of defining features of the genre, see J.J. Collins, "Introduction: Towards the Morphology of a Genre," *Semeia* 14 (1979): 21–59 and A. Yarbro Collins, "Early Christian Apocalypticism," *Semeia* 36 (1986): 1–7.

27. Graydon Snyder claims Hermas "is apocalyptic in form only." *The Apostolic Fathers: A New Translation and Commentary, Vol. VI, The Shepherd of Hermas* (ed. Robert M. Grant; London: Nelson, 1968), 9. More recently, J. Christian Wilson comments, "The book is virtually devoid of apocalyptic eschatology. About the best Hermas can offer us is one 100 foot long sea monster which has 'a head like a jar' and which does nothing but lie on the ground and stick out its tongue (*Vis.* IV:1:6–9). It is as if the author is trying his best to write an apocalypse but fails." Hermas represents, according to Wilson, "the twilight of apocalyptic." *Five Problems*, 41, 80–94.

28. Carolyn Osiek, "The Genre and Function of the *Shepherd of Hermas*," *Semeia* 36 (1986): 113–21. See also the analysis of David Hellholm, *Das Visionenbuch des Hermas als Apokalypse* (Lund: C. W. K. Gleerup, 1980).

29. Edith Humphrey, *The Ladies and the Cities: Transformation and Apocalyptic Identity in Joseph and Aseneth, 4 Ezra, the Apocalypse and The Shepherd of Hermas* (JSPSS 17; Sheffield, U. K.: Sheffield, 1995), 119–26.

30. For text, translation and commentary, see John T. Fitzgerald and L. Michael White, *The Tabula of Cebes* (Chico, Calif.: Scholars Press, 1983).

31. See C. Taylor, "Hermas and Cebes," published in three parts, *Journal of Philology* 27 (1901): 276–319; 28 (1903): 24–38; 94–98.

32. Fitzgerald and White, *Tabula of Cebes*, 18; Osiek, *Shepherd of Hermas*, 25.

33. These texts circulated independently of one another in antiquity, but have been collected, published, and studied together since the seventeenth century. See Bart D. Ehrman, "General Introduction," *The Apostolic Fathers* (2 vols; Cambridge: Harvard University Press, 2003), 1.1–16.

34. For a discussion of *1 Clement's* rhetoric and its imitation of contemporary *homonoia* speeches see Barbara Ellen Bowe, *A Church in Crisis: Ecclesiology and Paraenesis in Clement of Rome* (Minneapolis: Fortress, 1988).

35. The Greek text and English translation for *1 Clement* are from Ehrman, *Apostolic Fathers*, 1.18–151.

36. Grant and Graham briefly note striking parallels between *2 Clement* and *The Shepherd* and speculate that a Roman provenance for the homily would explain why it was ascribed to Clement. Robert M. Grant and Holt H. Graham, *First and Second Clement, The Apostolic Fathers* (vol. 2; New York: Nelson, 1965), 109.

37. Greek texts and translations (adapted) for *2 Clement* are from Ehrman, *Apostolic Fathers*, 1.154–99.

38. A point made by Karl Paul Donfried, *The Setting of Second Clement in Early Christianity* (Leiden: Brill, 1974), 115.

39. Grant and Graham note that repentance is "a central theme in chapters 8–18, but with no orderly development"; *First and Second Clement*, 110.

40. *2 Clement* preserves the saying also found in *Gospel of Thomas* 22:"When the two are one, and the outside like the inside, and the male with the female is neither male nor female" (12.2), but turns its interpretation toward erasure of sexual regard, not gender distinctions. His treatment of the saying culminates in a call for repentance. Donfried, *The Setting of Second Clement*, 153. See also Wayne Meeks, "The Image of the Androgyne: Some Uses of a Symbol in Earliest Christianity," *History of Religions* 12 (1974): 165–208.

41. For a thorough discussion of such issues, see Carolyn Osiek, *Rich and Poor in the Shepherd of Hermas: An Exegetical-Social Investigation* (CBQ Monograph Series 15; Washington: Catholic Biblical Association of America, 1983). Harry Maier also offers a perceptive analysis of Hermas's critique of the Roman social structures that make some Christians wealthier than others. See *The Social Setting of the Ministry as Reflected in the Writings of Hermas, Clement and Ignatius* (Waterloo: Wilfrid Laurier University Press, 1991), 55–86. See also James S. Jeffers, *Conflict at Rome: Social Order and Hierarchy in Early Christianity* (Minneapolis: Fortress Press, 1991).

42. Peter Lampe, *From Paul to Valentinus: Christians at Rome in the First Two Centuries* (trans. Michael Steinhauser; ed. Marshall D. Johnson; Minneapolis: Fortress, 2003), 94, see also 90–99; 218–36.

43. Dibelius attempted to sort out such elements, then concluded the *Shepherd* was a work of allegorical fiction; *Der Hirt*, 419–20. Robert Joly pursues a similar line of reasoning, *Hermas, Le Pasteur: Introduction, Texte Critique, Traduction et Notes* (2e ed. rev.; Paris: Les Éditions du Cerf, 1968), 17–21. Lampe concludes, "Hermas combines literary fiction with authentic autobiographical material"; *From Paul to Valentinus*, 220.

44. Throughout, the Greek text is from Bart D. Ehrman, *The Apostolic Fathers* (Vol. 2; Cambridge: Harvard University Press, 2003). Translations are my own unless otherwise noted.

45. See, for instance, Martin Leutzch, *Die Wahrnehmung sozialer Wirklichkeit im 'Hirten des Hermas,'* (Göttingen: Vandenhoeck & Ruprecht, 1989), 31–39 and Dibelius, *Der Hirt des Hermas,* 429. Lampe notes, "The motif of ἀναγνωρίζειν is a much-loved theme in the romances of the New Comedy. . . . All things considered, Hermas interweaves motifs from pagan light fiction, material from novels, into the text." Lampe, *From Paul to Valentinus,* 220.

46. Callimachus, *Hymn* 5.

47. Ovid, *Metamorphoses,* III.131–253.

48. Longus, *Daphnis and Chloe,* I.24.

49. Certain scribes seem to have resisted the reading. Codex Athous emends θέαν to θυγατέρα and the Ethiopic text emends it to "lady." See Ehrman, *Apostolic Fathers,* 2.177.

50. Codex Athous provides a telling variant reading here, with πορνείας in place of πονηρίας; Hermas is accused of desiring sexual immorality or fornication.

51. Hilhorst says flatly, "Obviously, Hermas's sin is that, upon seeing a beautiful woman bathing, he is overtaken by the desire to have sex with her"; "Erotic Elements," 198–99.

52. C.J. Jung, *Psychological Types of the Psychology of Individuation* (trans. H. Godwin Baynes; London: Kegan Paul, 1946), 277. Robert Joly offered a wry response to Jung, "Philologie et Psychanalyse: C. G. Jung et le "Pasteur" D'Hermas," *L'Antiquité Classique* 22 (1953): 422–28.

53. Cf. Matt 5:28, πᾶς βλέπων γυναῖκα πρὸς τὸ ἐπιθυμῆσαι αὐτὴν ἤδη ἐμοίχευσεν αὐτὴν ἐν τῇ καρδίᾳ αὐτοῦ; "But I say to you that everyone who looks at a woman with lust has already committed adultery with her in his heart" (NRSV); Exod 20:17.

54. Peter Brown, "Bodies and Minds: Sexuality and Renunciation in Early Christianity," in *Before Sexuality: The Construction of Erotic Experience in the Ancient Greek World* (ed. David M. Halperin, John J. Winkler, Froma Zeitlin; Princeton: Princeton University Press, 1990), 482; 479–93.

55. Edith Humphrey argues that the media of revelation are progressively intensified, thereby encouraging the reader's participation in the interpretive process: "The intensification of media or means of revelation in *Hermas,* from hearing to reading and writing, to seeing, to engagement in the vision, is, therefore, a powerful device of incorporation." Humphrey, *The Ladies and the Cities,* 140.

56. The description is Patricia Cox Miller's, from "'All the Words Were Frightful': Salvation by Dreams in The Shepherd of Hermas," *Vigiliae Christianae* 42 (1988): 332. See the discussion in expanded context in her *Dreams in Late Antiquity: Studies in the Imagination of a Culture* (Princeton: Princeton University Press, 1994).

57. Clement of Alexandria took Hermas's little book as a figure for the interpretative process, with letter by letter transcription indicating "bare

reading," but reading according to syllables signifying "gnostic unfolding." Clement of Alexandria, *Stromateis* 6.15.

58. See Osiek, *The Shepherd of Hermas*, 68; Dibelius, *Der Hirt des Hermas*, 463.

59. For a detailed theological analysis of the ecclesiology of the *Shepherd*, see Lage Pernveden, *The Concept of the Church in The Shepherd of Hermas*, (Lund, Sweden: C. W. K. Gleerup, 1966). Pernveden argues against interpreters who distinguish between the "ideal" church represented by the lady or the tower and the "real" church represented by human persons: "Instead of thinking of the Church in concepts like prototype and image, which imply the opposites celestial and earthly, invisible and visible, ideal and real, we have to imagine the Church as hidden and manifested. . . . it is always a matter of one and the same Church" (294–5).

60. See the brief but provocative analysis by Philippe Henne, "La polysémie allégorique dans le Pasteur d'Hermas," *Ephemerides Theologicae Lovanienses* 65.1 (1989):131–35.

61. Cogently argued by Steve Young, "Being a Man: The Pursuit of Manliness in *The Shepherd of Hermas*," *Journal of Early Christian Studies* 2.3 (1994): 237–55, though Young does not highlight questions of desire.

62. D'Angelo observes that she both looks like a man, heavily belted and prepared for work, and acts like one. Mary Rose D'Angelo, "'Knowing How to Preside Over His Own Household': Imperial Masculinity and Christian Asceticism in the Pastorals, Hermas, and Luke-Acts" in *New Testament Masculinities* (ed. Stephen D. Moore and Janice Capel Anderson), *Semeia* 45 (2003): 265–95. See Osiek's comment, *Shepherd of Hermas*, 77.

63. See the general discussion of *malakia* in Dale Martin, "Arsenokoites and Malakos: Meanings and Consequences," in *Biblical Ethics and Homosexuality* (ed. R. Brawley; Louisville, Ky.: Westminster/John Knox, 1996), 117–36, as well as D'Angelo's analysis of this passage in "Knowing How to Preside," 280.

64. Clement of Alexandria slightly rephrased Hermas, approvingly noting, "that which acts the man is Self-restraint." *Stromateis* 2.12.

65. Young, "Being a Man," 252.

66. See Pernveden on "The Religious and Ethical Dualism," 206–15; Snyder also offers useful commentary in *The Shepherd of Hermas*, 76–8.

67. The two ways tradition is exemplified in Christian texts such as Barnabas and Didache, not to mention Matthew 7:13–14; it appears in Hellenistic Jewish texts, with roots in both Torah and Wisdom texts; it is a common motif in Greco-Roman moralizing literature, often appearing as variations on the myth of Heracles before the two ways, told by Socrates and attributed to the sage Prodicus; Xenophon, *Memorabilia* 22.1.21–2.

68. A much studied aspect of Hermas. See J. Reiling, *Hermas and Christian Prophecy: A Study of the Eleventh Mandate* (Novum Testamentum Supplements 37; Leiden: Brill, 1973).

69. Scholars speculate about the antecedents of the term *dipsychos* and Hermas's relation to the book of James. See, for instance, O. J. F. Seitz, "Relationship

of the Shepherd of Hermas to the Epistle of James," *Journal of Biblical Literature* 63 (1944): 131–40 and "Antecedents and Signification of the Term *Dipsychos*," *Journal of Biblical Literature* 66 (1947): 211–19.

70. D'Angelo analyzes how the marriage, adultery, and divorce stipulations of *The Shepherd* "bear a tense relationship to the stipulations of the Julian law," which encouraged widows to remarry, but held a husband who did not divorce a wife caught in adultery to be guilty of pandering. D'Angelo, "Knowing How to Preside," 281–82.

71. Dibelius, *Der Hirt des Hermas*, 504–5; Osiek, *The Shepherd of Hermas*, 109–10.

72. Osiek discusses how the marriage questions serve as a "case analogy" for conversion; Osiek, *The Shepherd of Hermas*, 110; see also Snyder, *The Shepherd of Hermas*, 67; Dibelius, *Der Hirt*, 504–5.

73. For the concept of two spirits or two inhabitants of the human soul, Hermas has significant precedents, including Philo, "in every soul at its very birth there enter two powers (*dunameis*), the salutary and the destructive" (*Quest. in Ex.* I.23) and the Qumran Community Rule, "He has created Man to govern the world, and has appointed for him two spirits in which to walk until the time of his visitation: the spirits of truth and falsehood." For a survey in brief compass of a range of texts, see G.G. Stroumsa and Paula Fredriksen, "The Two Souls and the Divided Will," in *Self, Soul and Body in Religious Experience* (ed. A. I. Baumgarten, J. Assmann, and G. G. Stroumsa; Leiden: Brill, 1998), 198–217.

74. Also observed by Osiek, *The Shepherd of Hermas*, 148. Lampe notes that Stoic tradition lies behind *Mandate* 12's characterization of evil desire, but Osiek also points out that the discussion of good desire moves away from Stoic influence, perhaps reflecting Jewish two-ways teachings. See Lampe, *From Paul to Valentinus*, 230; Osiek, *The Shepherd of Hermas*, 148.

75. Knust provides a perceptive analysis of how such elements also formed part of the arsenal of early Christian polemic, and analyzes Hermas *Mand*. 11. See Jennifer Wright Knust, *Abandoned to Lust: Sexual Slander and Ancient Christianity* (New York: Columbia University Press, 2006), 135–41.

76. Snyder, *The Shepherd of Hermas*, 114.

77. Osiek, *Rich and Poor*, 78–90.

78. See the commentary by Osiek, *The Shepherd of Hermas*, 179.

79. Osiek, *The Shepherd of Hermas*, 180.

80. Giet, *Hermas et les Pasteurs*, 155.

81. For a discussion of Hellenistic views of how mixed gender signs could indicate good character, see Maud Gleason, *Making Men: Sophists and Self-Presentation in Ancient Rome* (Princeton: Princeton University Press, 1995), 59. Young observes, "followers, male and female alike, should become manly"; "Being a Man," 253.

82. An observation made by D'Angelo, "Knowing How to Preside," 279.

83. Emma Stafford observes that female representations of personified abstractions throughout ancient literary and artistic tradition have their root in

attitudes toward the feminine: "psychologically their desirable form conveys the desirability of the abstract values they embody." Emma J. Stafford, "Masculine values, feminine forms: on the gender of personified abstractions," in *Thinking Men: Masculinity and Self-Representation in the Classical Tradition* (ed. Lin Foxhall and John Salmon; London: Routledge, 1998), 53; 43–56. Also cited in D'Angelo, "Knowing How to Preside," 284.

84. See, for instance, Jonathan Walters, "Invading the Roman Body: Manliness and Impenetrability in Roman Thought," in *Roman Sexualities* (ed. Judith P. Hallett and Marilyn B. Skinner; Princeton: Princeton University Press, 1997), 29–43. Walters remarks, "A sexual protocol that proclaims itself to be about gender-appropriate behavior turns out to be part of a wider pattern of social status, where the violability or inviolability of the body is a privileged marker of such status" (41). See also Gleason on "manly modesty," in *Making Men*, 61. For discussions of the paradoxes and unpredictabilities of virginal desire, see Mary Foskett, *A Virgin Conceived: Mary and Classical Representations of Virginity* (Bloomington and Indianapolis: Indiana University Press, 2002), 1–73 as well as Dale Martin, "The Dangers of Desire," in *The Corinthian Body* (New Haven: Yale University Press, 1995), 198–227.

85. Otto Luschnat, "Die Jungfrauenszene in der Arkadienvision des Hermas," *Theologia Viatorum* XII (1973–74): 53–70. M. Dibelius, *Der Hirt des Hermas*, xxx.

86. Hilhorst, "Erotic Elements," 403.

87. Osiek, *The Shepherd of Hermas*, 68.

88. See again Steve Young's reading of Hermas's growth in manliness, which perceptively connects the text's concern with wealth and with the dangers of excessive involvement in business affairs to Hermas's obligation to rule household and house church by manfully maintaining rigid community boundaries. Young equates household and house church, or rather, takes the descriptions of Hermas's household to function as descriptions of a house church, over which Hermas is pastor—a role the text itself does not specify for him. Young, "Being a Man," 237–55. See D'Angelo's critique, "Knowing How to Preside," 267.

89. Patricia Cox Miller, "'All the Words Were Frightful,'" 335.

90. Michel Foucault, "Technologies of the Self," in *Ethics, Subjectivity and Truth: Essential Works of Foucault, 1954–84* (ed. Paul Rabinow; New York: New Press, 1997), 242; 1.223–51.

91. Foucault, "Technologies," 247.

Chapter Three

1. For the Greek text, I have relied on Richard Lipsius and Maximillian Bonnet, "Acta Pauli et Theclae," in *Acta Apostolorum Apocrypha, Part I, Acta Petri, Acta Pauli, Acta Petri et Pauli, Acta Pauli et Theclae, Acta Thaddaei* (ed. Richard Lipsius; Leipzig: 1891–1903; repr. Hildesheim: Georg Olms, 1959),

235–72. See also Leon Vouaux, *Les Actes de Paul et ses Lettres Apocryphes, Traduction et Commentaire* (Paris: Librairie Letouzey et Ané, 1913). The recent French translation by Willy Rordorf reflects his much anticipated critical text to be released in the Corpus Christianorum Series Apocryphorum: Willy Rordorf with Rodolphe Kasser, "Actes de Paul," in *Écrits apocryphes chrétiens* I (ed. François Bovon and Pierre Geoltrain; Gallimard, 1997), 1115–77. For English translations, J.K. Elliott, *The Apocryphal New Testament: A Collection of Apocryphal Christian Literature in an English Translation* (Oxford: Clarendon Press, 1993) and Wilhelm Schneemelcher, ed., *New Testament Apocrypha* (rev. ed. of collection by Edgar Hennecke; trans. R. McL. Wilson; Vol. 2; Louisville: Westminster/John Knox Press, 1992).

2. Schneemelcher estimates between 185 and 195 CE; Rordorf and Kasser suggest around 150; Hilhorst suggests a wider range, from 140–200. Wilhelm Schneemelcher, "The Acts of Paul: Introduction," in *New Testament Apocrypha* 2. 235; 213–37. Rordorf and Kasser, "Actes de Paul," I.1122. Hilhorst, "Tertullian on the Acts of Paul," in *The Apocryphal Acts of Paul and Thecla* (Kampen: Kok Pharos, 1996), 161; 150–63. Asia Minor is usually taken to be the provenance of the story: Tertullian claims the author was a presbyter in Asia Minor, and the story is set in Iconium and Pisidian Antioch, and mentions Seleucia. An overview of introductory issues is also provided in Hans-Josef Klauck, *The Apocryphal Acts of the Apostles: An Introduction* (transl. Brian McNeil; Waco: Baylor University Press, 2008), 47–50.

3. Rordorf and Kasser note their translation of the Thecla section is based on review of around fifty Greek manuscripts. For a concise summary of manuscripts and versions, see Kim Haines-Eitzen, "Engendering Palimpsests: Reading the Textual Tradition of the Acts of Paul and Thecla," in *The Early Christian Book* (ed. William E. Klingshirn and Linda Safran; Washington: Catholic University of America Press, 2007), 186; 177–93; along with introductions by Schneemelcher and Elliot.

4. For later veneration of Thecla, Stephen J. Davis, *The Cult of Saint Thecla: A Tradition of Women's Piety in Late Antiquity* (New York: Oxford University Press, 2001); Elizabeth A. Castelli, "Layers of Verbal and Visual Memory: Commemorating Thecla the Protomartyr," in *Martyrdom and Memory: Early Christian Culture Making* (New York: Columbia University Press, 2004), 134–71; Scott Fitzgerald Johnson, *The Life and Miracles of Thekla: A Literary Study* (Cambridge: Harvard University Press, 2006).

5. πίστις in the Pauline writings is the locus of divine transformative power. The root πιστ- occurs in 20 different forms 127 times in 111 verses spread throughout the seven undisputed Pauline letters.

6. Paul uses ἀνάστασις seven times in the undisputed writings. Four of these, all in 1 Corinthians 15, are to argue in favor of the literal resurrection of the dead (ἀνάστασις νεκρῶν), the ultimate personal transformation for believers (1 Co 15:12, 13, 21, 42). The other three use Jesus' resurrection to describe how divine power transforms: Jesus, from Son of David to Son of

God (Ro 1:4); believers, from life characterized by death to new life (Ro 6:5); and Paul himself, from Pharisee and persecutor to imitator of Christ's death and participant in Christ's resurrection (Phil 3:10).

7. See Beate Wehn, "'Blessed are the bodies of those who are virgins': Reflections on the Image of Paul in the *Acts of Thecla*," *Journal for the Study of the New Testament* 79 (2000): 152; 149–64.

8. See, for example, Melissa Aubin, "Reversing Romance? *The Acts of Thecla* and the Ancient Novel," in *Ancient Fiction and Early Christian Narrative* (ed. Ronald F. Hock, J. Bradley Chance, and Judith Perkins; Society of Biblical Literature Symposium Series. Atlanta: Scholars Press, 1998), 257–72; Willi Braun, "Physiotherapy of Femininity in the *Acts of Thecla*," in *Text and Artifact in the Religions of Mediterranean Antiquity: Essays in Honour of Peter Richardson* (ed. Stephen G. Wilson and Michel Desjardins; Waterloo, Ontario: Wilfrid Laurier University Press, 2002), 209–30; Stephen J. Davis, *The Cult of Saint Thecla*, 31–3.

9. See P. Toohey, "Love, Lovesickness, and Melancholia," *Illinois Classical Studies* 17 (1992): 265–86. Toohey focuses particularly on associations and distinctions between lovesickness and melancholia in antiquity, arguing that both may appear in either depressive or, more commonly, manic forms.

10. Longus, *Daphnis and Chloe*, Book II.7. in *Collected Ancient Greek Novels* (trans. Christopher Gill; ed. B. P. Reardon; Berkeley: University of California Press, 1989), 306.

11. Achilles Tatius, *Leucippe and Clitophon*, Book I.5, 6, 9, in *Collected Ancient Greek Novels* (trans. John J. Winkler), 179–82.

12. Heliodorus, *An Ethiopian Story*, Book 4.7, in *Collected Ancient Greek Novels*, (trans. J.R. Morgan), 429–30. So, too, Chaereas and Callirhoe, like Anthea and Habricomes, waste away after falling in love at first sight. See Chariton, *Chaereas and Callirhoe*, Book I.1, in *Collected Ancient Greek Novels* (trans. B. P. Reardon), 21–24 and Xenophon of Ephesus, *An Ephesian Tale*, Book 1.5, in *Collected Ancient Greek Novels* (trans. Graham Anderson), 131.

13. Braun, "Physiotherapy of Femininity," 213.

14. Peter Toohey argues that depictions of such "manic lovesickness" are in fact more common in ancient literature than those of "depressive lovesickness." "Lovesickness, displayed in a violent or manic fashion receives descriptions in almost all of the periods of ancient literature. It is a dominant amatory cliché" (Toohey, "Love, Lovesickness, and Melancholia," 275).

15. A phrase drawn from Peter Brooks: "[The erotic body in literature and art] is a tradition that also inevitably intersects with the political, since the erotic body both animates and disrupts the social order"; Peter Brooks, *Body Work: Objects of Desire in Modern Narrative* (Cambridge: Harvard University Press, 1993), 5–6.

16. Sigmund Freud, "Repression," in *The Standard Edition of the Complete Psychological Works of Sigmund Freud* (trans. James Strachey; London: Hogarth Press and the Institute for Psycho-Analysis, 1957), 14.146–58; and

"Resistance and Repression," in *Standard Edition of the Complete Psychological Works* (1963), 16.286–302.

17. Jacques Lacan, "The mirror stage as formative of the function of the I," in *Écrits: A Selection* (trans. Alan Sheridan; New York: Norton, 1977), 1–7; "The agency of the letter in the unconscious or reason since Freud," in *Écrits: A Selection*, 146–178.

18. Judith Butler, "Desire," in *Critical Terms for Literary Study* (ed. Frank Lentricchia and Thomas McLaughlin; 2nd ed.; Chicago: University of Chicago Press, 1995), 380–81.

19. Butler, "Desire," 380–81.

20. Brooks, *Body Work*, 20.

21. In Kristeva's dialogical reflection on the virgin Mary, she says flatly, "The fact remains, as far as the complexities and pitfalls of maternal experience are involved, that Freud offers only a massive *nothing* . . ."; Kristeva refers to "a motherhood that today remains, after the Virgin, without a discourse . . ." "Stabat Mater," in *Tales of Love* (trans. Leon S. Roudiez; New York: Columbia University Press, 1987) 255, 262; 234–63. See also Toril Moi, *Sexual/ Textual Politics: Feminist Literary Theory* (2nd ed.; London: Routledge, 1985, 2002), 149–72.

22. Catherine Clément and Julia Kristeva, *The Feminine and the Sacred* (Trans. Jane Marie Todd; New York: Columbia University Press, 2001), 56–57.

23. Clément and Kristeva, *The Feminine and the Sacred*, 57.

24. All included in Reardon, *Collected Ancient Greek Novels*.

25. Rosa Söder, *Die apokryphen Apostelgeschichten und die romanhafte Literatur der Antike* (Stuttgart, 1932; reprint ed., Darmstadt: Wissenschaftliche Buchgesellschaft, 1969), 187. Söder argued that the AAA should be included within the category of the Hellenistic novel because they are characterized by five essential novelistic elements: (1) the element of travel; (2) the aretological element; (3) the teratological element; (4) the tendentious element; and (5) the erotic element, as well as by five "special motifs." Others before Söder had explored the question of a literary relationship between the novels and the Apocryphal Acts. See Ernst von Dobschütz, "Der Roman in der altchristlichen Literatur," *Deutsche Rundschau* 111 (1902): 87–106 and Karl Kerenyi, *Die griechische-orientalische Romanliteratur in religionsgeschichtlicher Beleuchtung* (Tübingen, 1927; reprint ed., Darmstadt: Wissenschaftliche Buchgesellschaft, 1962). Virginia Burrus offers a careful survey of the scholarly literature to the mid-1980s in *Chastity as Autonomy: Women in the Stories of Apocryphal Acts* (Studies in Women and Religion, Vol. 23; Lewiston, Maine: Edwin Mellen, 1987).

26. Stevan L. Davies, *The Revolt of the Widows: The Social World of the Apocryphal Acts* (Carbondale: Southern Illinois University Press, 1980); Dennis Ronald MacDonald, *The Legend and the Apostle: The Battle for Paul in Story and Canon* (Philadelphia: Westminster Press, 1983); Burrus, *Chastity as Autonomy*. For a theoretically and methodologically sophisticated evaluation of these

works, and an assessment of arguments made against them, see Shelly Matthews, "Thinking of Thecla: Issues in Feminist Historiography," *Journal of Feminist Studies in Religion* 17.2 (2001): 29–55. For a favorable review of MacDonald's work, see Willy Rordorf, "Tradition and Composition in the Acts of Thecla: the State of the Question," *Semeia* 38 (1986): 43–52. Others remained unpersuaded. See Jean Daniel Kaestli, "Fiction littéraire et réalité sociale. Que peut-on savoir de la place des femmes dans le milieu de production des Actes apocryphes des Apôtres?," *Apocrypha/Le champ des apocryphes* 1 (1990): 279–302.

27. Jan Bremmer, "The Novel and the Apocryphal Acts: Place, Time and Readership," *Groningen Colloquia on the Novel* (Groningen: Egbert Forsten, 1998), 9.157–80.

28. Christine M. Thomas, "Stories Without Texts and Without Authors: The Problem of Fluidity in Ancient Novelistic Texts and Early Christian Literature," in *Ancient Fiction and Early Christian Narrative* (Society of Biblical Literature Symposium Series; Atlanta: Scholars Press, 1998), 278. For comparison to the Apocryphal Acts, Thomas recommends ancient fiction that focuses primarily on one figure, is episodic in structure—featuring a kind of "greatest hits" narrative organization—and is "workaday Greek" in style, such as the *Alexander Romance*, the *Life of Aesop*, the *Life of Homer*, or Jewish novellas such as *Joseph and Aseneth* and *Tobit*.

29. Judith Perkins, *The Suffering Self: Pain and Narrative Representation in the Early Christian Era* (London: Routledge, 1995), 46.

30. Judith Perkins, "This World or Another? The Intertextuality of the Greek Romances, the Apocryphal Acts and Apuleius' *Metamorphoses*," *Semeia* 80 (1997): 250.

31. Kate Cooper, *The Virgin and the Bride: Idealized Womanhood in Late Antiquity* (Cambridge: Harvard University Press, 1996), 27.

32. Cooper, *The Virgin and the Bride*, 55. See the critique of Cooper in Matthews, "Thinking of Thecla," 46–51.

33. Perkins's most recent book offers further complex comparisons of the ancient novels, the *Apocryphal Acts*, and other texts. She examines cultural constructions of Christian and elite imperial identities in relation to themes such as judgment, resurrection, gender, and time. Judith Perkins, *Roman Imperial Identities in the Early Christian Era* (London: Routledge, 2009).

34. Helen Morales, "The history of sexuality," in *The Greek and Roman Novel* (ed. Tim Whitmarsh; Cambridge Companion; Cambridge University Press, 2008), 43; 39–55.

35. See Katharine Haynes, *Fashioning the Feminine in the Greek Novel* (London: Routledge, 2003), 14, 39.

36. Virginia Burrus, "Mimicking Virgins: Colonial Ambivalence and the Ancient Romance," *Arethusa* 38 (2005): 55; 49–88. On a different point—the question of whether the female characters in the *Acts* primarily provide evidence of male debates over social power—Shelly Matthews argues

against Cooper (and Peter Brown) that, granting literary and rhetorical analysis as prerequisite, such texts may still yield information about historical women. See Matthews, "Thinking of Thecla," 46–51.

37. See Froma I. Zeitlin, "The Poetics of Eros: Nature, Art, and Imitation in Longus' *Daphnis and Chloe*," in *Before Sexuality: The Construction of Erotic Experience in the Ancient Greek World* (ed. David M. Halperin, John J. Winkler, and Froma I. Zeitlin; Princeton: Princeton University Press, 1990), 417–64. For a reading that traces stark differences in Chloe's experience of sexuality, see John Winkler, "The Education of Chloe: Hidden Injuries of Sex," in *The Constraints of Desire: The Anthropology of Sex and Gender in Ancient Greece* (London: Routledge, 1990), 101–26.

38. David Konstan argues that a symmetry or equilibrium of desire is more usual; *Sexual Symmetry: Love in the Ancient Novel and Related Genres* (Princeton, N.J.: Princeton University Press, 1994), 8.

39. See the analysis of erotic brinkmanship in B. P. Reardon, "Achilles Tatius and Ego-Narrative," in *Greek Fiction: The Greek Novel in Context* (ed. J. R. Morgan and Richard Stoneman; London: Routledge, 1994), 80–96.

40. For a further treatment of the theme of eros, see Massimo Fusillo, "Un paradigme thématique: l'eros," in *Naissance du Roman* (trans. from Italian, Marielle Abrioux; Paris: Éditions du Seuil, 1989), 195–258.

41. Schneemelcher, *Acts of Peter*, 313. Excerpts from the Greek text are taken from Richard Lipsius, "Acta Petri," in *Acta Apostolorum Apocrypha, Part I*, 78–104.

42. All references and English translations are from *The Acts of Andrew*, trans. Jean-Marc Prieur and Wilhelm Schneemelcher, in *New Testament Apocrypha* (ed. Wilhelm Schneemelcher; trans. R. McL. Wilson; Louisville: Westminster/John Knox Press, 1992), 2.101–51.

43. Greek text from Dennis Ronald MacDonald, *The Acts of Andrew and The Acts of Andrew and Matthias in the City of the Cannibals* (Atlanta: Scholars Press, 1990), 352–53.

44. Kate Cooper, *The Virgin and the Bride*, 52.

45. See François Bovon, "The Words of Life in the Acts of Andrew," in *The Apocryphal Acts of Andrew* (ed. Jan N. Bremmer; Leuven: Peeters, 2000), 81–95.

46. Prieur and Schneemelcher, *The Acts of Andrew*, (5), 129–30.

47. Prieur and Schneemelcher, *The Acts of Andrew*, (12), 132. Bovon comments on Stratocles' speech: "Christology is strangely absent here; the apostle alone offers a soteriological bridge. By contemplating what is taking place, the hearers attach themselves to the apostle and receive his intelligence." Bovon, "Words of Life," 91.

48. Bovon, "Words of Life," 92–93. See also Caroline Schroeder, "Embracing the Erotic in the Passion of Andrew, The Apocryphal Acts of Andrew, the Greek Novel, and Platonic Philosophy," in *The Apocryphal Acts of Andrew* (ed. Jan N. Bremmer; Leuven: Peeters, 2000), 110–26. Schroeder remarks, "The

results of true love and properly oriented desire in the *Passion of Andrew* are Platonic objectives: an understanding of the inner self, a unification with the divine, and a lasting sense of peace and rest. Although the relationships between the characters resemble relationships between the hero and heroines of the novels, the product of their love is a Platonic one," 114.

49. See the account of surviving contents in *The Acts of Peter*, trans. Wilhelm Schneemelcher, in *New Testament Apocrypha*, 2.271–321. See also the discussion of these episodes with attention to the suppression of children in Cornelia B. Horn, "Suffering Children, Parental Authority and the Quest for Liberation? A Tale of Three Girls in the *Acts of Paul (And Thecla), the Act(s) of Peter, The Acts of Nereus and Achilleus and The Epistle of Pseudo-Titus*," in *A Feminist Companion to the New Testament Apocrypha* (ed. Amy-Jill Levine with Maria Mayo Robbins; Cleveland: Pilgrim Press, 2006), 130; 118–145.

50. Here and subsequently, the translation is Schneemelcher's, *The Acts of Peter*, 285.

51. Brock remarks, "Predictably, in the *Acts of Peter* the blame for the attraction is placed directly upon the young girl." Ann Graham Brock, "Political Authority and Cultural Accommodation: Social Diversity in the *Acts of Paul* and the *Acts of Peter*," In *The Apocryphal Acts of the Apostles* (ed. François Bovon, Ann Graham Brock, Christopher R. Matthews; Boston: Harvard University Press, 1999), 155; 145–69.

52. Schneemelcher, *Acts of Peter*, 286.

53. Mary Foskett, *A Virgin Conceived: Mary and Classical Representations of Virginity* (Bloomington: Indiana University Press, 2002), 109.

54. In a later "elastic development" of the story that Christine Thomas describes, Peter's daughter becomes paradoxically both more active in defense of her own purity and more finally passive. Thomas summarizes the story of Peter's daughter in the *Acts of Nereus and Achilleus*: "As in the Coptic fragment, she becomes paralyzed at the prayers of her parents, but in the later version, she gradually recovers, only to be wooed by a certain *comes* Flaccus. She asks him to give her three days to consider his offer of marriage and, fasting and praying all the while, manages to die within that span of time (*Nereus* 15)." Christine M. Thomas, *The Acts of Peter, Gospel Literature, and the Ancient Novel: Rewriting the Past* (Oxford: Oxford University Press, 2003), 61.

55. Thomas explains, "In this sense, they might be called multiforms, that is, components of a set of individual performances of the same narrative" (Christine Thomas, *The Acts of Peter, Gospel Literature, and the Ancient Novel*, 64).

56. Schneemelcher, *Acts of Peter*, 287.

57. Schneemelcher, *Acts of Peter*, 287.

58. François Bovon and Eric Junod, "Reading the Apocryphal Acts of the Apostles," *Semeia* 38 (1986): 165–66. Jean-Daniel Kaestli similarly urges the necessity of studying each text in itself, "Les Principales Orientations de la Recherche sur les Actes Apocryphes des Apôtres," in *Les Actes Apocryphes Des Apôtres: Christianisme et Monde Pa en* (Paris: Labor et Fides, 1981), 49–67.

59. Massimo Fusillo, "Modern Critical Theories and the Ancient Novel," in *The Novel in the Ancient World*. (ed. Gareth Schmeling; Leiden: E.J. Brill, 1996), 291; 277–305.

60. See Elisabeth Esch-Ermeling, *Thekla—Paulusschülerin wider Willen? Strategien der Leserlenkung in den Theklaakten* (Neutestamentliche Abhandlungen 53; Münster: Aschendorff, 2008); Margaret P. Aymer, "Hailstorms and Fireballs: Redaction, World Creation, and Resistance in the *Acts of Paul and Thecla*," *Semeia* 75 (1997): 43–61; Aymer's analysis is deemed convincing by Gail Streete, *Redeeed Bodies: Women Martyrs in Early Christianity* (Louisville: Westminster John Knox Press, 2009), 42, 45, 87. Esch-Ermeling's and Streete's work became available to me late in the process of editing, and I have not adequately addressed their analyses.

61. MacDonald catalogues many parallels between the two sections as he argues that the duplications represent the folkloristic "law of contrast" and "law of repetition." MacDonald, *The Legend and the Apostle*, 28–31.

62. Without remarking on Onesiphorus' household, David Konstan draws attention to elements in the *Apocryphal Acts* that protect and affirm households and marital ties. "Acts of Love: A Narrative Pattern in the Apocryphal Acts," *Journal of Early Christian Studies* 6.1 (1998): 15–36. He concludes, "The double or ambiguous perspective of the Acts permits them a wide appeal, inasmuch as the image of radically celibate and independent women, youths and slaves is balanced or at least varied by the depiction of familial affection and integration" (35–36).

63. Betrayers of Paul known from 2 Tim 4:10 and 1:15.

64. Here and throughout, the Greek text is that of Lipsius, "Acta Pauli et Theclae," *Acta Apostolorum Apocrypha*, Part 1, 235–72. Translations are my own, with comparisons to Elliot, *The Apocryphal New Testament*; Schneemelcher, "Acts of Paul," in *New Testament Apocrypha*; and Rordorf, "Actes de Paul."

65. R.M. Grant, "The Description of Paul in the Acts of Paul and Thecla," *Vigiliae Christianae* 36 (1982): 1–4.

66. A.J. Malherbe, "A Physical Description of Paul," *Harvard Theological Review* 79 (1986): 170–75; repr. in Malherbe, *Paul and the Popular Philosophers* (Minneapolis: Fortress, 1989), 165–70.

67. János Bollók, "The Description of Paul in the Acta Pauli," in *The Apocryphal Acts of Paul and Thecla* (ed. Jan N. Bremmer; Kampen: Kok Pharos Publishing House, 1996), 1–15.

68. Jan N. Bremmer, "Magic, martyrdom and women's liberation in the Acts of Paul and Thecla," in *The Apocryphal Acts of Paul and Thecla*, 39.

69. Burrus, "Mimicking Virgins," 56, n. 16.

70. Perhaps echoing the description of Stephen in Acts 6:15.

71. Wehn argues that ἀνάστασις implies more than a theological doctrine of life after death, but also a rising up of Thecla more broadly: "I believe that we are compelled to translate ἀνάστασις in the *Acts of Thecla* with the two concepts of *rising up (Augstehen)* and *resurrection (Auferstehen)*. The hope of

resurrection is manifested in Thecla's conduct, in the radical departures that mark her life of faith, and also in the actions of the persons who support Thecla when danger is greatest, making possible experiences of resurrection." Beate Wehn, "'Blessed are the bodies of those who are virgins': Reflections on the Image of Paul in the *Acts of Thecla*," *Journal for the Study of the New Testament* 79 (2000): 152; 149–64.

72. Haines-Eitzen, "Engendering Palimpsests," 188–89.

73. Brooks, *Body Work*, 25.

74. Rordorf, "Actes de Paul," III.7, 1131.

75. Roland Barthes, *A Lover's Discourse: Fragments* (trans. Richard Howard; New York: Hill and Wang, 1978), 189; 192.

76. Scholars debate whether the pair maliciously misrepresent Paul's gospel, but the judgment of Voaux still seems persuasive: "Mais l'auteur ne les fait-il pas exagérer à dessein? Ils ont saisi la pensée et compris la colère de Thamyris, et flairent un bonne occasion; aussi renchérissent-ils sur sa plainte, et prétendent-ils que l'apôtre ferrait de la chasteté la condition expresse de la résurrection. Ce serait le seul passage du livre où serait exprimée si nettement, non plus le conseil très pressant, mais la nécessité de la continence." Léon Vouaux, *Les Actes de Paul*, 171. Rordorf comments: "cette affirmation encratite vient des ennemis de Paul et durcit son point de vue; l'apôtre des Actes de Paul na pas interdit le marriage." Rordorf, "Actes de Paul," 1132.

77. For a discussion of Paul as practitioner of "erotic magic," see Magda Misset-Van de Weg, "Answers to the Plights of an Ascetic Woman Named Thecla," in *A Feminist Companion to the New Testament Apocrypha* (ed. Amy-Jill Levine with Maria Mayo Robbins; Cleveland: Pilgrim Press, 2006), 148–51.

78. McInerney remarks, "By giving away her bracelets and her mirror, objects which are strongly identified both with her social class and her gender, Thecla purchases the right to go on listening to Paul's words. She has not yet, apparently, earned the right to speak words of her own." Maud Burnett McInerney, *Eloquent Virgins from Thecla to Joan of Arc* (New York: Palgrave MacMillan, 2003), 39.

79. Foskett, *A Virgin Conceived*, 107–8.

80. στέργω, Liddell and Scott 1996,1639. But see Maximilla's claim in *The Acts of Andrew* that she is "kindled and inflamed "with this form of affection (ἐξάπτει καὶ φλέγει τῇ πρὸς αὐτό στοργῇ); Greek text from MacDonald, *The Acts of Andrew*, 352–53.

81. Haines-Eitzen, "Engendering Palimpsests," 190. For the Syriac version, which carefully places many other people in the prison scene with Paul and Thecla, see William Wright, *Apocryphal Acts of the Apostles: Edited from Syriac Manuscripts in the British Museum and Other Libraries With English Translations and Notes* (Amsterdam: Philo Press, 1968), 125–26.

82. Anne Carson, "Putting Her In Her Place: Woman, Dirt, and Desire," in *Before Sexuality*, 135–69. Anne Ellis Hansen's essay in the same volume carries the discussion into the medical writers of the later Roman period,

"The Medical Writers' Woman," 309–34. See also Dale Martin, "The Dangers of Desire," in *The Corinthian Body* (New Haven: Yale University Press, 1995), 198–228, especially 219–22.

83. Aubin, "Reversing Romance?," 264.

84. David Konstan, *Sexual Symmetry*, 32.

85. Vorster comments, "The 'no' of society to non-marriage can nowhere better be seen than in Thecla's mother herself, condemning Thecla in anaphoric outcry. The similarly sounding ἄνομος and ἄνυμφος linked by the epanaphoric κατακαίω emphasizes the social antagonism against those exposing the fragility of the social body." Johannes N. Vorster, "Construction of Culture through the Construction of Person: The *Acts of Thecla* as an Example," in *The Rhetorical Analysis of Scripture: Essays from the 1995 London Conference* (ed. Stanley E. Porter and Thomas H. Olbricht; Journal for the Study of the New Testament Supplement Series 146; Sheffield: Sheffield, 1997), 465; 445–82.

86. Cornelia B. Horn, "Suffering Children, Parental Authority and the Quest for Liberation?," 125.

87. I have here translated Ὡς ἀνυπομονήτου μου οὔσης as "Thinking that I might not endure . . ." rather than the frequent translation choice, "As if I were not able to endure . . ." The "As if" might convey indignation from a character on her way to more autonomy (So Bremmer, "Magic, martyrdom and women's liberation," 49). But in the immediate context, there is no active self-assertion against Paul; Paul's gaze is what Thecla urgently seeks and welcomes. "Because . . ." or "Thinking that I might not endure . . ." seem more plausible translations, though all are grammatically possible. One may take ὡς plus the genitive absolute as expressing the reason for the action ("Because I am not able to endure . . ."), a presumed but false condition, ("As if I were not able to endure . . ."), or a conclusion existing in Paul's imagination, ("Thinking that I am not able to endure . . ."). "ὡς," BDAG (3rd ed., 2000), 1103–6.

88. "In short, nowhere does it appear more clearly that man's desire finds meaning in the desire of the other, not so much because the other holds the key to the object desired, as because the first object of desire is to be recognized by the other." Jacques Lacan, "The function and field of speech and language in psychoanalysis," *Ecrits: A Selection* (trans. Alan Sheridan; New York: Norton, 1977), 58.

89. Fusillo discusses René Girard's treatment of love triangles and their implications for the ancient novel in *Naissance du Roman*, 235–44.

90. McInerney's *Eloquent Virgins* offers an astute analysis of Thecla's transformation from passive listener to one with the power of speech; 39–44.

91. Davis discusses connections between itineracy and transvestitism, *The Cult of Saint Thecla*, 31–33.

92. Gail Streete, "Buying the Stairway to Heaven: Perpetua and Thecla as Early Christian Heroines," in *A Feminist Companion to the New Testament Apocrypha*

(ed. Amy-Jill Levine with Maria Mayo Robbins; Cleveland: Pilgrim Press, 2006), 199; 186–205. Streete offers more extensive analysis in *Redeemed Bodies*.

93. Helen Morales, "The History of Sexuality," 53.

94. Wehn explores echoes of the Abraham and Isaac stories of exposing wives to sexual assault in a strange land, concluding that such echoes strengthen the narrative critique of Paul's abandonment of Thecla by associating him with other "morally dubious men." Wehn, "Reflection on the Image of Paul in the Acts of Thecla," 158–59.

95. McInerney remarks "The power to define herself in words is immediately linked to the ability to defend herself from the threat of assault." McInerney, *Eloquent Virgins*, 41.

96. Calef provides a lively analysis of Thecla in light of the "test" or "ordeal" scenes in the ancient novel. Susan A. Calef, "Thecla 'Tried and True' and the Inversion of Romance," in *A Feminist Companion to the New Testament Apocrypha* (ed. Amy-Jill Levine with Maria Mayo Robbins; Cleveland: Pilgrim Press, 2006), 163–85.

97. MacDonald, *The Legend and the Apostle*, 41.

98. McInerney, *Eloquent Virgins*, 42.

99. Clément and Kristeva, *The Feminine and the Sacred*, 57.

100. See helpful discussion by Misset-Van de Weg, "Answers to the Plights of an Ascetic Woman Named Thecla," 156–62.

101. Later iconography often depicts Thecla in the *orans* position. See Davis, *The Cult of Saint Thecla*.

102. So Roland Barthes: "*retentissement* / reverberation: Fundamental mode of amorous subjectivity: a word, an image reverberates painfully in the subject's affective consciousness. . . . it is a *coup de theatre*, the 'favorable moment' of a painting: pathetic scene of the ravaged, prostrated subject." *A Lover's Discourse*, 200.

103. As oft noted, Paul's commission is in striking contrast to the pastoral epistles' version of Paul: "Let a woman learn in silence with full submission. I permit no woman to teach or to have authority over a man; she is to keep silent" (I Tim 2:11–12 NRSV).

104. Manuscripts and versions preserve alternate endings to the text. In one, Thecla is threatened again with rape and escapes into a rock; in another, she does not die but is absorbed into the ground (Lipsius, 44–45).

105. Wehn, "Blessed are the bodies of those who are virgins," 164; Vorster, "Construction of Culture through the Construction of Person," 462.

106. Sometimes attributed to "Pseudo-Basil." Gilbert Dagron, ed. and trans., *Vie et Miracles de Sainte Thècle: Texte Grec, Traduction et Commentaire* (Brussells: Société des Bollandistes, 1978). Dagron points out many misogynistic tendencies in the *Life*.

107. Scott Fitzgerald Johnson, *The Life and Miracles of Thekla: A Literary Study*; Castelli, "Layers of Verbal and Visual Memory," 135.

108. For a broad analysis of the literary development and expansion of Thecla's legend see Stephen J. Davis, *The Cult of Saint Thecla*. See also Monika Pesthy, "Thecla among the Fathers of the Church," in *The Apocryphal Acts of Paul and Thecla*, 164–78; Catherine Burrus and Lucas Van Rompay, "Thecla in Syriac Christianity: Preliminary Observations," *Hugoye* 5.2 (2002):1–14.

109. Johnson, *The Life and Miracles of Thekla*, 36.

110. I again rely on Johnson's translation, *The Life and Miracles of Thekla*, 60.

111. See Johnson for further analysis of Alexander's "interception" of Thecla, *The Life and Miracles of Thekla*, 45–48.

112. Castelli, "Layers of Verbal and Visual Memory," 154.

113. Dennis MacDonald and Andrew D. Scrimgeour, "Pseudo-Chrysostom's Panegyric to Thecla: The Heroine of the *Acts of Paul* in Homily and Art," *Semeia* 38 (1986): 156; 151–59. Greek text: Michel Aubineau, "Le Panégyrique de Thècle, Attribué a Jean Chrysostome (*BHG* 1720): la fin retrouvée d'un texte mutilé," *Analecta Bollandiana* 93.3–4 (1975): 349–62. See also Léonie Hayne, "Thecla and the Church Fathers," *Vigiliae Christianae* 48 (1994): 209–18.

114. Aymer, for instance, argues that "Thecla is used by the redactor as the quintessential 'lover' of Christ, who falls in love with the beautiful one, goes through many trials to be with her lover, and finally is able to consummate that love." There is however, no language in the tale to support so eroticized a rendering of Thecla's devotion to Christ. See Margaret P. Aymer, "Hailstorms and Fireballs," 43–61.

115. Argued by Eung Chun Park, "ΑΓΝΕΙΑ as a Sublime Form of ΕΡΩΣ in the *Acts of Paul and Thecla*," in *Distant Voices Drawing Near: Essays in Honor of Antoinette Clark Wire* (ed. Holly Hearon; Collegeville: Liturgical, 2004), 215–26.

116. Judith Butler, "Desire," *Critical Terms for Literary Study*, 380–81.

117. Butler, "Desire," 381.

118. Konstan, *Sexual Symmetry*; Massimo Fusillo, *Naissance du Roman*, 212–29.

119. For a discussion of how the antifamilial discourse of the Apocryphal Acts is aimed particularly at marriage, see Andrew S. Jacobs, "A Family Affair: Marriage, Class, and Ethics in the Apocryphal Acts of the Apostles," *Journal of Early Christian Studies* 7 (1999): 105–38.

120. See again the analyses by Aubin, "Reversing Romance" and Braun, "Physiotherapy of Femininity." Braun characterizes his reading as a "female-to-male conversion story," 222.

121. Musonius Rufus, *Diatribe* 4; Plutarch, *Mulierum Virtutes* 244E–245C; both discussed by Jeremy McInerny, "Plutarch's Manly Women," in *Andreia: Studies in Manliness and Courage in Classical Antiquity* (ed. Ralph M. Rosen and Ineke Sluiter; Leiden: Brill, 2003), 319–44.

122. Virginia Burrus remarks, of both Thecla and Leukippe: "The girl's defiance, in which spectacular passivity combines with unexpected strength of resistance, complicates her femininity, as 'transvestite' passages in both texts

highlight; the lover's distinctly unheroic helplessness and unsteady loyalty likewise render his masculinity markedly ambivalent." "MimickingVirgins," 64.

Chapter Four

1. "Longinus" is the conventional name used for the author of *Peri Hupsous*, though the attribution is uncertain, and some scholars prefer "Pseudo-Longinus." From the Renaissance until the mid-twentieth century, the treatise was usually dated to the third century CE. More recent scholars tend to date it to the first century CE. See the discussion in Richard Macksey, "Longinus Reconsidered," *Modern Language Notes* 108 (1993): 913–34.

2. Translation of Sappho by John Winkler, "Double Consciousness in Sappho's Lyrics," in *The Constraints of Desire: The Anthropology of Sex and Gender in Ancient Greece,*" (New York: Routledge, 1990), 178; 162–87. Plutarch also admired the poem and quotes fragments of it, for instance at *Eroticus* 17.762 and *On Moral Progress* 136.

3. 'Longinus,' "On Sublimity," in *Ancient Literary Criticism: The Principal Texts in New Translations* (trans. D. A. Russell; New York: Oxford University Press, 1972), 472; 460–503. All subsequent English quotations of Longinus are from this translation and will be noted parenthetically in the text.

4. Neil Hertz, "A Reading of Longinus," *The End of the Line: Essays on Psychoanalysis and the Sublime,"* (New York: Columbia University Press, 1986), 6; 1–20 For a discussion of Sappho's ode, see Winkler, "Double Consciousness," 178–80.

5. Donald Russell remarks in his edition of the Greek text, "No translation of the title is likely to please everybody." After exploring the reasons, he concedes, "The translator is therefore fairly free to use 'sublimity,' 'greatness,' 'grandeur,' 'elevation,' 'magnificence,' etc., as occasion demands." 'Longinus,' *On The Sublime: Edited With Introduction and Commentary* (ed. D.A. Russell; Oxford: Clarendon, 1972), 57.

6. Alexander Pope, *Essay on Criticism* (1709), 111. 680.

7. Hertz, "A Reading of Longinus."

8. Phrases from Virginia Burrus, "Mimicking Virgins: Colonial Ambivalence and the Ancient Romance," *Arethusa* 38 (2005): 69.

9. "Constructing Narrative: An Interview with Peter Brooks Conducted by John S. Rickard and Harold Schweizer," in Peter Brooks, *Psychoanalysis and Storytelling* (Oxford, UK & Cambridge, MA: Blackwell, 1994), 105–6.

10. For reviews of the state of the questions, see Edith M. Humphrey, *Joseph and Aseneth* (Sheffield: Sheffield, 2000), 17–37; Randall D. Chesnutt, *From Death to Life: Conversion in Joseph and Aseneth* (JSPSS16; Sheffield: Sheffield, 1995), 20–95; Christoph Burchard, "The Present State of Research on Joseph and Aseneth," in *New Perspectives on Ancient Judaism* (ed. J. Neusner, P. Borgen, E.S. Frerichs and R. Horsley; Lanham, Md.: University Press of America, 1987), 31–52.

11. Marc Philonenko, *Joseph et Aséneth: Introduction, Texte Critique, Traduction et Notes* (Leiden: Brill, 1968); Christoph Burchard, *Untersuchungen zu Joseph und Aseneth* (Tübingen: J. C. B. Mohr, 1965). Christoph Burchard has now published a critical edition of an eclectic text based on the *b* family: Christoph Burchard, *Joseph und Aseneth: Kritisch Herausgegeben* (Leiden: Brill, 2003). An English translation of Philonenko's Greek text is available in D. Cook, "Joseph and Aseneth," in *The Apocryphal Old Testament* (ed. H. F. D. Sparks; Oxford: Clarendon, 1984), 465–503. Burchard's English translation has also long been available: "*Joseph and Aseneth:* A New Translation and Introduction," in *The Old Testament Pseudepigrapha* (ed. James H. Charlesworth; New York: Doubleday, 1985), 2.177–247. Joseph and Aseneth survives in eight versions, along with the Greek manuscripts.

12. See Chesnutt's discussion of the value of the longer text in *From Death to Life*, 20–95.

13. Angela Standhartinger, "From Fictional Text to Socio-Historical Context," *SBL Seminar Papers 1996* (SBLSP 33; Atlanta: Scholar's Press, 1996), 302–18; *Das Frauenbild Im Judentum Der Hellenistischen Zeit: Ein Beitrag anhand von 'Joseph und Aseneth'* (Leiden: Brill, 1995), 219–25.

14. Ross Shepard Kraemer, "Recasting *Aseneth:* The Enhancement of Traditional Elements in the Longer Reconstruction," *When Aseneth Met Joseph: A Late Antique Tale of the Biblical Patriarch and His Egyptian Wife, Reconsidered* (New York: Oxford University Press, 1998), 80; 50–88.

15. Kraemer, *When Aseneth Met Joseph*, 206–10.

16. Humphrey, *Joseph and Aseneth*, 23–26.

17. Christoph Burchard, "The Text of *Joseph and Aseneth* Reconsidered," *Journal for the Study of the Pseudepigrapha* 14.2 (2005): 83–96.

18. Christoph Burchard, *Joseph und Aseneth: Kritisch Herausgegeben*.

19. See, for example, Chesnutt, *From Death to Life*, 36–37; Humphrey, *Joseph and Aseneth*, 28–31; Howard Clark Kee, "The Socio-Cultural Setting of Joseph and Aseneth," *New Testament Studies* 29 (1983): 394–413. Of those who assume an Egyptian provenance, Bohak has little company in positing a considerably earlier date, arguing that the text is to be understood as an allegorical defense for the building of an alternate temple at Heliopolis in the mid-second century BCE; see Gideon Bohak, *Joseph and Aseneth and the Jewish Temple in Heliopolis* (Atlanta: Scholars Press, 1996).

20. Kraemer, *When Aseneth Met Joseph*, 291–92.

21. Kraemer, *When Aseneth Met Joseph*, 304.

22. Kraemer is not the first to suggest the text may be from a late-ancient Christian hand. Batiffol, who published the first full Greek text of the tale in 1889–1890, suggested it was a fifth-century Christian work. See discussion in Chesnutt, *From Death to Life*, 39–40.

23. Harold Attridge, in a very favorable review, remarks that not all of Kraemer's comparisons with adjurations and mystical ascents are equally convincing, and that dating and authorship issues will likely remain

controversial, but calls her challenge to the reigning consensus, "overall solid and serious." Harold Attridge, review of Ross S. Kraemer, *When Aseneth Met Joseph: A Late Antique Tale of The Biblical Patriarch and His Egyptian Wife, Reconsidered, Hebrew Studies* 41 (2000), 313–316. Randall Chesnutt concludes that despite Kraemer's re-evaluation, "the work still seems best understood as a product of non-Christian Hellenistic Judaism around the turn of the eras." Chesnutt, review of Ross S. Kraemer, *When Aseneth Met Joseph, Journal of Biblical Literature* 119 (2000):760–62. Timothy Horner, on the other hand, says Kraemer's arguments have convinced him of *Aseneth's* late date:"In my estimation, she has added a text to the late antique library. That is no small achievement." Horner, review of Ross S. Kraemer, *When Aseneth Met Joseph, Journal of Early Christian Studies* 9 (1999): 602–03. See also George J. Brooke, "Men and Women as Angels in *Joseph and Aseneth, Journal for the Study of the Pseudepigrapha* 14.2 (2005): 159–77.

24. John J. Collins, "Joseph and Aseneth: Jewish or Christian?" *Journal for the Study of the Pseudepigrapha* 14.2 (2005): 97–112.

25. Kraemer, *When Aseneth Met Joseph*, 294.

26. Richard Pervo, "Joseph and Aseneth and the Greek Novel," *SBL Seminar Papers, 1976* (SBLSP 14; Missoula: Scholars Press, 1976), 171; 171–82. See also his *Profit With Delight: The Literary Genre of the Acts of the Apostles* (Philadephia: Fortress, 1987), 119–21.

27. For a recent argument, see Susan Docherty, "*Joseph and Aseneth*: Rewritten Bible or Narrative Expansion," *Journal for the Study of Judaism* 35 (2004): 27–47. Gruen suggests that though *Joseph and Aseneth* draws little of its plot from the Genesis Joseph narratives, it does continue the ambiguities of the Genesis portrait of Joseph: at once a pious hero, a favorite of the divine, yet given to arrogance and excessive disdain. Erich S. Gruen, "The Hellenistic Images of Joseph," in *Heritage and Hellenism: The Reinvention of Jewish Tradition* (Berkeley: University of California Press, 1998), 73–109. For rabbinic retellings of the Joseph traditions, see James L. Kugel, *In Potiphar's House: The Interpretive Life of Biblical Texts* (San Francisco: HarperSanFrancisco, 1990).

28. See Kraemer's treatment of Wisdom and the Strange Woman; *When Aseneth Met Joseph*, 22–27.

29. See Edith McEwan Humphrey, *The Ladies and the Cities: Transformation and Apocalyptic Identity in Joseph and Aseneth, 4 Ezra, the Apocalypse and The Shepherd of Hermas* (JSPSS 17; Sheffield: Sheffield, 1995), 30–56; Humphrey, *Joseph and Aseneth*, 40–46; Kraemer, *When Aseneth Met Joseph*, 19–49.

30. For discussion of intertextuality as "transposition" rather than "the banal sense of 'study of sources,'" see Julia Kristeva, *Revolution in Poetic Language* (New York: Columbia University Press, 1984), 59–60 and "Word, Dialogue and Novel," in *The Kristeva Reader* (ed. Toril Moi; New York: Columbia University Press, 1986), 34–61; see also Thas Morgan, "The Space of Intertextuality," in *Intertextuality and Contemporary American Fiction* (ed. Patrick

O'Donnell and Robert Con Davis; Baltimore: Johns Hopkins University Press, 1989), 239–79.

31. Chesnutt, *From Death to Life*, 165; 153–271. For broad studies of the question of Jewish missionizing with divergent conclusions, see Martin Goodman, *Mission and Conversion: Proselytizing in the Religious History of the Roman Empire* (Oxford: Clarendon, 1994) and Louis Feldman, "Was Judaism a Missionary Religion in Ancient Times?" in *Jewish Assimilation, Acculturation and Accommodation: Past Traditions, Current Issues and Future Prospects* (Lanham, Md.: University Press of America, 1992), 24–37.

32. Chesnutt echoes views of earlier scholars, such as Burchard, but develops them more thoroughly through sociological models of "conversion." *From Death to Life*, 153-271. Cohen similarly treats Aseneth as an example of "venerating the God of the Jews and denying or ignoring all other Gods." Shaye J. D. Cohen, *The Beginnings of Jewishness: Boundaries, Varieties, Uncertainties*, (Berkeley: University of California Press, 1999), 150. In an older work, Nickelsburg argued that the text, with its syncretistic elements, might itself be taken as missionary, appealing to Gentiles to convert. George W. E. Nickelsburg, *Jewish Literature Between the Bible and the Mishnah: A Historical and Literary Introduction* (Philadelphia: Fortress, 1981), 258–65. Gruen, on the other hand, argues that there is little evidence of "missionary purpose" in the text, though strong interest in relations of Jew and Gentile in the Diaspora. Gruen, "The Hellenistic Images of Joseph," 94–95.

33. This summary draws on the analysis of the Greek romances by Judith Perkins, *The Suffering Self: Pain and Narrative Representation in the Early Christian Era* (London: Routledge, 1995), 41–76. See also Richard Pervo, "Aseneth and Her Sisters: Women in Jewish Narrative and in the Greek Novels," in *Women Like This: New Perspectives on Jewish Women in the Greco-Roman World* (ed. Amy-Jill Levine; Atlanta: Scholars Press, 1991), 145–60 and the comparative treatment of *Ethiopian Story* and *Joseph and Aseneth* by Virginia Burrus, "Mimicking Virgins," 49–88.

34. Lawrence M. Wills, *The Jewish Novel in the Ancient World* (Ithaca: Cornell University Press, 1995), 13–14. Wills also offers a translation and introduction to the text, which he titles, "The Marriage and Conversion of Aseneth," in Lawrence M. Wills, *Ancient Jewish Novels: An Anthology* (New York: Oxford University Press, 2002), 121–62. Wills suggests, though not, I think, convincingly, that *Joseph and Aseneth* is the product of two layers of story: an earlier national hero romance had the mystical union theme introduced later; 178–84.

35. For analysis, see Athalya Brenner, ed., *A Feminist Companion to Esther, Judith and Susanna* (Sheffield: Sheffield, 1995); Toni A. Craven, *Artistry and Faith in the Book of Judith* (Society of Biblical Literature, 1983); Amy-Jill Levine, "Hemmed in on Every Side: Jews and Women in the Book of Susanna," *The Feminist Companion to the Bible* (ed. Athalya Brenner; Sheffield: Sheffield, 1995); Sidnie Ann White, "Esther: a Feminine Model for the Jewish

Diaspora," in *Gender and Difference* (ed. Peggy L. Day; Minneapolis: Fortress, 2006).

36. Philonenko, *Joseph et Aséneth*, 79–98.

37. Humphrey, *Joseph and Aseneth*, 41; 45–46

38. Pervo, "Joseph and Aseneth and the Greek Novel," 175–77.

39. See, for instance, Richard I. Pervo, "Aseneth and Her Sisters," 145–60; also *Profit with Delight*.

40. Virginia Burrus examines virginity as "a site of articulated cultural ambivalence" in "Mimicking Virgins," 53. For a broad discussion of ancient views of virginity, see Dale Martin, "The Dangers of Desire," in *The Corinthian Body* (New Haven: Yale University Press, 1995), 198–228, especially 219–22; and Foskett, *A Virgin Conceived*, 23–73. See also Anne Carson, "Putting Her In Her Place: Woman, Dirt, and Desire," and Anne Ellis Hansen, "The Medical Writers' Woman," in *Before Sexuality: The Construction of Erotic Experience in the Ancient Greek World* (ed. David M. Halperin, John J. Winkler, and Froma I Zeitlin; Princeton, N.J.: Princeton University Press, 1990), 135–69; 309–34.

41. Humphrey, *Joseph and Aseneth*, 80–113.

42. Whose name differs from the "Potiphera" of Genesis.

43. Throughout, the Greek text is from Burchard, *Joseph und Aseneth: Kritisch Herausgegeben*. Translations are my own, with reference to those by Burchard, "Joseph and Aseneth," in *Old Testament Pseudepigrapha*, and Wills, *Ancient Jewish Novels: An Anthology*.

44. Mieke Bal, *Narratology: Introduction to the Theory of Narrative* (2nd edition; Toronto: University of Toronto Press, 1999), 36.

45. See Longinus on "Amplification," *On Sublimity*, 12.1–2.

46. Richard I. Pervo, "Aseneth and Her Sisters," 149.

47. Kraemer points out how Aseneth's rooms encode a dual association with Woman Wisdom, whose rooms are filled with all precious and pleasant riches (Prov 24:3) and the Strange Woman, whose rooms are filled with death (Prov 9:18); *When Aseneth Met Joseph*, 23.

48. The description has strong similarities to the tower in *The Shepherd of Hermas*, a foursquare structure made of large fitted stones, with gates and guards (*Vis* 9.2 [79])—clearly, both descriptions are intended to convey the grandeur of the structures.

49. Humphrey notes that the prolix description and insistence upon virginity gain comic dimensions. She remarks also on virginity as an ambivalent trait, "indicating alternately misandry and a valued chastity." Humphrey, *Joseph and Aseneth*, 86, 90.

50. For Longinus on mimesis as complex relationship with literary authority, see Tim Whitmarsh, *Greek Literature and the Roman Empire: The Politics of Imitation* (New York: Oxford University Press, 2001), 59–60.

51. Pervo remarks with a light touch on Aseneth's characterization: "Aseneth is never a helpless, simpering virgin. . . . Her regal behavior and insistence

upon the husband of her choice nicely contrast with her subsequent dejection and thus help the plot. . . . By resolutely and intemperately rejecting her father's plans and by stomping out of the hall in anger, she sets up the plot. Girls who blow up at their fathers *should* get into trouble in ancient novels, and Aseneth's trouble turns out to be neither better nor worse than the usual fate of heroines: love at first sight." Richard I. Pervo, "Aseneth and Her Sisters," 150.

52. Longinus offers a pointed contrast between strategies of amplification and a more Demosthenic abruptness at *On Sublimity*, 12.5.

53. See, for instance, Kraemer, *When Aseneth Met Joseph*, 156–67; Philonenko, *Joseph et Aséneth*, 79–82.

54. Burchard also points out that the language credits Joseph with prophetical insights, like those Philo describes: "To a prophet nothing is unknown, because he has intelligible light in him and shadowless rays" (Philo, *Spec. Leg.* 4:192). Burchard, *Joseph and Aseneth*, 209, note r.

55. Perhaps again recalling a Song of Songs image of the lover "gazing in at the windows, looking through the lattice" (2:9b NRSV).

56. "You have ravished my heart, my sister, my bride . . . How sweet is your love, my sister, my bride?" (Song of Songs 4:9a, 10a NRSV). Readers may also recall Egyptian royal marriages between siblings.

57. Wills reads this scene as an engagement, saying Joseph "thus agrees with her father to marry her." The reading seems, however, to flatten the ambiguity of language. Wills, *The Jewish Novel*, 171.

58. Michael Penn, "Identity Transformation and Authorial Identification in *Joseph and Aseneth*," *Journal for the Study of the Pseudepigrapha* 13.2 (2002): 174; 171–183.

59. Chesnutt notes other places in the text where the formulation "it is not proper for a man (woman) who worships God to . . ." is used (8.5, 7; 21.1; 23.9, 12; 29.3). Chesnutt, *From Death to Life*, 99.

60. Chesnutt notes, "As Burchard and Philonenko have noted, this triad echoes the biblical formula 'grain, wine and oil,' and, like that formula, is a summary of the staples of life. It provides a representative expression for the Jewish way of life vis-à-vis Gentile existence." Chesnutt, *From Death to Life*, 132. See also his "Perceptions of Oil in Early Judaism and the Meal Formula in *Joseph and Aseneth*," *Journal for the Study of the Pseudepigrapha* 14.2 (2005):113–32.

61. So Penn, "Identity Transformation," 174.

62. So Philo remarks, "we must rejoice with them [proselytes], as if, though blind at the first they had recovered their sight and had come from the deepest darkness to behold the most radiant light." Philo, *On the Virtues*, 179 (trans. F. H. Colson; Cambridge: Harvard University Press, 1939), 8.273. Or Paul, "Therefore we have been buried with him by baptism into death, so that, just as Christ was raised from the dead by the glory of the Father, so we too might walk in newness of life" (Rom 6:3–4 NRSV).

63. Longinus discusses the rhetorical (sublime) effect of changes of speaking voice at 26.2. See discussion by Yun Lee Too, *The Idea of Ancient Literary Criticism*, (Oxford: Clarendon Press, 1998), 195–200.

64. Pervo, "Aseneth and her sisters," 151.

65. However formulaic her speeches, Chesnutt notes that there is no hint that Aseneth is following prescribed initiatory procedure, but rather is acting autonomously. Chesnutt, *From Death to Life*, 121. Kraemer, on the other hand, likens Aseneth's behaviors and prayers to late-ancient formulae for adjuration of angels. Kraemer, *When Aseneth Met Joseph*, 89–109.

66. The depiction of God as creator has an intriguing further parallel in Longinus who, in an unusual and noteworthy citation of Jewish scripture by a Greek rhetorician, refers to Genesis 1. Longinus urges, "Much better than the Battle of the Gods are the passages which represent divinity as genuinely unsoiled and great and pure" (9.8). He adds: "Similarly, the lawgiver of the Jews, no ordinary man—for he understood and expressed God's power in accordance with its worth—writes at the beginning of his *Laws*: 'God said'—now what?—'Let there be light,' and there was light; 'Let there be earth,' and there was earth" (9.9).

67. The cosmology is strikingly similar to Hermas, *Similitudes* 9.3.3 and *Visions* 3.2.4ff.

68. Mary Foskett reviews the range of ways Aseneth uses *parthenos* in the prayer and concludes, "Aseneth repeatedly identifies herself as a *parthenos*, a self-designation that connotes not boastfulness and arrogance, but humility, vulnerability, and ignorance. The *parthenos* of former privilege has been transformed into a *parthenos* of *tapeinosis* (cf. 13.1, 21.21)." Foskett, *A Virgin Conceived*, 102.

69. Wills assumes the prayer to be a late addition to an earlier national hero tale; *The Jewish Novel*, 184.

70. The tearing apart of the heavens is reminiscent of *The Shepherd of Hermas*, *Vision* 1.1.4.

71. Kraemer, *When Aseneth Met Joseph*, 197.

72. Humphrey's earlier study analyzes not only Aseneth, but several literary instances of the transfigured Woman-Building, "The building, like the woman herself, is a symbol of the faithful as a whole, either Jewish or Christian, hence she is a figure of solidarity. . . . In each case, this narrative event moves a symbolic female figure from an aspect of weakness to a picture of glory, but does this in a specific way to specific ends." Edith McEwan Humphrey, *The Ladies and the Cities*, 19.

73. Bohak, *Joseph and Aseneth and the Jewish Temple in Heliopolis*; Kraemer, *When Aseneth Met Joseph*, 38–39; 167–72.

74. Humphrey, *Joseph and Aseneth*, n. 52, p. 54.

75. Chesnutt remarks, "By having Aseneth eat from the honeycomb [said to be the same food as that eaten by the angels of God in paradise] the author places this convert on a par with the Jew by birth, and indeed with the

angels of God, who eat the same immortal food." Chesnutt, *From Death to Life*, 131.

76. See Anathea Portier-Young, "Sweet Mercy Metropolis: Interpreting Aseneth's Honeycomb," *Journal for the Study of the Pseudepigrapha* 14.2 (2005): 133–57.

77. Penn, "Identity Transformation," 176.

78. Song of Songs 4:1–7; 7:1–5. See also Sirach 24:13–17. Of particular relevance may be Song of Songs 8:10: "I was a wall, and my breasts were like towers; then I was in his eyes as one who brings peace" (NRSV). Humphrey notes that the detail of mountain-like breasts is in neither the *b* nor the *d* family of texts, and that Burchard has added the detail from text family *a* to his eclectic text. Humphrey, *Joseph and Aseneth*, 73. The addition seems, however, coherent with the breast imagery developed throughout the story.

79. Longinus also remarks on the technique of using a continuous series of tropes to describe *men's* bodies (32.5), another instance of his general point, "that tropes are naturally grand, that metaphors conduce to sublimity, and that passages involving emotion and description are the most suitable field for them" (32.6).

80. See Penn, "Identity Transformation," for examples of Greco-Roman parallels, 176–77.

81. Penn, "Identity Transformation," 177.

82. Burrus, "Mimicking Virgins," 73.

83. For detailed analysis of the chiasmic structure of Aseneth's Psalm, see Humphrey, "Chiasmus and Transformation in Joseph and Aseneth," in *The Ladies and the Cities*, 30–56; esp. 40–42.

84. See thoroughgoing criticism of the longer version's compromise of Aseneth's autonomy by Standhartinger, *Das Frauenbild*, and by Kraemer, *When Aseneth Met Joseph*.

85. Pervo notes, "the love of God is what makes realization of her romantic passion possible;" "Aseneth and Her Sisters," 152.

86. Yun Lee Too, *The Idea of Ancient Literary Criticism*, 187–217.

87. Levi's visions of "letters written in heaven by the finger of God" may connect him to Aseneth's "fingers of a fast-writing scribe" (20.5) and to the heavenly books of life (15:4; 15:12).

88. Chesnutt remarks on the strong correspondences between Aseneth's earlier revelatory experiences and the mysticism of Levi. Randall D. Chesnutt, "Revelatory Experiences Attributed to Biblical Women in Early Jewish Literature," in *Women Like This*, 115; 107–25.

89. Burrus argues that in *Joseph and Aseneth*, as in *An Ethiopian Story*, virginity itself is "converted"—an analysis that captures well the strikingly nonerotic way the tale represents postconversion marriage and social relations. Yet the complex cluster of associations with "virginity" in Aseneth's story seem to me more inverted or displaced than continued or "converted" in Part Two of the story. Virginia Burrus, "Mimicking Virgins," 82.

90. See Burrus' provocative analysis of the cultural ambivalence of the story's outcome (and that of *An Ethiopian Story*): ". . . the union of alien virgins conveys a mixed message, effecting neither the false universalism of cultural transcendence nor the illusory purity of ethnic integrity, but rather slyly subverting both hegemonic claims." "Mimicking Virgins," 84.

Conclusion

1. Ross Shepard Kraemer, *When Aseneth Met Joseph: A Late Antique Tale of the Biblical Patriarch and His Egyptian Wife, Reconsidered* (New York: Oxford University Press, 1998), 194.
2. Simon Goldhill. *Foucault's Virginity: Ancient Erotic Fiction and the History of Sexuality* (Cambridge: Cambridge University Press, 1995), 44–45.

Bibliography

Ancient Primary Texts

Bovon, François and Pierre Geoltrain. *Écrits apocryphe chrétiens*. Paris: I. Gallimard, 1997.

Burchard, Christoph. "Ein vorläufiger griechischer Text Von *Joseph Und Aseneth*." *Dielheimer Blätter zum Alten Testament und seiner Rezeption in der Alten Kirche* 14 (1979): 2–53 and 16 (1982): 37–39.

————. "Joseph and Aseneth." Pages 177–247 in *The Old Testament Pseudepigrapha*, vol. 2. Edited by James H. Charlesworth. New York: Doubleday, 1985.

————. *Joseph und Aseneth: Kritisch Herausgegeben*. With assistance from Carsten Burfeind and Uta Barbara Fink. Leiden: Brill, 2003.

Cook, D. "Joseph and Aseneth." Pages 465–503 in *The Apocryphal Old Testament*. Edited by H. F. D. Sparks. Oxford: Clarendon Press, 1984.

Copenhaver, Brian. *Hermetica*. Cambridge: Cambridge University Press, 1992.

Ehrman, Bart D. *The Apostolic Fathers*. 2 vols. Loeb Classical Library. Cambridge: Harvard University Press, 2003.

Elliott, J.K. *The Apocryphal New Testament: A Collection of Apocryphal Christian Literature in an English Translation Based on M.R. James*. Oxford: Clarendon, 1993.

Epictetus. *Discourses and Enchiridion*. Translated by Thomas Wentworth Higginson. New York: Walter J. Black, 1944.

Fitzgerald, John T., and L. Michael White. *The Tabula of Cebes*. Chico, Calif.: Scholars Press, 1983.

Galen. *Selected Works*. Translated by P. N. Singer. New York: Oxford University Press, 1997.

Grant, Robert, ed. *The Apostolic Fathers: A New Translation and Commentary*. 6 vols. London: Nelson, 1966.

Hennecke, E., and W. Schneemelcher, eds. *New Testament Apocrypha*. 2 vols. Rev. ed. Translated by R. McL. Wilson. Philadelphia: Westminster/John Knox, 1991.

Joly, Robert. *Hermas, Le Pasteur: Introduction, Texte Critique, Traduction et Notes*. 2e Edition Revue et Augmentée. Paris: Les Éditions du Cerf, 1968.

Lightfoot, J.B., and J.R. Harmer. *The Apostolic Fathers*. 2nd ed. Revised by Michael W. Holmes. Grand Rapids: Baker, 1989.

Lindemann, Andreas, and Henning Paulsen. *Die Apostolischen Väter*. Tübingen: J. C. B. Mohr, 1992.

Lipsius, R. A., and M. Bonnet. *Acta Apostolorum Apocrypha*. Leipzig: 1891–1903. Reprinted Hildesheim: G. Olms, 1959.

Longinus. *On the Sublime: Edited with Introduction and Commentary*. Edited and translated by D. A. Russell. Oxford: Clarendon, 1972.

———. *On The Sublime*. Translated by W. Hamilton Fyfe. Cambridge: Harvard University Press, 1973.

———. "On Sublimity." Pages 460–503 in *Ancient Literary Criticism: The Principal Texts in New Translations*. Translated by D. A. Russell. New York: Oxford University Press, 1972.

Lutz, Cora E. "Musonius Rufus, the Roman Socrates. Introduction, Texts and Translation." *Yale Classical Studies* 10 (1967): 3–147.

MacDonald, Dennis Ronald. *The Acts of Andrew and The Acts of Andrew and Matthias in the City of the Cannibals*. Atlanta: Scholars Press, 1990.

Marcus Aurelius. *The Meditations of Marcus Aurelius Antoninus*. Translated by A. S. L. Farquharson. New York: Oxford University Press, 1989.

Ovid. *Metamorphoses*. Translated by A. D. Melville. New York: Oxford University Press, 1986.

Philo. Translated by F. H. Colson. 10 vols. Loeb Classical Library. Cambridge: Harvard University Press, 1939.

Philonenko, Marc. *Joseph et Aseneth: Introduction, Texte Critique, Traduction et Notes*. Sbp 13. Leiden: E.J. Brill, 1968.

Plutarch. Translated by W. C. Helmbold. 14 vols. Loeb Classical Library. Cambridge: Harvard University Press, 1939.

———. *Essays*. Translated by Robin Waterfield. New York: Penguin, 1992.

———. *Selected Essays and Dialogues*. Translated by Donald Russell. New York: Oxford University Press, 1993.

Pomeroy, Sarah B., ed. *Plutarch's Advice to the Bride and Groom and A Consolation to His Wife*. New York: Oxford University Press, 1999.

Reardon, B.P., ed. *Collected Ancient Greek Novels*. Berkeley: University of California Press, 1989.

Roberts, Alexander and James Donaldson, eds., *The Ante-Nicene Fathers*. 1885–1887. 10 vols. Repr., Peabody, Mass: Hendrickson, 1994.

Seneca. *Moral Essays*. Translated by John W. Basare. New York: Putnam's, 1928.

Snyder, Graydon F. *The Shepherd of Hermas. The Apostolic Fathers: A New Translation and Commentary.* Vol. 6. London: Thomas Nelson & Sons, 1968.

Vouaux, Léon. *Les Actes de Paul et ses Lettres Apocryphes: Introduction, Textes, Traduction et Commentaire.* Paris: Librairie Letouzey et Ané, 1913.

Whittaker, Molly, ed. *Der Hirt des Hermas.* Berlin: Akademie Verlag, 1967.

Wills, Lawrence M., ed. and transl. *Ancient Jewish Novels: An Anthology.* Oxford: Oxford University Press, 2002.

Wright, William. *Apocryphal Acts of the Apostles: Edited from Syriac Manuscripts in the British Museum and Other Libraries With English Translations and Notes.* Amsterdam: Philo, 1968.

Secondary Texts

Anderson, Graham. *Ancient Fiction: The Novel in the Graeco-Roman World.* London: Croom Helm/Barnes and Noble, 1984.

Aptowitzer, V. "Asenath, the Wife of Joseph: A Haggadic Literary-Historical Study." *Hebrew Union College Annual* 1 (1924): 239–306.

Attridge, Harold. "Review of Ross S. Kraemer, *When Aseneth Met Joseph.*" *Hebrew Studies* 41 (2000): 313–16.

Aubin, Melissa. "Reversing Romance? *The Acts of Paul and Thecla* and the Ancient Novel." Pages 257–72 in *Ancient Fiction and Early Christian Narrative.* Edited by Ronald F. Hock, J. Bradley Chance, and Judith Perkins. Atlanta: Scholars Press, 1998.

Aubin, Paul. *Le Probléme de la Conversion.* Paris: Beauchesne et ses Fils, 1962.

Aubineau, Michel. "Le Panégyrique de Thècle, Attribué a Jean Chrysostome (BHG 1720): la fin retrouvée d'un texte motile." *Analecta Bollandiana* 93 (1975): 349–62.

Aune, David C. "Mastery of the Passions: Philo, 4 Maccabees and Earliest Christianity." Pages 125–58 in *Hellenization Revisited: Shaping a Christian Response within the Greco-Roman World.* Edited by Wendy E. Helleman. Lanham, Md: University Press of America, 1994.

Austin-Broos, Diane. "The Anthropology of Conversion: An Introduction." Pages 1–12 in *The Anthropology of Religious Conversion.* Edited by Andrew Buckser and Stephen D. Glazier. Lanham, Md: Rowman & Littlefield, 2003.

Aymer, Margaret P. "Hailstorms and Fireballs: Redaction, World Creation, and Resistance in the Acts of Paul and Thecla." *Semeia* 79 (1997): 45–61.

Baer, Richard A., Jr. *Philo's Use of the Categories Male and Female.* Leiden: Brill, 1970.

Bailey, Jon Nelson. "*Metanoia* in the Writings of Philo Judaeus." *Society of Biblical Literature Seminar Papers* 28 (1991): 135–41.

Bal, Mieke. *Narratology: Introduction to the Theory of Narrative.* 2nd ed. Toronto: University of Toronto Press, 1999.

———. *On Story-Telling: Essays in Narratology.* Edited by David Jobling. Sonoma, Calif.: Polebridge, 1991.

Balot, Ryan K. "Foucault, Chariton, and the Masculine Self." *Helios* 25 (1998): 139–62.

Barnard, L.W. "The Shepherd of Hermas in Recent Study." *The Heythrop Journal* 9 (1968): 29–36.

Barthes, Roland. *A Lover's Discourse: Fragments.* Translated by Richard Howard. New York: Hill and Wang, 1978.

Bauckham, R.J. "The Great Tribulation in the Shepherd of Hermas." *Journal of Theological Studies* new series 25 (1974): 27–40.

Bohak, Gideon. *Joseph and Aseneth and the Jewish Temple in Heliopolis.* Atlanta: Scholars Press, 1996.

Bollók, János. "The Description of Paul in the Acta Pauli." Pages 1–15 in *The Apocryphal Acts of Paul and Thecla.* Edited by Jan N. Bremmer. Kampen: Kok Pharos, 1996.

Boughton, Lynne Courter. "From Pious Legend to Feminist Fantasy: Distinguishing Hagiographical License from Apostolic Practice in the Acts of Paul/Acts of Thecla." *Journal of Religion* 71 (1991): 362–83.

Bovon, François. *New Testament Traditions and Apocryphal Narratives.* Translated by Jane Haapiseva-Hunter. Princeton Theological Monographs 36. Allison Park, Pa: Pickwick, 1995.

———. "The Words of Life in the Acts of Andrew." Pages 81–95 in *The Apocryphal Acts of Andrew.* Edited by Jan N. Bremmer. Leuven: Peeters, 2000.

Bovon, François, and Eric Junod. "Reading the Apocryphal Acts of the Apostles." *Semeia* 38 (1986): 161–71.

Bovon, François, et. al. *Les Actes Apocryphes Des Apôtres: Christianisme Et Monde Païen.* Geneva: Labor et Fides, 1981.

Bowe, Barbara Ellen. *A Church in Crisis: Ecclesiology and Paraenesis in Clement of Rome.* Minneapolis: Fortress Press, 1988.

Boyarin, Daniel. "Body Politic among the Brides of Christ: Paul and the Origins of Christian Sexual Renunciation." Pages 459–78 in *Asceticism.* Edited by V. Wimbush and R. Valantasis. New York: Oxford University Press, 1995.

Braun, Willi. "Physiotherapy of Femininity in the Acts of Thecla." Pages 209–30 in *Text and Artifact in the Religions of Mediterranean Antiquity: Essays in Honour of Peter Richardson.* Edited by Stephen G. Wilson and Michel Desjardins. Waterloo, Ontario: Wilfred Laurier University Press, 2002.

Braund, Susanna Morton, and Christopher Gill. *The Passions in Roman Thought and Literature.* Cambridge: Cambridge University Press, 1997.

Bremmer, Jan N. *The Apocryphal Acts of Paul and Thecla: An Introduction.* Kampen, Netherlands: Kok Pharos, 1996.

———. "The Novel and the Apocryphal Acts: Place, Time, and Readership." Pages 157–80 in *Groningen Colloquia on the Novel,* Vol. 9. Groningen: Egbert Forsten, 1998.

Bremmer, Jan. N., Wout J. van Bekkum, and Arie L. Molendijk, eds. *Cultures of Conversions.* Leuven: Peeters, 2006.

————. *Paradigms, Poetics and Politics of Conversion.* Leuven: Peeters, 2006.

Brenner, Athalya, ed. *A Feminist Companion to Esther, Judith and Susanna.* Sheffield: Sheffield Academic Press, 1995.

Brock, Ann Graham. "Political Authority and Cultural Accommodation: Social Diversity in the *Acts of Paul* and the *Acts of Peter.*" Pages 145–69 in *The Apocryphal Acts of the Apostles.* Edited by François Bovon, Ann Graham Brock, Christopher R. Matthews. Boston: Harvard University Press, 1999.

Brooke, George J. "Men and Women as Angels in Joseph and Aseneth." *Journal for the Study of the Pseudepigrapha* 14.2 (2005): 159–77.

Brooks, Peter. *Body Work: Objects of Desire in Modern Narrative.* Cambridge: Harvard University Press, 1993.

————. *Psychoanalysis and Storytelling.* Oxford: Blackwell, 1994.

————. *Reading for the Plot.* New York: Alfred A. Knopf, 1984.

Brown, Peter. "Bodies and Minds: Sexuality and Renunciation in Early Christianity." Pages 479–93 in *Before Sexuality: The Construction of Erotic Experience in the Ancient Greek World.* Edited by David M. Halperin, John J. Winkler, Froma Zeitlin. Princeton: Princeton University Press, 1990.

————. *The Body and Society: Men, Women and Sexual Renunciation in Early Christianity.* New York: Columbia University Press, 1988.

Brown, Milton Perry. *The Authentic Writings of Ignatius.* Durham, N. C.: Duke University Press, 1963.

Brox, Norbert. *Der Hirt Des Hermas.* Gottingen: Vandenhoeck & Ruprecht, 1991.

Bruce, Steve. "Sociology of Conversion: The Last Twenty-Five Years." Pages 1–11 in *Paradigms, Poetics and Politics of Conversion.* Edited by Jan N. Bremmer, Wout J. van Bekkum, and Arie L. Molendijk. Leuven: Peeters, 2006.

Buckser, Andrew and Stephen D. Glazier. *The Anthropology of Religious Conversion.* Lanham, Md: Rowman & Littlefield, 2003.

Burchard, Christoph. "The Importance of Joseph and Aseneth for the Study of the New Testament: A General Survey and a Fresh Look at the Lord's Supper." *New Testament Studies* 33 (1987): 102–34.

————. "The Present State of Research on Joseph and Aseneth." Pages 31–52 in *Religion, Literature, Society: Ancient Israel.* Edited by Jacob Neusner, et. al. Lanham, Md: University Press of America, 1987.

————. "The Text of *Joseph and Aseneth* Reconsidered." *Journal for the Study of the Pseudepigrapha* 14.2 (2005): 83–96.

————. *Untersuchungen zu Joseph und Aseneth.* Tübingen: J. C. B. Mohr, 1965.

Burrus, Catherine, and Lucan Van Rompay. "Thecla in Syriac Christianity: Preliminary Observations." *Hugoye* 5.2 (2002): 1–14.

Burrus, Virginia. *Chastity as Autonomy: Women in the Stories of the Apocryphal Acts.* Lewiston, Maine: Edwin Mellen, 1987.

————. "Mimicking Virgins: Colonial Ambivalence and the Ancient Romance." *Arethusa* 38 (2005): 49–88.

———. *The Sex Lives of Saints: An Erotics of Ancient Hagiography.* Philadelphia: University of Pennsylvania Press, 2004.

Burrus, Virginia and Catherine Keller, eds. *Toward a Theology of Eros: Transfiguring Passion at the Limits of Discipline.* New York: Fordham University Press, 2006.

Butler, Judith. "Desire." Pages 369–86 in *Critical Terms for Literary Study.* Edited Frank Lentricchia and Thomas McLaughlin. 2nd edition. Chicago: University of Chicago Press, 1995.

Carson, Anne. "Putting Her in Her Place: Woman, Dirt, and Desire." Pages 135–69 in *Before Sexuality: The Construction of Erotic Experience in the Ancient Greek World.* Edited by David M. Halperin, John J. Winkler, and Froma I. Zeitlin. Princeton: Princeton University Press, 1990.

Castelli, Elizabeth A. *Martyrdom and Memory: Early Christian Culture Making.* New York: Columbia University Press, 2006.

Chadwick, Henry. "Review of Norbert Brox, *Der Hirt Des Hermas.*" *Journal of Ecclesiastical History* 47 (1996): 119.

Chesnutt, Randall D. *From Death to Life: Conversion in Joseph and Aseneth.* JSPSS 16. Sheffield: Sheffield Academic Press, 1995.

———. "From Text to Context: The Social Matrix of *Joseph and Aseneth.*" Pages 285–302 in *Society of Biblical Literature Seminar Papers 1996.* Society of Biblical Literature Seminar Papers 33. Atlanta: Scholars Press, 1996.

———. "Perceptions of Oil in Early Judaism and the Meal Formula in Joseph and Aseneth." *Journal for the Study of the Pseudepigrapha* 14.2 (2005): 113–32.

———. "Revelatory Experiences Attributed to Biblical Women in Early Jewish Literature." Pages 107–25 in *Women Like This: New Perspectives on Jewish Women in the Greco-Roman World.* Edited by Amy-Jill Levine. Atlanta: Scholars Press, 1991.

———. Review of Ross S. Kraemer, *When Aseneth Met Joseph.* *Journal of Biblical Literature* 199 (2000): 760–62.

———. "The Social Setting and Purpose of Joseph and Aseneth." *Journal for the Study of the Pseudepigrapha* 2 (1988): 21–48.

Clark, Elizabeth A. "Engendering the Study of Religion." Pages 217–42 in *The Future of the Study of Religion: Proceedings of Congress 2000.* Edited by Slavica Jakelic and Lori Pearson. Leiden: Brill, 2004.

Clark, Kenneth Willis. "The Sins of Hermas." Pages 102–19 in *Early Christian Origins: Studies in Honor of Harold R. Willoughby.* Chicago: Quadrangle Books, 1961.

Clément, Catherine and Julia Kristeva. *The Feminine and the Sacred.* Translated by Jane Marie Todd. New York: Columbia University Press, 2001.

Cobb, L. Stephanie. *Dying to Be Men: Gender and Language in Early Christian Martyr Texts.* New York: Columbia University Press, 2008.

Cohen, Shaye J. D. *The Beginnings of Jewishness: Boundaries, Varieties, Uncertainties.* Berkeley: University of California Press, 1999.

Coleborne, W. "A Linguistic Approach to the Problem of Structure and Composition of the Shepherd of Hermas." *Colloquium* 3 (1967): 133–42.

————. "*The Shepherd* of Hermas: A Case for Multiple Authorship and Some Implications." *Studia Patristica* 10 (1970): 65–70.

Collins, Adela Yarbro. "Early Christian Apocalypticism." *Semeia* 36 (1986): 1–7.

Collins, John J. "Introduction: Towards the Morphology of a Genre." *Semeia* 14 (1979): 21–59.

————. "*Joseph and Aseneth*: Jewish or Christian?" *Journal for the Study of the Pseudepigrapha.* 14.2 (2005): 97–112.

Cooper, Kate. *The Virgin and the Bride: Idealized Womanhood in Late Antiquity.* Cambridge: Harvard University Press, 1996.

Corrington, Gail Peterson. "Salvation, Celibacy, and Power: 'Divine Women' in Late Antiquity." Pages 321–25 in *Society of Biblical Literature Seminar Papers 1985.* Society of Biblical Literature Seminar Papers 24. Atlanta: Scholars Press, 1985.

Craven, Toni A. *Artistry and Faith in the Book of Judith.* Atlanta: Society of Biblical Literature, 1983.

Dagron, Gilbert. *Vie et Miracles de Sainte Theclè: Texte Grec, Traduction et Commentaire.* Brussels: Société des Bollandistes, 1978.

D'Angelo, Mary Rose. "'Knowing How to Preside Over His Own Household': Imperial Masculinity and Christian Asceticism in the Pastorals, Hermas, and Luke-Acts." in *New Testament Masculinities.* Edited by Stephen D. Moore and Janice Capel Anderson. *Semeia* 45 (2003): 265–95.

Davies, Stevan L. *The Revolt of the Widows: The Social World of the Apocryphal Acts.* Carbondale, Ill.: Southern Illinois University Press, 1980.

Davis, Stephen J. *The Cult of St. Thecla: A Tradition of Women's Piety in Late Antiquity.* New York: Oxford University Press, 2001.

————. "A 'Pauline' Defense of Women's Right to Baptize? Intertextuality and Apostolic Authority in the Acts of Paul." *Journal of Early Christian Studies* 8 (2000): 453–59.

De Lauretis, Teresa. *Alice Doesn't: Feminism, Semiotics, Cinema.* Bloomington, Ind.: Indiana University Press, 1984.

Décobert, Christian. "La Conversion Comme Aversion." *Archives de Sciences Sociales Des Religions* 104 (1998): 33–60.

Dibelius, M. *Der Hirt des Hermas. Die Apostolischen Vater.* Vol. 4. Tübingen: J. C. B. Mohr [Paul Siebeck], 1923.

Dillon, John. *The Middle Platonists: A Study of Platonism 80 BC to AD 220.* London: Duckworth, 1977.

Dobschütz, Ernst von. "Der Roman in der altchristlichen Literatur." *Deutsche Rundschau* 111 (1902): 87–106.

Docherty, Susan. "*Joseph and Aseneth*: Rewritten Bible or Narrative Expansion." *Journal for the Study of Judaism in the Persian, Hellenistic, and Roman Periods* 35 (2004): 27–47.

————. "Joseph the Patriarch: Representations of Joseph in Early Post-Biblical Literature." Pages 194–216 in *Borders, Boundaries, and the Bible.* Edited by Martin O'Kane. JSOTSS 313. Sheffield: Sheffield Academic Press, 2002.

Donfried, Karl Paul. *The Setting of Second Clement in Early Christianity*. Leiden: Brill, 1974.

Douglas, Reed Conrad. "Liminality and Conversion in Joseph and Aseneth." *Journal for the Study of the Pseudepigrapha* 3 (1988): 31–42.

Du Bois, Page. *Sappho is Burning*. Chicago: University of Chicago Press, 1995.

Dunn, Peter W. "Women's Liberation, the *Acts of Paul*, and Other Apocryphal Acts of the Apostles: A Review of Some Recent Interpreters." *Apocrypha* 4 (1993): 245–61.

Esch-Ermeling, Elisabeth. *Thekla-Paulusschülerin wider Willen? Strategien der Leserlenkung in den Theklaakten*. Neutestamentliche Abhandlungen 53. Münster: Aschendorff, 2008.

Feldman, Louis. *Jewish Assimilation, Acculturation and Accommodation: Past Traditions, Current Issues and Future Prospects*. Lanham, Md.: University Press of America, 1992.

Finn, Thomas D. *From Death to Rebirth: Ritual and Conversion in Antiquity*. New York: Paulist Press, 1997.

Foskett, Mary. *A Virgin Conceived: Mary and Classical Representations of Virginity*. Bloomington, Ind.: Indiana University Press, 2002.

Foucault, Michel. *The Care of the Self*. Translated by Robert Hurley. *The History of Sexuality*. Vol. 3. New York: Vintage Books, 1988.

———. *Ethics: Subjectivity and Truth*. Edited by Paul Rabinow. Translated by Robert Hurley. *Essential Works of Foucault 1954–84*. New York: The New Press, 1997.

———. *The Use of Pleasure*. Translated by Robert Hurley. *The History of Sexuality*. Vol. 2. New York: Vintage Books, 1990.

Francis, James A. *Subversive Virtue: Asceticism and Authority in the Second-Century Pagan World*. University Park, Pa.: Pennsylvania State University Press, 1995.

Fredriksen, Paula. "Paul and Augustine: Conversion Narratives, Orthodox Traditions, and the Retrospective Self." *Journal of Theological Studies* 37 (1986): 3–34.

Fredrikson, Nadia Ibrahim. "L'Esprit saint et les esprits mauvais dans le *Pasteur* D'Hermas: Sources et Prolongements." *Vigiliae Christianae* 55 (2001): 262–80.

Freud, Sigmund. *The Standard Edition of the Complete Psychological Works of Sigmund Freud*. Translated by James Strachey. London: Hogarth Press and the Institute for Psycho-Analysis, 1957–1963.

Fulkerson, Laurel. "*Metameleia* and Friends: Remorse and Repentance in Fifth- and Fourth-Century Athenian Orators." *Phoenix* 58 (2004): 241–59.

Fusillo, Massimo. "Modern Critical Theories and the Ancient Novel." Pages 277–305 in *The Novel in the Ancient World*. Edited by Gareth Schmeling. Leiden: Brill, 1996.

———. *Naissance du Roman*. Paris: Éditions du Seuil, 1991.

———. "Un paradigme thématique: l'eros." Pages 195–258 in *Naissance du Roman*. Transl., Marielle Abrioux. Paris: Éditions du Seuil, 1989.

Gaca, Kathy L. *The Making of Fornication: Eros, Ethics, and Political Reform in Greek Philosophy and Early Christianity.* Berkeley: University of California Press, 2003.

Gallagher, E. "Conversion and Community in Late Antiquity." *Journal of Religion* 73 (1993): 1–15.

Gaventa, Beverly. *From Darkness to Light: Conversion in the New Testament.* Philadelphia: Fortress Press, 1986.

Genette, Gerard. *Narrative Discourse: An Essay in Method.* Translated by Jane E. Lewin. Ithaca, N.Y.: Cornell University Press, 1980.

———. *Narrative Discourse Revisited.* Translated by Jane E. Lewin. Ithaca, N.Y.: Cornell University Press, 1988.

Giet, Stanislas. "L'Apocalypse d'Hermas et la Pénitence." *Studia Patristica* 3 (1961): 214–18.

———. *Hermas et les Pasteurs: Les trois auteurs du Pasteur d'Hermas.* Paris: Presses Universitaires du France, 1963.

———. "Les Trois Auteurs Du Pasteur D'Hermas." *Studia Patristica* 8.2 (1966): 10–23.

Gill, Christopher. *The Structured Self in Hellenistic and Roman Thought.* New York: Oxford University Press, 2006.

Girard, René. *Deceit, Desire, and the Novel: Self and Other in Literary Structure.* Translated by Yvonne Freccero. Baltimore, Md.: Johns Hopkins University Press, 1965.

Gleason, Maud W. *Making Men: Sophists and Self-Preservation in Ancient Rome.* Princeton: Princeton University Press, 1995.

Glenny, W. Edward. "1 Corinthians 7:29–31 and the Teaching of Continence in the Acts of Paul and Thecla." *Grace Theological Journal* 11 (1990): 53–70.

Goldhill, Simon. *Foucault's Virginity: Ancient Erotic Fiction and the History of Sexuality.* Cambridge: Cambridge University Press, 1995.

Goodman, Martin. *Mission and Conversion: Proselytizing in the Religious History of the Roman Empire.* Oxford: Clarendon, 1994.

Grant, Robert M. "The Description of Paul in the Acts of Paul and Thecla." *Vigiliae Christianae* 36 (1982): 1–4.

———. *Ignatius of Antioch.* Volume 4. *The Apostolic Fathers.* London: Nelson, 1966.

Grant, Robert M. and Holt H. Graham. *First and Second Clement.* Volume 2 *The Apostolic Fathers.* New York: Nelson, 1965.

Green, Joel B. *Body, Soul, and Human Life: The Nature of Humanity in the Bible.* Grand Rapids: Baker Academic, 2008.

Gruen, Erich S. *Heritage and Hellenism: The Reinvention of Jewish Tradition.* Berkeley: University of California Press, 1998.

Guerlac, Suzanne. "Longinus and the Subject of the Sublime." *New Literary History* 16 (1985): 275–90.

Hadot, Pierre. *Philosophy as a Way of Life: Spiritual Exercises from Socrates to Foucault.* Edited by Arnold I. Davidson. Translated by Michael Chase. Oxford: Blackwell, 1995.

Haines-Eitzen, Kim. "Engendering Palimpsests: Reading the Textual Tradition of the Acts of Paul and Thecla." Pages 177–93 in *The Early Christian Book*. Edited by William E. Klingshirn and Linda Safran. Washington: Catholic University Press of America, 2007.

Hallett, Judith, and Marilyn B. Skinner, eds. *Roman Sexualities*. Princeton: Princeton University Press, 1997.

Halperin, David M., John J. Winkler, and Froma I. Zeitlin, eds. *Before Sexuality: The Construction of Erotic Experience in the Ancient Greek World*. Princeton: Princeton University Press, 1990.

Hanson, Ann Ellis. "The Medical Writers' Woman." Pages 309–37 in *Before Sexuality: The Construction of Erotic Experience in the Ancient Greek World*. Edited by David M. Halperin, John J. Winkler, and Froma I. Zeitlin. Princeton: Princeton University Press, 1990.

Harpham, Geoffrey Galt. *The Ascetic Imperative in Culture and Criticism*. Chicago: University of Chicago Press, 1987.

Hauck, Robert J. "The Great Fast: Christology in the *Shepherd* of Hermas." *Anglican Theological Review* 75 (1993): 187–98.

Hayne, Léonie. "Thecla and the Church Fathers." *Vigiliae Christianae* 48 (1994): 209–18.

Haynes, Katharine. *Fashioning the Feminine in the Greek Novel*. London: Routledge, 2003.

Heikkinen, J. W. "Notes on 'Epistrepho' and 'Metanoeo.'" *The Ecumenical Review* 19 (1967): 313–16.

Helleman, Wendy, ed. *Hellenization Revisited: Shaping a Christian Response within the Greco-Roman World*. Lanham, Md.: University Press of America, 1994.

Hellholm, David. *Das Visionenbuch des Hermas als Apokalypse*. Lund: C. W. K. Gleerup, 1980.

Henne, Phillippe. *L'unité Du Pasteur D'Hermas: Tradition et Rédaction*. Cahrb 31. Paris: J. Gabalda, 1992.

———. "La Penitence et la Redaction du Pasteur D'Hermas." *Revue Biblique* 98 (1991): 358–97.

———. "La Polysemie Allegorique dans Le Pasteur D'Hermas." *Ephemerides Theologicae Lovanienses* 65 (1989): 131–35.

Hertz, Neil. *The End of the Line: Essays on Psychoanalysis and the Sublime*. New York: Columbia University Press, 1986.

Hilhorst, A. "Erotic Elements in the Shepherd of Hermas." Pages 193–204 in *Groningen Colloquia on the Novel*. Vol. 4. Groningen: Egbert Forsten, 1998.

———. "Tertullian on the Acts of Paul." Pages 150–63 in *The Apocryphal Acts of Paul and Thecla*. Kampen: Kok Pharos, 1996.

Hinchman, Lewis P. and Sandra K. Hinchman, *Memory, Identity, Community: The Idea of Narrative in the Human Sciences*. SUNY Press, 1997.

Hock, Ronald, Brad Chance, and Judith Perkins, eds. *Ancient Fiction and Early Christian Narrative*. SBL Symposium Series 6. Atlanta: Scholars Press, 1998.

Holtz, T. "Christliche Interpolationen in 'Joseph und Aseneth.'" *New Testament Studies* 14 (1968): 482–97.

Horner, Timothy. "Review: *When Joseph Met Aseneth.*" *Journal of Early Christian Studies* 9 (1999): 602–03.

Hubbard, Moyer. "Honey for Aseneth: Interpreting a Religious Symbol." *Journal for the Study of the Pseudepigrapha* 16 (1997): 97–110.

Humphrey, Edith M. *Joseph and Aseneth.* Guides to Apocrypha and Pseudepigrapha. Edited by Michael A. Knibb. Sheffield: Sheffield Academic Press, 2000.

———. *The Ladies and the Cities: Transformations and Apocalyptic Identity in Joseph and Aseneth, 4 Ezra, the Apocalypse and the Shepherd of Hermas.* JSPSS 17. Sheffield: Sheffield Academic Press, 1995.

———. "On Bees and Best Guesses: The Problem of *Sitz Im Leben* from Internal Evidence as Illustrated by Joseph and Aseneth." *Currents in Research: Biblical Studies* 7 (1999): 223–36.

Hunter, David G. "The Language of Desire: Clement of Alexandria's Transformation of Ascetic Discourse." *Semeia* 57 (1991): 95–111.

Jacobs, Andrew S. "A Family Affair: Marriage, Class, and Ethics in the Apocryphal Acts of the Apostles." *Journal of Early Christian Studies* 7 (1999): 105–38.

Jaeger, Werner. *Paideia: the Ideals of Greek Culture.* Translated by Gilbert Highet. New York: Oxford University Press, 1943.

———. Review of Eduard Norden, *Agnostos Theos.* Reprinted in *Scripta Minora* I. Rome: Edizioni di Storia e Litteratura, 1960.

James, William. *Varieties of Religious Experience.* New York: Modern Library, 1902.

Jeffers, James S. *Conflict at Rome: Social Order and Hierarchy in Early Christianity.* Minneapolis: Fortress Press, 1991.

Johnson, Scott Fitzgerald. *The Life and Miracles of Thekla: A Literary Study.* Cambridge: Harvard University Press, 2006.

Joly, Robert. "Philologie et Psychanalyse: C.G. Jung et le 'Pasteur' D'Hermas." *L'Antiquité Classique* 22 (1953): 422–428.

Jung, Carl J. *Psychological Types of the Psychology of Individuation.* Translated by H. Godwin Baynes. London: Kegan Paul, 1946.

Kaestli, Jean Daniel. *Les Actes Apocryphes Des Apôtres: Christianisme et Monde Païen.* Paris: Labor et Fides, 1981.

———. "Les Actes Apocryphes Et La Reconstitution De L'histoire Des Femmes Dans Le Christianisme Ancien." *Foi et Vie* 88 (1989): 71–79.

———. "Fiction littéraire et réalité sociale. Que peut-on savoir de la place des femmes dans le milieu de production des Actes apocryphes des Apôtres?" *Apocrypha/ Le champ des apocryphes* 1 (1990): 279–302.

Kaster, Robert A. *Emotion, Restraint, and Community in Ancient Rome.* New York: Oxford University Press, 2005.

Kee, Howard C. "The Socio-Cultural Setting of *Joseph and Aseneth.*" *New Testament Studies* 29 (1983): 394–413.

———. "The Socio-Religious Setting and Aims of 'Joseph and Asenath.'" Pages 183–192 in *Society of Biblical Literature Seminar Papers 1976*. Society of Biblical Literature Seminar Papers 10. Missoula, MT: Scholars Press, 1976.

Kerenyi, Karl. *Die greichische-orientalische Romanliteratur in religionsgeschichtlicher Beleuchtung*. Darmstadt: Wissenschaftliche Buchgesellschaft, 1962.

Kirkland, Alastair. "The Literary History of The Shepherd off [*sic*] Hermas Visions I to IV. *The Second Century* 9 (1992): 87–102.

Kittel, G., and G. Friedrich, eds. *Theological Dictionary of the New Testament*. Translated by G. W. Bromiley. 10 vols. Grand Rapids: Eerdmans, 1964–1976.

Klauck, Hans-Josef. *The Apocryphal Acts of the Apostles: An Introduction*. Translated by Brian McNeil. Waco: Baylor University Press, 2008.

Knust, Jennifer Wright. *Abandoned to Lust: Sexual Slander and Ancient Christianity*. New York: Columbia University Press, 2006.

Konstan, David. "Acts of Love: A Narrative Pattern in the Apocryphal Acts." *Journal of Early Christian Studies* 6 (1998): 15–36.

———. "Philo's *De Virtutibus* in the Perspective of Classical Greek Philosophy." *Studia Philonica Annual* 18 (2006): 59–72.

———. *Sexual Symmetry: Love in the Ancient Novel and Related Genres*. Princeton: Princeton University Press, 1994.

Kraemer, Ross S. *When Aseneth Met Joseph: A Late Antique Tale of the Biblical Patriarch and his Egyptian Wife, Reconsidered*. New York: Oxford University Press, 1998.

———. "When Aseneth Met Joseph: A Postscript." *For a Later Generation*. Edited by Beverly A. Bow, Randal A. Argall, and Rodney A. Werline. Harrisonburg, Va.: Trinity, 2000.

Kraemer, Ross Shepard and Mary Rose D'Angelo, eds. *Women and Christian Origins*. New York: Oxford University Press, 1999.

Kristeva, Julia. *Desire in Language*. Translated by Alice Jardine, Thomas Gora, and Leon S. Roudiez. Edited by Leon S. Roudiez. New York: Columbia University Press, 1980.

———. *The Kristeva Reader*. Edited by Toril Moi. New York: Columbia University Press, 1986.

———. *Revolution in Poetic Language*. New York: Columbia University Press, 1984.

———. *Tales of Love*. Translated by Leon S. Roudiez. New York: Columbia University Press, 1987.

Kugel, James L. *In Potiphar's House: The Interpretive Life of Biblical Texts*. San Francisco: HarperSanFrancisco, 1990.

Lacan, Jacques. *Écrits: A Selection*. Translated by Alan Sheridan. New York: Norton, 1977.

———. *The Seminar of Jacques Lacan, Book XI: The Four Fundamental Concepts of Psychoanalysis*. Edited by Jacques-Alain Miller. Translated by Alan Sheridan. New York: Norton, 1981.

Lake, Kirsopp. "The Shepherd of Hermas and Christian Life in Rome in the Second Century." *Harvard Theological Review* 4 (1968): 25–46.

Lalleman, Pieter J. "The Canonical and the Apocryphal Acts of the Apostles." *Groningen Colloquia on the Novel* 9 (1998):181–91.

Lamb, Jonathan. "Longinus, the Dialectic, and the Practice of Mastery." *English Literary History* 60 (1993): 545–67.

Lampe, Peter. *From Paul to Valentinus: Christians at Rome in the First Two Centuries.* Translated by Michael Steinhauser. Edited by Marshall D. Johnson. Minneapolis: Fortress Press, 2003.

Lane Fox, Robin. *Pagans and Christians.* New York: HarperSanFrancisco, 1986.

Lawson, John. *A Theological and Historical Introduction to the Apostolic Fathers.* New York: MacMillan, 1961.

Leutzch, Martin. *Die Wahrnehmung sozialer Wirklichkeit im 'Hirten des Hermas.'* Göttingen: Vandenhoeck & Ruprecht, 1989.

Levine, Amy-Jill, ed. *A Feminist Companion to the New Testament Apocrypha.* Cleveland: Pilgrim Press, 2006.

———. "Hemmed in on Every Side: Jews and Women in the Book of Susanna." *The Feminist Companion to the Bible.* Edited by Athalya Brenner. Sheffield: Sheffield Academic Press, 1995.

———. *Women Like This: New Perspectives on Jewish Women in the Greco-Roman World.* Atlanta: Scholars Press, 1991.

Lieber, Andrea. "I set a table before you: the Jewish eschatological character of Aseneth's conversion meal." *Journal for the Study of the Pseudepigrapha* 14.1 (2004): 63–77.

Lieu, Judith. "The 'Attraction of Women' in/To Early Judaism and Christianity: Gender and the Politics of Conversion." *Journal for the Study of the New Testament* 72 (1998): 5–22.

Lluis-Font, Pedro. "Sources de la doctrine d'Hermas sur les deux esprits." *Revue D'Ascétique et de Mystique* 39 (1963): 83–98.

Lofland, J. and N. Skonovd. "Conversion Motifs." *Journal for the Scientific Study of Religion* 20 (1981): 373–85.

Lofland, J. and R. Stark. "Becoming a World Saver: A Theory of Conversion to a Deviant Perspective." *American Sociological Review* 30 (1965): 862–75.

Long, A.A. *From Epicurus to Epictetus: Studies in Hellenistic and Roman Philosophy.* Oxford: Clarendon Press, 2006.

Luschnat, Otto. "Die Jungfrauenszene in der Arkadienvision des Hermas." *Theologia Viatorum* 12 (1973–74): 53–70.

MacDonald, Dennis R. "The Apocryphal Acts of Apostles." *Semeia* 38 (1986): 9–171.

———. *The Legend and the Apostle: the Battle for Paul in Story and Canon.* Philadelphia: Westminster Press, 1983.

———. *There is No Male and Female: the Fate of a Dominical Saying in Paul and Gnosticism.* Philadelphia: Fortress Press, 1987.

MacDonald, Dennis R., and Andrew D. Scrimgeour. "Pseudo-Chrysostom's Panegyric to Thecla: The Heroine of the Acts of Paul in Homily and Art." *Semeia* 38 (1986): 151–59.

MacDonald, Margaret Y. "Rereading Paul: Early Interpreters of Paul on Women and Gender." Pages 236–53 in *Women and Christian Origins*. Edited by Ross S. Kraemer and Mary Rose D'Angelo. New York: Oxford, 1999.

Macksey, Richard. "Longinus Reconsidered." *Modern Language Notes* 108 (1993): 913–34.

MacMullen, Ramsay. *Christianizing the Roman Empire* a.d. *100–400*. New Haven: Yale University Press, 1984.

———. "Conversion: A Historian's View." *The Second Century* 5 (1985–1986): 67–81.

Maier, Harry. *The Social Setting of the Ministry as Reflected in the Writings of Hermas, Clement and Ignatius*. Waterloo, Ontario: Wilfrid Laurier University Press, 1991.

Makaryk, Irena R., general editor and compiler. *Encyclopedia of Contemporary Literary Theory: Approaches, Scholars, Terms*. Toronto: University of Toronto Press, 1993.

Malherbe, A. J. "A Physical Description of Paul." *Harvard Theological Review* 79 (1986): 170–75.

Marguerat, Daniel, and Ken McKinney. "The Acts of Paul and the Canonical Acts: A Phenomenon of Rereading." *Semeia* 80 (1997): 169–83.

Martin, Dale. "Arsenokoites and Malakos: Meanings and Consequences." Pages 117–36 in *Biblical Ethics and Homosexuality*. Edited by R. Brawley. Louisville: Westminster John Knox Press, 1996.

———. *The Corinthian Body*. New Haven: Yale University Press, 1995.

———. "Paul without Passion: On Paul's rejection of desire in sex and marriage." Pages 201–15 in *Constructing Early Christian Families*. Edited by Halvor Moxnes. London: Routledge, 1997.

———. *Sex and the Single Savior: Gender and Sexuality in Biblical Interpretation*. Louisville: Westminster John Knox Press, 2006.

Matthews, Shelly. *First Converts: Rich Pagan Women and the Rhetoric of Mission in Early Judaism and Christianity*. Stanford: Stanford University Press, 2001.

———. "Thinking of Thecla: Issues in Feminist Historiography." *Journal of Feminist Studies in Religion* 17 (2001): 39–55.

McInerney, Maud Burnett. *Eloquent Virgins from Thecla to Joan of Arc*. New York: Palgrave MacMillan, 2003.

McKnight, Scot. *Turning to Jesus: the Sociology of Conversion in the Gospels*. Louisville: Westminster John Knox Press, 2002.

Meeks, Wayne. "The Image of the Androgyne: Some Uses of a Symbol in Earliest Christianity." *History of Religions* 12 (1974): 165–208.

Meyerhoff, Barbara G., Linda A. Camino and Edith Turner. "Rites of Passage: An Overview." Pages 380–87 in *Encyclopedia of Religion* 12. New York: Macmillan, 1987.

Miller, Patricia Cox. "All the Words Were Frightful: Salvation by Dreams in the Shepherd of Hermas." *Vigiliae Christianae* 42 (1988): 327–38.

———. "The Blazing Body: Ascetic Desire in Jerome's Letter to Eustochium." *Journal of Early Christian Studies* 1 (1993): 21–45.

———. *Dreams in Late Antiquity: Studies in the Imagination of a Culture*. Princeton: Princeton University Press, 1994.

Moi, Toril. *Sexual/Textual Politics: Feminist Literary Theory*. 2nd ed. London: Routledge, 1985, 2002.

Morgan, J.R. "The Ancient Novel at the End of the Century: Scholarship Since the Dartmouth Conference." *Classical Philology* 91 (1996): 63–73.

Morgan, Thaïs. "The Space of Intertextuality." Pages 239–79 in *Intertextuality and Contemporary American Fiction*. Edited by Patrick O'Donnell and Robert Con Davis. Baltimore: Johns Hopkins University Press, 1989.

Moore, Stephen D., and Janice Capel Anderson. *New Testament Masculinities*. Semeia Studies 45. Atlanta: Society of Biblical Literature, 2003.

———. "Taking it Like a Man: Masculinity in 4 Maccabees." *Journal of Biblical Literature* 117 (1998): 249–73.

Morgan, J. R., and Richard Stoneman. *Greek Fiction: The Greek Novel in Context*. London: Routledge, 1994.

Morgan-Wynne, J.E. "The 'delicacy' of the Spirit in the Shepherd of Hermas and in Tertullian." *Studia Patristica* 21 (1989): 154–57.

Moxnes, Halvor. "God and His Angel in the Shepherd of Hermas." *Studia Theologia* 28 (1974): 49–56.

Nagy, Gregory, ed. *Greek Literature, Volume 8: Greek Literature in the Roman Period and in Late Antiquity*. New York: Routledge, 2001.

Nave, Guy. *The Role and Function of Repentance in Luke-Acts*. Atlanta: Society of Biblical Literature, 2002.

Nickelsburg, George W. E. *Jewish Literature between the Bible and the Mishnah: A Historical and Literary Introduction*. Philadelphia: Fortress Press, 1981.

Nock, Arthur Darby. *Conversion: The Old and New in Religion from Alexander the Great to Augustine of Hippo*. Oxford: Clarendon, 1933.

Norden, Eduard. *Agnostos Theos*. Stuttgart: B.G. Teubner, 1912.

North, Helen. *Sophrosyne: Self-Knowledge and Self-Restraint in Greek Literature*. Ithaca: Cornell University Press, 1966.

Nussbaum, Martha C. *The Therapy of Desire: Theory and Practice in Hellenistic Ethics*. Princeton: Princeton University Press, 1994.

O'Brien, D.P. "The Cumaean Sibyl as the Revelation-bearer in the Shepherd of Hermas." *Journal of Early Christian Studies* 5 (1997): 473–96.

Osiek, Carolyn. "The Genre and Function of the Shepherd of Hermas." *Early Christian Apocalypticism: Genre and Setting. Semeia* 36 (1986): 113–21.

———. "The Oral World of Early Christianity in Rome: The Case of Hermas." Pages 151–72 in *Judaism and Christianity in First-Century Rome*. Edited by Karl P. Donfried and Peter Richardson. Grand Rapids: Eerdmans, 1998.

————. *Rich and Poor in the Shepherd of Hermas: An Exegetical-Social Investigation.* CBQ Monograph Series 15. Washington, D. C.: Catholic Biblical Association of America, 1983.

————. *The Shepherd of Hermas: A Commentary.* Hermeneia. Minneapolis: Fortress Press, 1999.

————. "Wealth and Poverty in the *Shepherd of Hermas.*" *Studia Patristica* 17 (1982): 725–30.

Osiek, Carolyn and Margaret M. MacDonald. *A Woman's Place: House Churches in Earliest Christianity.* Minneapolis: Fortress Press, 2005.

Park, Eung Chun. "ΑΓΝΕΙΑ as a Sublime form of ΕΡΩΣ in the Acts of Paul and Thecla." Pages 215–26 in *Distant Voices Drawing Near: Essays in Honor of Antoinette Clark Wire.* Edited by Holly Hearon. Collegeville, Minn.: Liturgical Press, 2004.

Penn, Michael. "Identity Transformation and Authorial Identification in Joseph and Aseneth." *Journal for the Study of the Pseudepigrapha* 13 (2002): 171–83.

Perkins, Judith. *Roman Imperial Identities in the Early Christian Era.* London: Routledge, 2009.

————. *The Suffering Self.* London: Routledge, 1995.

————. "This World or Another? The Intertextuality of the Greek Romances, the Apocryphal Acts and Apuleius' Metamorphoses." *Semeia* 80 (1997): 247–60.

Pernveden, Lage. *The Concept of the Church in The Shepherd of Hermas.* Lund: C. W. K. Gleerup, 1966.

Pervo, Richard I. "Aseneth and Her Sisters: Women in Jewish Narrative and in the Greek Novels." Pages 145–60 in *"Women Like This": New Perspectives on Jewish Women in the Greco-Roman World.* Edited by Amy-Jill Levine. Atlanta: Scholars Press, 1991.

————. "Early Christian Fiction." Pages 239–54 in *Greek Fiction: The Greek Novel in Context.* Edited by J. R. Morgan and Richard Stoneman. London: Routledge, 1994.

————. "Joseph and Asenath and the Greek Novel." Pages 171–81 in *Society of Biblical Literature Seminar Papers 1976.* Society of Biblical Literature Seminar Papers 10. Missoula, Mont.: Scholars Press, 1976.

————. *Profit With Delight: the Literary Genre of the Acts of the Apostles.* Philadelphia: Fortress Press, 1987.

Pesthy, Monika. "Thecla among the Fathers of the Church." Pages 164–78 in *The Apocryphal Acts of Paul and Thecla.* Edited by Jan N. Bremmer. Kampen: Kok Pharso, 1996.

Portier-Young, Anathea E. "Sweet Mercy Metropolis: Interpreting Aseneth's Honeycomb." *Journal for the Study of the Pseudepigrapha* 14.2 (2005): 133–57.

Rahner, Karl. *Theological Investigations. Vol. XV. Penance in the Early Church.* London: Darton, Longman & Todd, 1956.

Rambo, Lewis R. "Anthropology and the Study of Conversion." Pages 146–59 in *The Anthropology of Religious Conversion.* Edited by Andrew Buckser and Stephen D. Glazier. Lanham, Md: Rowman & Littlefield, 2003.

———. "Current Research on Religious Conversion." *Religious Studies Review* 8 (1982): 146–59.

———. *Understanding Religious Conversion.* New Haven: Yale University Press, 1993.

Reardon, B.P. "Achilles Tatius and Ego-Narrative." Pages 80–96 in *Greek Fiction: The Greek Novel in Context.* Edited by J.R. Morgan and Richard Stoneman. London: Routledge, 1994.

Reiling, J. *Hermas and Christian Prophecy: A Study of the Eleventh Mandate.* NovTSup, 37. Leiden: Brill, 1973.

Richardson, James T. "The Active vs. Passive Convert: Paradigm Conflict in Conversion/Recruitment Research." *Journal for the Scientific Study of Religion* 24 (1985): 119–236.

Richlin, Amy. "Zeus and Metis: Foucault, Feminism, Classics." *Helios* 18 (1991): 160–80.

Rimmon, Shlomith. "A Comprehensive Theory of Narrative: Genette's *Figures III* and the Structuralist Study of Fiction." *Poetics and Theory of Literature* 1 (1976): 33–62.

Rist, J. M. *Stoic Philosophy.* Cambridge: Cambridge University Press, 1969.

Rordorf, Willy. "Tradition and Composition in the Acts of Thecla: The State of the Question." *Semeia* 38 (1986): 43–52.

Rosen, Ralph M. and Ineke Sluiter, eds. *Andreia: Studies in Manliness and Courage in Classical Antiquity.* Leiden: Brill, 2003.

Russell, D.A. "Longinus Revisited." *Mnemosyne* 34 (1981): 72–86.

Schmeling, Gareth, ed. *The Novel in the Ancient World.* Leiden: Brill, 1996.

Schoedel, William R. *Ignatius of Antioch: A Commentary on the Letters of Ignatius of Antioch.* Philadelphia: Fortress Press, 1985.

Schroeder, Caroline. "Embracing the Erotic in the Passion of Andrew: The Apocryphal Acts of Andrew, the Greek Novel, and Platonic Philosophy." Pages 110–26 in *The Apocryphal Acts of Andrew.* Edited by Jan N. Bremmer. Leuven: Peeters, 2000.

Seitz, O. J. F. "Antecedents and Signification of the Term *Dipsychos.*" *Journal of Biblical Literature* 66 (1947): 211–19.

———. "Relationship of the Shepherd of Hermas to the Epistle of James," *Journal of Biblical Literature* 63 (1944): 131–40.

Söder, Rosa. *Die Apokryphen Apostelgeschichte Und Die Romanhafte Literatur Der Antike.* Stuttgart: W. Kohlhamer, 1932.

Sollors, Werner, ed. *The Return of Thematic Criticism.* Cambridge: Harvard University Press, 1993.

Sorabji, Richard. *Emotion and Peace of Mind: From Stoic Agitation to Christian Temptation.* The Gifford Lectures. New York: Oxford University Press, 2000.

Stafford, Emma J. "Masculine values, feminine forms: on the gender of personi-
fied abstractions." Pages 43–56 in *Thinking Men: Masculinity and Self-
Representation in the Classical Tradition*. Edited by Lin Foxhall and John Salmon.
New York: Routledge, 1998.

Standhartinger, Angela. *Das Frauenbild im Judentum der Hellenistischen Zeit: Ein
Beitrag anhand von "Joseph und Aseneth."* Leiden: Brill, 1995.

———. "From Fictional Text to Socio-Historical Context." Pages 302–18 in
SBL Seminar Papers, 1996. Society of Biblical Literature Seminar Papers 33.
Atlanta: Scholars Press, 1996.

Stark, Rodney. *The Rise of Christianity*. New York: HarperSanFrancisco, 1997.

Stark, Rodney and Roger Finke. *Acts of Faith: Explaining the Human Side of
Religion*. Berkeley: University of California Press, 2000.

Stoops, Robert F. Jr., ed. *The Apocryphal Acts of the Apostles in Intertextual Perspectives. Semeia* 80 (1997).

Streete, Gail. *Redeemed Bodies: Women Martyrs in Early Christianity*. Louisville:
Westminster John Knox, 2009.

Stroumsa, Guy G. "Dreams and Visions in Early Christian Discourse." Pages
189–212 in *Dream Cultures: Explorations in the Comparative History of Dreaming*.
Edited by David Shulman and Guy G. Stroumsa. New York: Oxford
University Press, 1999.

———. "From Repentance to Penance in Early Christianity: Tertullian's *De
paenitentia* in Context." Pages 167–78 in *Transformations of the Inner Self in Ancient
Religions*. Edited by Jan Assmann and Guy G. Stroumsa. Leiden: Brill, 1999.

Stroumsa, Guy G., and Paula Fredriksen, "The Two Souls and the Divided Will."
Pages 198–217 in *Self, Soul and Body in Religious Experience*. Edited by
A. I. Baumgarten, J. Assmann, and G. G. Stroumsa. Leiden: Brill, 1998.

Tatum, James, ed. *The Search for the Ancient Novel*. Baltimore, Md.: Johns Hopkins
University Press, 1994.

Taylor, C. "Hermas and Cebes." *Journal of Philology* 27 (1901): 276–319; 28 (1903):
24–38, 94–98.

Thomas, Christine M. *The Acts of Peter, Gospel Literature, and the Ancient Novel:
Rewriting the Past*. New York: Oxford, 2003.

———. "Stories Without Texts and Without Authors: The Problem of Fluidity in
Ancient Novelistic Texts and Early Christian Literature." Pages 273–91 in
Ancient Fiction and Early Christian Narrative. Edited by Ronald F. Hock,
J. Bradley Chance, and Judith Perkins. Atlanta: Scholars Press, 1998.

Too, Yun Lee. *The Idea of Ancient Literary Criticism*. Oxford: Clarendon Press, 1998.

Toohey, P. "Love, Lovesickness, and Melancholia." *Illinois Classical Studies* 17
(1992): 265–86.

Viswanathan, Gauri. *Outside the Fold: Conversion, Modernity, and Belief*. Princeton:
Princeton University Press, 1998.

Vorster, Johannes N. "Construction of Culture through the Construction of
Person: *The Acts of Thecla* as an Example." Pages 445–73 in *The Rhetorical*

Analysis of Scripture. Edited by Stanley Porter. Sheffield: Sheffield Academic Press, 1997.

Walsh, George B. "Sublime Method: Longinus on Language and Imitation." *Classical Antiquity* 7 (1988): 252–69.

Walters, Jonathan. "Invading the Roman Body: Manliness and Impenetrability in Roman Thought." Pages 29–43 in *Roman Sexualities.* Edited by Judith P. Hallett and Marilyn B. Skinner. Princeton: Princeton University Press, 1997.

Weg, Magda Misset-van de. "'Blessed Are the Bodies of the Virgins . . .'" Pages 233–49 in *Begin with the Body.* Edited by Jonneke Bekkenkamp. Louvain: Peeters, 1998.

Wehn, Beate. "'Blessed are the bodies of those who are virgins': Reflections on the Image of Paul in the *Acts of Thecla.*" *Journal for the Study of the New Testament* 79 (2000): 149–64.

White, Sidnie Ann. "Esther: A Feminine Model for the Jewish Diaspora." In *Gender and Difference.* Edited by Peggy L. Day. Minneapolis: Fortress Press, 2006.

Whitmarsh, Tim. *Ancient Greek Literature.* Malden, Mass.: Polity Press, 2004.

———, ed. *The Cambridge Companion to the Greek and Roman Novel.* Cambridge: Cambridge University Press, 2008.

———. "Dialogues in Love: Bakhtin and His Critics on the Greek Novel." Pages 107–29 in *The Bakhtin Circle and Ancient Narrative.* Edited by R. Bracht Branham. Groningen: Barkhuis Publishing & Groningen University Library, 2005.

———. *Greek Literature and the Roman Empire: The Politics of Imitation.* Oxford: Oxford University Press, 2001.

Wills, Lawrence M. *The Jewish Novel in the Ancient World.* Ithaca: Cornell University Press, 1995.

Wilson, J.C. *Five Problems in the Interpretation of the Shepherd of Hermas: Authorship, Genre, Canonicity, Apocalyptic, and the Absence of the Name 'Jesus Christ.'* Lewiston, Maine: Mellen Biblical Press, 1995.

———. *Toward a Reassessment of the Shepherd of Hermas: Its Date and Its Pneumatology.* Lewiston, Maine: Mellen Biblical Press, 1993.

Wilson, Walter T. "Pious Soldiers, Gender Deviants, and the Ideology of Actium: Courage and Warfare in Philo's *De Fortitudine.*" *Studia Philonica Annual* 17 (2005): 1–32.

Winkler, John J. *The Constraints of Desire: The Anthropology of Sex and Gender in Ancient Greece.* New York: Routledge, 1990.

Winston, David. "Philo's Doctrine of Repentance." Pages 29–40 in *The School of Moses: Studies in Philo and Hellenistic Religion.* Edited by John Peter Kenny. Atlanta: Scholar's Press, 1995.

Wire, Antoinette Clark. "The Social Functions of Women's Asceticism in the Roman East." Pages 308–28 in *Images of the Feminine in Gnosticism.* Edited by Karen L. King. Harrisburg: Trinity Press International, 2000.

Young, Steve. "Being a Man: The Pursuit of Manliness in the Shepherd of Hermas." *Journal of Early Christian Studies* 2 (1994): 237–55.

Zeitlin, Froma I. "The Poetics of Eros: Nature, Art, and Imitation in Longus' *Daphnis and Chloe*." Pages 417–64 in *Before Sexuality: The Construction of Erotic Experience in the Ancient Greek World.* Edited by David M. Halperin, John J. Winkler, and Froma I. Zeitlin. Princeton: Princeton University Press, 1990.

Zock, Hetty. "Paradigms in Psychological Conversion Research." Pages 41–58 in *Paradigms, Poetics and Politics of Conversion.* Edited by Jan N. Bremmer, Wout J. van Bekkum, and Arie L. Molendjik. Leuven: Peeters, 2006.

Index